Can't Believe it's Kosher!

Jewish Tradition for Today's Lifestyle

Congregation Beth Israel Sisterhood
Milwaukee, Wisconsin

About the Cover

The floating figures on the cover may bring to mind the playfulness of Marc Chagall. I tried to convey a dreamy lightness of spirit which is the heart and soul of a warm and busy kitchen.

In fact, "the kitchen" is a character in my house — a friend and companion in creativity. Cooking should make us jump, giggle and sigh with contentedness.

Recipes will become wishes fulfilled for your family. Eat in good health, enjoy and, most important of all, float!

Cindy Cooper

Congregation Beth Israel Sisterhood
6880 North Green Bay Avenue
Milwaukee, Wisconsin 53209

Phone: (414) 351-1800   Fax: (414) 351-1803
Toll-Free: (866) 331-1818

Website: www.cantbelieveitskosher.com
E-mail: cookbook@cantbelieveitskosher.com

Library of Congress Catalog Card Number 00-092489

ISBN 0-9700071-0-8

Printed in the USA by

WIMMER
The Wimmer Companies
Memphis
1-800-548-2537

Who We Are

We are proud to publish a cookbook that reflects contemporary and traditional Jewish cooking. Food has always played an important role in the celebration of Jewish life.

The desire to create fresh, healthy and easy to prepare dishes that honor the age old Jewish dietary laws has provided a challenging incentive for choosing the recipes, contributed by Beth Israel members and friends, presented in this book. The modern Jewish cook has many choices available to create this new type of kosher cuisine. Lactose-free products and new meat-free items have unleashed flavors previously unknown to our mothers and grandmothers. New kosher products, which multiply daily, have also helped shorten the time needed to prepare many traditional dishes.

Our community's strong ties to family traditions are beautifully represented in these recipes, some of which have been handed down from generation to generation. We hope the recipes and information presented here will inspire new families as well as older generations to create culinary delights to be enjoyed by all.

This book is a product of the Sisterhood of Congregation Beth Israel of Milwaukee, Wisconsin. Our congregation has been an integral part of the community since 1885. The Sisterhood is the sole support of the synagogue's extensive Judaica library and its services and supports other synagogue programs. We also maintain the kosher kitchen which is available to the community for citywide events.

Our Sisterhood is affiliated with the Women's League for Conservative Judaism, an international organization dedicated to preserving Jewish ideals and traditions. We provide monetary support, through the Women's League, to the Jewish Theological Seminary in New York City and Israel, and to the University of Judaism in Los Angeles.

Many thanks go to all those who gave their time and expertise to bring this, Beth Israel Sisterhood's third cookbook, to fruition.

Cookbook Committee

Project Director and Editor:
Beverly Feiges

Computer Editor:
Terri Minkin

Associate Computer Editors:
Ruby Carneol & Anita Nagurka

Text Writer:
Phyllis Lensky

Proofreaders:
Suzanne Davidson & Betty Jacobs

Art and Cover Design:
Cindy Cooper

Steering Committee:

Suzanne Davidson	Phyllis Lensky
Bunny Dolnick	Susan Marcus
Betty Jacobs	Millie Polisky
Miriam Kahn	Gladys Shukur

Marketing Committee:

Jerry Dorf	Jack Marcus
Jennie Elias	Barbara Perchonok
Paul Elias	Fred Perchonok
Dr. Lewis Feiges	Mary Anne Selby
Dr. Burton Friedman	Michael Spanjar

Website Development:
Howard Feiges
Kerri Huxley
Anita Nagurka

Table of Contents

All recipes have been tested and written to make them easy to follow and, wherever possible, easy to prepare. Recipes comply with the laws of *kashrut*, the Jewish dietary laws, which include the separation of meat and milk. Each recipe indicates a notation of "Meat," "Dairy" or "Parve." "Parve" contains neither meat nor dairy products and may be used with either meat or dairy meals. The recipes appropriate for Passover which are not included specifically in the Passover section are indicated with a star (✡).

What is "Jewish Food"?

For those of us who live in the United States, "Jewish food" is usually associated with mouth-watering delicacies such as gefilte fish, chopped liver, chicken soup and matzo balls and, of course, bagels and lox. These foods, along with kishke, knishes and kugels (also known as Jewish "K" rations) are familiar dishes on the tables of Ashkenazi Jews or those whose ancestors come from Eastern Europe. However, the dispersion of Jews over the centuries and their enforced exile from their countries of birth broadened the scope of their cooking. Living in countries far from their homeland, they adapted their cooking to include the native ingredients while still conforming to the laws of *kashrut* (dietary laws).

Sephardic Jews encompass those who lived mainly in countries such as Spain, Portugal, Turkey, Iran, Iraq, Syria, Lebanon and North Africa. The Jews of India, known as B'nai Yisroel — Children of Israel — have lived there for several thousand years and a small Jewish community also existed in China. Each of them has their particular customs associated with food preparation and holiday menus. For instance, in the United States, it is traditional to serve potato *latkes* (pancakes) at Chanukah, while in Israel the food of choice is *sufganiyot,* a jelly-filled doughnut. Rice is a staple of the Sephardi diet, as well as for the Indian Jews. Potatoes are a basic for those from Eastern Europe. The blintz, a thin filled pancake, also makes its appearance as an enchilada, a blini, a crêpe or an egg roll, depending on the country of origin.

Cholent, a Sabbath dish of meat, potatoes, beans, onions and water, cooked on a low flame all night and eaten at the Sabbath lunch, can be found in many variations depending on the country. Many of Eastern European origin eat *charoset* at the Passover seder, made from a mixture of apples, nuts and wine. Sephardi Jews, however, may use dates and figs as the main ingredient.

Though customs may differ and ingredients may change, the one thing that remains constant about "Jewish food" is that it is creative and delicious. We have tried to include a collection of the best recipes representative of these cultures.

The Meaning of Kashrut (Kosher)

The laws of kashrut define an important aspect of Jewish life. We spend considerable amounts of time shopping, preparing and consuming food, and mealtime plays a central part in our daily, Shabbat and holiday routines. For Jews, the importance is placed not on living to eat but on eating to live, and how to do it in a fit *(kasher)* manner. The laws of kashrut provide discipline and define what we can eat and how it should be prepared and served. Kosher food has not been "blessed" by a rabbi, nor is kashrut a health code for food. Rather, kashrut was commanded by God and brings holiness into our lives. Our table becomes an altar, and we are constantly reminded of our tradition and our connection to Jews all over the world.

Briefly, the laws of kashrut describe what can be eaten: only those animals that chew their cud and have a cloven hoof; fish that have both fins and scales; birds such as chicken, turkey, goose and duck; fresh vegetables, fruits, nuts and grains. Animals and fish that do not fit the above description, such as pigs, rabbits and shellfish, are forbidden. A specially trained person, the *shochet,* is responsible for the ritual slaughtering of animals and fowl. Ingesting animal blood is also forbidden, and special steps are taken to remove it in the kashering process before the meat is cooked. Many of us may remember how our grandmothers soaked and salted the meat when they returned from the market. Today, most meat is kashered and ready for use when we purchase it at our favorite kosher butcher shop.

Since the observance of kashrut forbids serving milk with meat, the kosher kitchen has two sets of dishes, pots and pans, silverware and other utensils. Parve foods contain neither meat nor dairy products and may be used with either meat or dairy meals. In addition, the kashrut laws of Passover prohibit using any leavened products or other *chometz.* To accommodate these rules, special sets of dishes and silverware are used during this holiday period.

In order to assure the kashrut of foods, various organizations oversee the preparation of food products at their source. Their certification is called a *hechsher* and is usually denoted by a symbol such as the widely known Ⓤ or Ⓚ. More and more products with kosher certification appear on store shelves each year.

For a detailed description of the rules of kashrut, refer to *A Guide to Jewish Religious Practice* by Rabbi Isaac Klein and consult a rabbi.

Jewish Holidays
2001~2010

	Purim	Passover	Shavuot	Rosh Hashanah	Yom Kippur	Sukkot	Chanukah
2001	March 9	April 8-15	May 28-29	Sept. 18-19 5762	Sept. 27	Oct. 2-10*	Dec. 10-17
2002	February 26	March 28-April 4	May 17-18	Sept. 7-8 5763	Sept. 16	Sept. 21-29*	Nov. 30-Dec. 7
2003	March 18	April 17-24	June 6-7	Sept. 27-28 5764	Oct. 6	Oct. 11-19*	Dec. 20-27
2004	March 7	April 6-13	May 26-27	Sept. 16-17 5765	Sept. 25	Sept. 30-Oct. 8*	Dec. 8-15
2005	March 25	April 24-May 1	June 13-14	Oct. 4-5 5766	Oct. 13	Oct. 18-26*	Dec. 26-Jan.3
2006	March 14	April 13-20	June 2-3	Sept. 23-24 5767	Oct. 2	Oct. 7-15*	Dec. 16-23
2007	March 4	April 3-10	May 23-24	Sept. 13-14 5768	Sept. 22	Sept. 27-Oct. 5*	Dec. 5-12
2008	March 21	April 20-27	June 9-10	Sept. 30-Oct.1 5769	Oct. 9	Oct. 14-22*	Dec. 22-29
2009	March 10	April 9-16	May 29-30	Sept. 19-20 5770	Sept. 28	Oct. 3-11*	Dec. 12-19
2010	Feb. 28	March 30-April 6	May 6-7	Sept. 9-10 5771	Sept. 18	Sept. 23-Oct. 1*	Dec. 2-9

Simchat Torah is the Last Day of Sukkot
All Holidays Begin at Sundown of Previous Evening

How the Jewish (Lunar)
Months Coincide
with the Secular (Solar) Months

Tishrei: September - October
Cheshvan: October - November
Kislev: November - December
Tevet: December - January
Shevat: January - February
Adar: February - March

Nisan: March - April
Iyar: April - May
Sivan: May - June
Tammuz: June - July
Av: July - August
Elul: August - September

Holidays
&
Festivals

Shabbat (The Sabbath)

All the hustle and bustle of the week build toward that special day of rest we call Shabbat, a day in which we put aside the workday world for a day of physical and spiritual renewal. The house has been cleaned, delicious food has been prepared for the traditional three Shabbat meals (dinner, lunch and *seudah shelishit* — the third traditional meal), and a beautiful table is set. The woman of the house, surrounded by her children, lights the Shabbat candles 18 minutes before sundown on Friday. Men who have their own households or whose wives are away during Shabbat are also bound by the commandment to light Shabbat candles.

One of the joys of Shabbat is sharing it with family and friends. We begin the celebration with the wonderful melodies of *Shalom Aleichem,* followed by the reading of *Eyeshet Chayil* (A Woman of Valor) from Proverbs and the blessing of the children.

Central to the Shabbat meal is the *Kiddush,* the blessing over wine or grape juice, chanted by the head of the household. Prior to the *Hamotzi,* the blessing over two loaves of challah, it is customary to wash your hands and recite a blessing. After *Hamotzi,* the challah is cut and sprinkled with salt and each person at the table receives a piece. We conclude the meal with the *Birkat Hamazon,* a series of blessings in which we thank the Almighty for providing us with food and satisfying our appetites.

Following Shabbat morning services in the synagogue, we enjoy a wonderful Shabbat lunch, preceded by hand washing, *Kiddush* and the *Hamotzi,* concluding with the *Birkat Hamazon.* By this time we are all ready to indulge in that wonderful luxury of Shabbat — a refreshing nap!

When the first three stars of the evening appear in the sky, Shabbat is over. We mark the conclusion with the lovely *Havdallah* service which emphasizes the light and sweetness of Shabbat by incorporating a candle with multiple wicks, sweet-smelling spices and a blessing over wine. As we go out into the night, wishing each other *Shavuah Tov* (a good week), we are refreshed, invigorated and ready to begin a new week.

Suggested Shabbat Menu

Traditional	Alternative
Wine	Wine
Challah (pages 47, 48)	Challah (pages 47, 48)
Tuna Gefilte Fish (page 130)	Vegetarian Chopped Liver (page 26)
Chicken Soup with Noodles (page 61)	Garden Vegetable Soup (page 70)
Pineapple Ginger Chicken (page 153)	Tofu Pot Roast (page 172)
Microwave Barley and Rice Casserole (page 191)	Fruited Couscous Salad (page 94)
Crunchy Green Beans (page 206)	Deep Dark Chocolate Cake (page 230)
Sunshine Cake (page 234)	

Rosh Hashanah

From the beginning of the month of Elul in the late summer or fall of the year, we engage in a period of introspection, examining our faults and shortcomings and reflecting on the past year. On the evening of the 29th of Elul, Rosh Hashanah, the "head of the year," officially begins. This holiday celebrates not only the beginning of the Jewish new year but also the "birthday of the world" and its creation. The blowing of the *shofar,* a ram's horn, is central to the synagogue service and is a call to repentance. Rosh Hashanah begins the Ten Days of Repentance, culminating with Yom Kippur, the Day of Atonement.

Many traditions have become associated with this holiday. In some communities it is customary to serve a stuffed fish head, since Rosh Hashanah is called the head of the year. Apples and round challahs filled with raisins are dipped in honey, followed by a special blessing requesting a "good and sweet year." Sour foods like dill pickles are not usually served. On the second night of Rosh Hashanah we eat a new fruit. Pomegranates are especially favored because their many seeds suggest abundance for the year ahead.

Each night of Rosh Hashanah and at lunch on the first and second day, a festive meal is served. Candles are lit each evening of the holiday, and a special holiday *Kiddush* is recited. On the first night of the festival, the Shehecheyanu** prayer is recited during both candle lighting and the *Kiddush.* Friends and family greet each other with *"L'shanah tovah tikatevu* - may you be inscribed for a good year."

** Shehecheyanu Prayer

Blessed art thou, O Lord our God, King of the Universe, Who has kept us in life and sustained us and enabled us to reach this season.

Suggested Menu for Rosh Hashanah

Wine
Raisin Challah (page 48)
Apples and Honey
Baked Gefilte Fish Loaf (page 130)
Chicken Soup with Kreplach (page 61)
Traditional Brisket (page 132)
Tzimmes (page 210)
Acini de Pepe (page 184)
Marinated Vegetable Salad (page 89)
Honey Cake with Cherries (page 236)
One-Bowl Apple Cake (page 219)

Yom Kippur

Ten days after Rosh Hashanah, we begin the holiest day of the Jewish calendar — Yom Kippur, the Day of Atonement. During the past ten days of repentance, we should have made amends for any hurt we may have caused our family and friends, even inadvertently, and asked their forgiveness. God can forgive sins we have committed against Him, but we must directly ask forgiveness from others.

In order to make the daylong fast of Yom Kippur easier, the dinner before the *Kol Nidre* service in the synagogue usually omits foods that are overly spicy or sweet. As on Shabbat and other holidays, candles are lit before sunset, the appropriate blessings are recited and we light a yahrzeit candle to remember family members who have died. Many people dress in white as a symbol of purity, and it is a tradition to wear nonleather shoes. Another important tradition is the giving of *tzedakah* (charity). We also wish our friends and family *"gmar hatimah tovah* — may you be sealed in the Book of Life for good."

Yom Kippur affords us a wonderful opportunity to reflect on the past year and give serious thought to how we can improve in the year ahead. Beginning in the evening with the *Kol Nidre* service and continuing all through the following day, we are engaged in prayer, introspection and repentance. When we conclude the services at the end of the day with a prayer to be "sealed in the Book of Life" and hear the blasts of the *shofar,* we feel invigorated and refreshed as we join with family and friends in a traditional breakfast meal. Tired, but fulfilled, we arrive home in time to follow the tradition of beginning to build the *sukkah.*

Suggested Menu for Yom Kippur Break Fast

Juice and Coffee
Herring with Cranberries (page 33)
Bagels and Rye Bread
Lox Spread (page 109)
Egg Salad Spread (page 26)
Swiss Cheese Kugel (page 183)
Fresh Fruit with Tangy Dressing (page 101)
Cardamom Coffee Cake (pages 247, 248)

Sukkot

Two weeks after Rosh Hashanah it's time to begin celebrating Sukkot, one of the *Shelosh Regalim* (three pilgrimage holidays — Sukkot, Pesach and Shavuot), when Jews came to celebrate at the Temple in Jerusalem. This holiday is actually known by three names: the Festival of the Ingathering, commemorating the fall harvest; the Season of Rejoicing; and the Feast of Tabernacles.

One of the major symbols of the holiday is the *sukkah,* a temporary building with a roof of branches, evergreen boughs or corn stalks through which we can see the stars. The *sukkah* reminds us of the temporary structures our ancestors lived in while they wandered in the desert and the huts in which the Israelites lived during the harvest season. Building a *sukkah,* in which we eat for the first seven days of the holiday, is often a family affair. A festive atmosphere is created with brightly colored decorations and fruits and vegetables of the season. Though the *sukkah* remains standing during the next two days, it is not a requirement to eat in it.

The *etrog* (citron) and *lulav* (palm, myrtle and willow bound together in a special way) are waved during special parts of the prayer service in the synagogue and in the *sukkah* during the week of Sukkot.

The eighth day of Sukkot is known as Shemini Atzeret, and it is customary to have a memorial service. The following day we join in the joyous celebration of Simchat Torah, the rejoicing of the Torah. There is dancing and singing and the children march through the synagogue with flags and apples. The annual cycle of reading the Torah is concluded and begins again.

Suggested Menu for Sukkot

Wine
Raisin Challah (page 48)
Gezundte Vegetable Soup (page 71)
Sweet and Sour Turkey Meatballs with Noodles (page 162)
Oriental Coleslaw Delight (page 91)
Raspberry Mold (page 102)
Banana Pineapple Cake (page 221)

Chanukah

The eight-day celebration of Chanukah, a minor holiday usually celebrated in December, commemorates the victory of a small band of rebels — the Maccabees — against the Syrian king, Antiochus IV. Led by Judah Maccabee and his brothers, they fought for the right to continue to live as Jews, resisting the king's efforts to assimilate them into the dominant Greek culture. With the temple defiled, it was necessary to cleanse and rededicate it. Unfortunately, only a single cruse of pure oil, enough for one day, was available to rekindle the lamp in the Temple. But a miracle occurred, and the lamp burned for eight days until more oil could be prepared. To commemorate this miracle, each night of the festival we kindle an additional light on a chanukiah, an eight-branch candelabra or oil lamp, until all eight candles are lit. The candles are lit from left to right with a special ninth candle called the *shammash* and are placed in a window so the miracle of Chanukah is evident to all who pass by.

The emphasis on oil has produced the custom of preparing foods cooked in oil. Ashkenazi Jews eat potato *latkes* (pancakes). *Sufganiyot,* doughnuts filled with jelly, are a popular Chanukah treat in Israel. The story of Judith, who plied King Holofernes with wine and cheesecakes before she slew him, is also the basis for serving dairy foods during Chanukah.

The festive nature of Chanukah has given rise to the custom of giving Chanukah *gelt* (money) and other gifts to the children, along with singing songs and playing games with the *dreidel,* a four-sided spinning top.

Suggested Menu for Chanukah

Baba Ghanoush (page 32)
Hummus (page 30)
Pita
Short-Cut Potato Latkes (page 213)
Applesauce
Vegetable Stuffed Cabbage (page 167)
Chanukah Cookies (pages 247,248)

Tu B'Shevat

It's the Jewish Arbor Day, the New Year of the Trees, celebrating nature's rebirth and the budding of the trees. Though it's still winter for many of us in the United States and Europe, it is the beginning of spring in Israel. Many people commemorate this holiday by making a donation to the Jewish National Fund, which has been so prominent in the reforestation of Israel. It is also an opportunity to think about the environment and how we can preserve it.

Tu B'Shevat, which really means the 15th of the month of Shevat, is celebrated with the custom of eating 15 different varieties of fruits. In keeping with this custom, a new tradition, the Tu B'Shevat seder, has developed. Friends and family join together at a table laden with at least 15 varieties of fruits like pomegranates, dates, figs, carob and grapes and a selection of red and white wines to participate in special readings and the joy of eating nature's bounty. Recommended wines are sauterne, rosé, Tokay and Malaga. The white wine symbolizes the slumber that descends upon nature in the Fall when the sun's rays are weakened. The red wine predicts the awakening of nature in the Spring with the growth and blossoming.

Suggestions for Platters

Fresh Fruit	Dried Fruit	Canned Fruit	Nuts
Tangerines	Raisins	Spiced Crabapples	Walnuts
Grapefruit	Figs *	Cherries	Pecans
Coconut	Apricots	Pineapple	Cashews
Oranges	Pears	Peaches	Almonds
Grapes *	Peaches	Plums	Sunflower Seeds
Pomegranates *	Prunes	Pears	Chestnuts
Kumquats	Dates *	Spiced Apple Rings	Hazelnuts
Pineapple		Cranberries	
		Olives *	

Participants ought to taste the fruits which are starred. They are mentioned in the Bible as especially connected with Israel.

Purim

Every little girl's heroine is Queen Esther, one of the main characters in the Purim story. The wife of King Achasheurus of Persia and the niece of Mordecai, she persuaded her husband to foil the plot of the wicked prime minister, Haman, who was intent on eliminating all the Jews from the land. Her heroism and her uncle's cunning saved the Jews from extinction and Haman and his associates received their just punishment — death by hanging.

Purim is an especially joyous holiday. Both children and adults dress in costumes and masks and come to synagogue to fulfill the mitzvah of hearing *Megillat Esther,* the Scroll of Esther, read in the evening and the following morning. The sound of noisemakers and shouting drowns out the name of Haman each time it is mentioned in the reading of the *Megillah.* Following the reading, festivities take place, including the traditional Purim *seudah,* a meal replete with delicious food and, of course, Hamantashen, the three-cornered filled pastries that are so much a part of this holiday. Special playlets and songs are often written especially for the *seudah,* all with a humorous twist.

One of the nicest customs of Purim is the commandment to send *mishloach manot,* gifts of food and drink, to friends and relatives. A minimum of two portions of food, ready to eat, should be sent to at least one person to fulfill the mitzvah. Hamantashen are often included, and baking, preparing the packages and delivering them are a wonderful activity for the children. It is also a mitzvah to give charity on Purim to help those in need.

As we put away the costumes and finish all the wonderful goodies we have received, a glance at the calendar tells us that we have exactly one month to prepare for another holiday that begins with "P" — Passover!

Tasty Treats for "Mishloach Manot"

Hamantaschen (page 249)
Chocolate Chip Meringue Squares (page 258)
Mandelbread (page 292)
Lemon Bars (page 261)
Viennese Raspberry Bars (page 261)

Passover

No other holiday on the Jewish calendar requires as much preparation as Passover. As soon as Purim is over, Jewish families all over the world plunge into the scrupulous cleaning required for the observance of this eight-day holiday (seven days in Israel). Though not every Jewish family may adhere to all the rules and customs of Passover, it nevertheless remains the most widely observed Jewish holiday. All traces of *chometz* — food substances forbidden on Passover — are removed from the house. These include any products that could ferment or leaven and, in particular, products made from wheat, barley, rye, oats and spelt. Any alcoholic beverages made from fermented grains are also forbidden. There are some differences in permitted foods between Ashkenazic and Sephardic Jews. Stoves, refrigerators, cupboards and closets are scoured and cleaned thoroughly.

Special sets of dishes, silverware, pots and pans and other kitchen utensils especially for the eight days of the holiday are hauled out of their storage spaces. Cupboards bulge with boxes of *matzo*, a specially baked unleavened bread used all week. Favorite foods are cooked, and a general hustle and bustle is felt throughout the house as we approach the 14th of Nisan, usually in late March or early April.

Passover commemorates not only the Hebrews' liberation from slavery in Egypt but also the beginning of their nationhood. On the first two nights of the holiday (in Israel, only one night), we gather with family and friends at a *Seder*, a special ritualistic meal which combines singing, prayers and the reading of the *Haggadah*, a book composed by the Rabbis of old which contains passages from the Torah and the many miracles God performed for our ancestors. A special seder plate containing the symbols of the celebration sits in the center of the table along with the Elijah's Cup and three pieces of matzo. The middle matzo is called the *afikomen* and is hidden during the Seder for the children to find. The youngest child usually asks the Four Questions, meant to stimulate further questions and discussion, since the Seder is supposed to be a learning experience and a time for each of us to feel that we, personally, were brought out of Egypt from slavery to freedom.

Suggested Seder Menu

Bubbie's Gefilte Fish (page 131)
Homemade Horseradish (page 129)
Chicken Soup with Matzo Balls (page 61)
Orange Turkey Breast (page 160)
Potato Kugel (pages 212, 281)
Yummy Yams (page 209)
Flourless Chocolate Cake (page 228)
Caramel Pecan Squares (page 295)

Lag B'Omer

From the second day of Passover until Shavuot, we count the *Omer* — the 49 days between these two holidays. Lag B'Omer is literally the 33rd day of the *Omer*. One of the pleasant things about this holiday is lifting the prohibitions against hair cutting and shaving, entertainment and music and weddings, activities that are forbidden during this period of semi-mourning.

The origins of the holiday are somewhat obscure, but scholars have speculated that it has a military origin, coinciding with some events during the Bar Kochba revolt. In Israel, bonfires are lit and families go on picnics.

Yom Hazikaron/Yom Haatzmaut/ Yom Yerushalayim

Yom Hazikaron, Remembrance Day, is a day on which we memorialize the approximately 14,000 Israelis killed in the various Israeli-Arab wars. At 11 A.M. in Israel all traffic, conversation and business halts for a two-minute period of silence. It is a somber day, always coming the day before we celebrate Israel's independence.

The next day the mood immediately changes to one of jubilation as Israelis especially, and Jews throughout the Diaspora, celebrate Yom Haatzmaut, Israel's Independence Day. On the 5th of Iyar (May 14, 1948), the British Mandate of Palestine ended and the State of Israel was established. After 2,000 years Israel had truly become a Jewish homeland. In Israel there are usually huge parades and much festivity. In the United States communities all over the country sponsor special celebrations with entertainment, dancing, food booths and special services.

Yom Yerushalayim is the newest Jewish holiday. It was declared after Israel recaptured the Old City of Jerusalem in the 1967 Six Day War. Though the armistice agreement at the end of the War of Independence in 1948 provided that Israelis would have access to the Western Wall to pray, this clause had never been honored by Jordan, and Jews had not been allowed to enter the Old City. Jews could now go to the Wall to pray, and the city of Jerusalem was united once again.

Shavuot

For many Jews today, Shavuot is synonymous with the ceremony of Confirmation. Yet its significance is far more important than that modern ritual. As one of the three pilgrimage holidays, Shavuot was originally celebrated as the end of the spring harvest, concluding *sefirat ha omer,* the 49-day period between the second day of Passover and Shavuot. According to tradition, with the exception of Lag B'Omer, which falls during that period, it is a time of semi-mourning during which traditional Jews do not get haircuts or celebrate weddings.

Shavuot is also called the Festival of First Fruits. However, its greatest significance is that it celebrates the most important event in Jewish history — the giving of the Torah. The Talmud teaches us that God gave the Ten Commandments to the Jews on the 6th of Sivan, the first night of Shavuot. To commemorate this event, many Jews gather together in synagogues or private homes for a *tikkun layl shavuot,* an all-night study session, ending in the early morning with the *Shacharit* service. In Israel thousands flock to the *Kotel* (Western Wall) for the morning services. At services in the synagogue it is also the custom to read the Book of Ruth, a beautiful story about a woman with devotion to the Torah and deep affection for her mother-in-law, Naomi.

What would a Jewish holiday be without food? Of course there are culinary traditions associated with Shavuot. In most households it is the custom to serve dairy dishes and blintzes, cheesecake and other rich dairy desserts. With the arrival of spring and a festive atmosphere in homes and synagogues decorated with fruits and flowers, Shavuot is a joyous and welcome holiday.

Suggested Menu for Shavuot

Luscious Lavash (page 30)
Ivory Gazpacho (page 74)
Hearts of Romaine Salad (page 83)
Mango Salsa Salmon (page 122)
Mushroom Quiche (page 113)
Wisconsin Cheesecake (page 224)

Yom Hashoah and Tisha B'Av

Yom Hashoah and Tisha B'Av commemorate many of the saddest periods in Jewish history. Sometime between mid-April and early May, on the 27th of Nisan, Yom Hashoah — Holocaust Remembrance Day — is observed. This date was set by the Israeli Knesset, and in that country at 11:00 A.M. sirens are sounded, individuals stop what they are doing, traffic halts and everyone stands at attention. In the United States, many synagogues have established special prayer and memorial services, and special speakers who are often Holocaust survivors participate. Holocaust memorials have been erected as a continuing reminder of the greatest Jewish tragedy of modern times.

In 586 B.C.E., on the 9th of Av, the Babylonians destroyed the First Temple, and on that same day in 70 C.E. the Romans burned down the Second Temple. Three weeks prior to the 9th of Av in 70 C.E. the Romans breached the walls of Jerusalem and destroyed the city. For this reason, the three weeks leading up to Tisha B'Av are observed as a time of mourning and weddings are prohibited. During the last nine days of this three-week period, the spirit of mourning is heightened and Jews do not cut their hair, shave or drink wine. They eat no meat except on Shabbat. The observance of Tisha B'Av concludes with a daylong fast and synagogue services during which *Eicha* (Lamentations) is read while participants sit in a darkened atmosphere on low stools or the floor. During the fast, it is forbidden to bathe, wear perfume or leather shoes or participate in any other normal activities that are not permitted during a period of mourning.

Appetizers,
Relishes
&
Beverages

Quick Appetizer Tips

◆ Layer cream cheese, lox and minced red onion on flour tortilla. Roll tightly and slice in 1-inch pieces to make spirals.

◆ Use flavored yogurt as a dip for fresh fruit.

◆ Mix flaked leftover fish or smoked fish with mayonnaise, chopped celery and relish. Serve with crackers.

◆ Mash sardines with mustard and ketchup. Serve with crackers.

◆ Pour bottled salsa over softened cream cheese and serve with crackers.

◆ Instead of crackers, you can use cucumber slices, celery, endive spears or apple slices.

◆ Make a quick trail mix with nuts, soy nuts, dried cranberries, mini chocolate chips, cherries or other dried fruits, and sunflower seeds.

◆ For a quick vegetable dip, use 1 cup mayonnaise and curry powder to taste. Serve with cooked cold artichokes or raw vegetables.

◆ Spray corn tortillas lightly with nonstick vegetable oil spray. Cut into wedges and bake at 350° until crispy, about 10 minutes. Sprinkle with salt.

Beef Teriyaki Satay *(Meat)*

1	pound boneless steak, 1-inch thick	2	tablespoons sugar
1	(13½-ounce) can pineapple tidbits, drained (reserve syrup)	1	tablespoon cooking sherry
¼	cup pineapple syrup	¼	teaspoon ground ginger
¼	cup soy sauce	1	clove garlic, minced
			Small skewers

- ◆ Slice meat into strips, 3 inches by ⅛ inch.
- ◆ In a deep bowl combine syrup with remaining ingredients except pineapple. Mix well.
- ◆ Add meat and stir to coat. Marinate for 1 hour in refrigerator.
- ◆ Lace meat loosely in accordion style on small skewers, threading pineapple as you weave in and out. Broil to desired doneness, turning to brown all sides.

Yield: *8 to 10 servings*

Sweet-Sour Meatballs *(Meat)*

2	pounds ground meat	½	cup water
	Oil	¼	cup lemon juice
1	(11-ounce) can tomato mushroom sauce	½	cup sugar
		1	onion, chopped fine

- ◆ Form meat into balls. Brown in a skillet in oil; set aside.
- ◆ Mix remaining ingredients in a 3-quart pot; bring to a boil. Drop meatballs into hot sauce. Simmer for 1 hour.

Yield: *10 to 12 servings*

Oriental Wings *(Meat)*

3	pounds chicken wings	¼	teaspoon pepper
½	cup sugar	¾	cup water
3	tablespoons cornstarch	⅓	cup lemon juice
1	teaspoon salt	¼	cup soy sauce
½	teaspoon ground ginger		

♦ Preheat oven to 400°. Cut off wing tips and discard. Divide each wing in half by cutting through the joint with a sharp knife or poultry shears. Place in a single layer on a rack in a broiler pan and bake for 30 minutes, turning once. Drain fat.

♦ Mix sugar, cornstarch, salt, ginger and pepper in a small saucepan. Stir in water, lemon juice and soy sauce. Cook, stirring constantly until mixture thickens and boils for 3 minutes. Brush part of the sauce over the chicken wings. Continue baking, turning and brushing several times with mixture for 40 minutes, or until richly glazed. Serve hot.

Yield: *12 servings*

Note: *You may microwave sauce on high until bubbly, then microwave at half the power for 3 minutes until thickened.*

Mock Chopped Liver *(Parve)*

3	eggs, hard-boiled and peeled	2½	cups fresh green beans
	Oil	¼	cup chopped walnuts
3	small onions, sliced		Pinch of salt and pepper

♦ Set eggs aside in refrigerator to cool for 1 hour.

♦ Cover bottom of small skillet with oil. Heat oil and sauté onions until tender.

♦ Steam or boil green beans until soft. Set aside to cool to room temperature.

♦ Blend all ingredients in food processor. Mash together in a mixing bowl with a fork. Add salt and pepper. Refrigerate for at least 2 hours before serving.

Yield: *2 cups*

Mom's Chopped Liver *(Meat)*

L'dor V'dor — *"From generation to generation"*

2 pounds beef liver	½ cup water
1 pound calf's liver	1 tablespoon sugar
Salt and pepper to taste	6 extra large eggs, hard-boiled
½ cup margarine	and peeled
3 extra large onions, quartered	2 medium carrots, peeled

- ◆ Lightly salt and pepper liver and broil until cooked through, but not overdone. Let cool.
- ◆ Melt margarine in skillet with cover.
- ◆ Separate onions into pieces and add to margarine. When onions begin to cook, add water, sugar and a little salt and pepper. Cover and steam until onions become translucent.
- ◆ Cut eggs into quarters.
- ◆ Peel and divide cooled liver and tear into small pieces to go through grinder.
- ◆ Grind liver, hard-boiled eggs, and onions with liquid. Be sure to grind liver, then eggs, then liver, then onion mixture, then liver, in that order. (If you grind onions and eggs in succession it will splatter.) Finish by grinding carrots to clean grinder and add more color and taste to the dish.
- ◆ Add more sugar, salt and pepper to taste.
- ◆ Serve with rye bread, matzo or crackers.

Yield: *12 servings*

Note: *A food processor with chopping blade may be used instead of grinder.*

Vegetarian Chopped Liver *(Parve)*

The secret is peas.

1	tablespoon oil (or vegetable spray)	1	(15-ounce) can baby peas, drained
1	large white onion, chopped		Salt and pepper to taste
1	cup walnuts		

- ◆ Sauté chopped onion in pan.
- ◆ Place walnuts in food processor and chop very well. Add drained peas and sautéed onions. Combine in processor until well blended. Add salt and pepper to taste.
- ◆ Place in covered container and refrigerate for several hours or overnight.
- ◆ Serve with crackers, bread or pita.

Yield: *8 servings*

Egg Salad Spread *(Parve)*

12	eggs, hard-boiled and peeled	1	bunch scallions, chopped
¾	cup mayonnaise, divided	1	(2-ounce) can sliced black olives
	Salt, pepper, lemon pepper, to taste	1	(14-ounce) jar artichoke hearts, chopped fine
1	(2-ounce) jar black caviar (optional)		Paprika, for garnish

- ◆ Chop eggs. Make egg salad using ½ cup mayonnaise, salt, pepper and lemon pepper.
- ◆ Spray a round or oblong dish with vegetable spray and place egg salad in it. Place in refrigerator to mold several hours or overnight.
- ◆ Unmold egg salad on a plate and layer top with caviar, scallions, olives and artichokes. Cover with thin layer of mayonnaise and sprinkle with paprika.
- ◆ Refrigerate until ready to serve. Serve with cocktail rye or crackers.

Yield: *20 appetizer servings*

Note: *Leftovers make great sandwiches.*

Tuna Antipasto *(Parve)*

Guests can't stop eating this one!

3	(6-ounce) cans white albacore tuna in water, rinsed and drained	1	(6-ounce) jar marinated artichokes, rinsed, drained and cut up
1	(4-ounce) jar sliced mushrooms, rinsed and drained	6	baby carrots, sliced
		½	cup midget gherkin sweet pickles, sliced
1	(2-ounce) can sliced black olives, rinsed and drained	¾	cup chili sauce
⅓	cup pimiento-stuffed green olives, sliced	½	cup ketchup
		1	teaspoon prepared horseradish, or to taste
		1	tablespoon lemon juice

◆ In a large bowl, break up tuna with a fork. Add mushrooms, black and green olives, artichokes, carrots and pickles.

◆ In a separate bowl, combine remaining ingredients; add to tuna mixture and refrigerate.

◆ Serve on crackers, pita or cocktail rye bread.

Yield: *12 servings*

Note: *This recipe may be prepared a day ahead.*

Oven-Roasted Garlic *(Parve)*

4	medium garlic heads	12	ounces water
¼	cup olive oil		

◆ Preheat oven to 350°. Using a sharp knife, remove the top of the garlic head to expose inner cloves. Brush heads with olive oil and place in a shallow casserole. Fill dish with 1 inch of water and cover.

◆ Bake for 45 to 60 minutes until garlic is soft and light brown. Check garlic for softness, since oven temperature may vary.

◆ Serve with crusty bread. Remove the garlic from its skin with a knife and spread onto bread.

Yield: *8 servings*

Mediterranean Tapenade *(Parve)*

1	pound eggplant, halved lengthwise	2	ounces sliced pimientos, rinsed and drained
1	(15-ounce) can garbanzo beans, drained	2	tablespoons chopped parsley
¼	cup olive oil	2	teaspoons chopped garlic
10	ounces pimiento-stuffed green olives, rinsed and drained	1	teaspoon chopped fresh rosemary
			Salt and pepper, to taste

◆ Preheat oven to 450°. Place eggplant cut side down on greased baking sheet. Roast until soft, about 35 minutes. Allow to cool.

◆ Scrape pulp into food processor. Add garbanzo beans and oil to processor and purée until smooth.

◆ Transfer to a medium bowl. Add remaining ingredients to processor and coarsely chop.

◆ Combine olive and eggplant mixtures. Season with salt and pepper, if necessary.

◆ Serve with breadsticks or crackers.

Yield: *12 to 15 servings*

Olive Tapenade *(Parve)*

1	(6-ounce) can niçoise or Greek pitted olives, drained	4	tablespoons fresh chopped parsley, no stems
1	(6-ounce) can green pitted olives, drained	2	tablespoons extra virgin olive oil
1	tablespoon chopped garlic		

◆ Place olives in food processor and process until fine.

◆ Mix chopped olives with the other ingredients and place in the refrigerator for a few hours or overnight.

◆ Serve at room temperature with crackers, toasted French bread or toasted pita.

Yield: *12 servings*

Note: *You may also hand chop olives if a food processor is not available. Tapenade keeps about a week.*

Bruschetta *(Parve)*

3	large ripe tomatoes, peeled, seeded and cut up		Freshly ground black pepper
½	large red onion, diced	¼	cup extra virgin olive oil, and additional oil for brushing
1	cucumber, peeled, seeded and diced	1	tablespoon red wine vinegar
1	cup fresh basil leaves, shredded	1	baguette
	Coarse salt	2-3	peeled garlic cloves, for rubbing

◆ To peel tomatoes, cut out core on one end. On other end make an 'X' with a sharp knife. Plunge into boiling water for about 30 seconds. With slotted spoon, remove tomato from water and slip off skin under cold running water. To remove seeds, cut tomatoes in half and squeeze gently in palm of hand.

◆ In a large bowl, combine tomatoes, onions, cucumbers, and basil. Season lightly with salt and pepper.

◆ Add olive oil and vinegar; toss well to combine. Let stand at room temperature for at least 1 hour, but no longer than 3.

◆ Preheat broiler or grill pan.

◆ Cut baguette diagonally into ½-inch-thick slices. Brush both sides lightly with olive oil. Grill or broil on both sides until toasted. Rub garlic cloves over warm bread slices.

◆ Put a spoonful of tomato mixture over bread and let sit for 15 minutes before serving.

Yield: *8 to 12 servings*

Note: *You may use a drained 14½-ounce can of diced tomatoes instead of fresh tomatoes.*

Luscious Lavash *(Dairy)*

1	sheet lavash	½	pound fresh mushrooms, sliced
½	pound Havarti or Fontina cheese		

- ◆ Preheat broiler. Place lavash on ungreased cookie sheet. Cut cheese into pieces and place all over the lavash. Scatter mushrooms over the cheese.
- ◆ Broil until cheese is well melted. Remove from oven and cut crosswise into squares to serve.

Yield: *6 servings*

Note: *Lavash is a large, round Syrian flat bread the consistency of a cracker.*

Hummus *(Parve)*

An Israeli staple.

1	(15-ounce) can garbanzo beans, drained		Pinch salt
	Juice of 1 lemon	¼	teaspoon cumin (optional)
3	tablespoons tahini	1	tablespoon chopped parsley
2-3	cloves garlic, crushed		Paprika

- ◆ Place beans, lemon juice, tahini, garlic, salt and cumin in blender or food processor. Blend to a creamy paste. If paste seems too thick, add lemon juice to thin it to the consistency of a creamy mayonnaise.
- ◆ Decorate the dish with chopped parsley and paprika.
- ◆ Serve with pita bread or raw vegetables.

Yield: *8 to 10 servings*

Note: *Tahini (crushed sesame seeds) may be found in the ethnic section of the grocery store.*

Mediterranean Olive Oil Dip *(Parve)*

Better than butter!

1	large tomato, peeled, seeded, and chopped	2	cloves garlic, minced
½	cup light virgin olive oil	1	teaspoon chopped fresh basil

◆ To peel and seed tomato, see Bruschetta recipe.

◆ Combine all ingredients in small bowl. Dip or spoon onto fresh Italian bread.

Yield: *6 to 8 servings*

Caponata *(Parve)*

2	large eggplants	3	ribs celery, diced
¾	cup olive oil	¼	cup capers
2	onions, chopped	½	cup pine nuts
3	cloves garlic, crushed	¼	cup red wine vinegar
1	(20-ounce) can plum tomatoes, chopped	2	tablespoons sugar
1	(6-ounce) can pitted black olives, drained and chopped		Salt and pepper to taste

◆ Wash and cube unpeeled eggplant. Sauté in oil until soft. Remove and set aside. Sauté onions and garlic in same oil. Add tomatoes, olives and celery. Cook until celery is tender, 15 minutes. Add eggplant, capers and pine nuts.

◆ In another pan heat vinegar and sugar until dissolved. Pour over eggplant mixture. Season to taste and cook, uncovered, an additional 20 minutes.

◆ Serve hot or cold as relish with dinner or on French bread rounds as cocktail dish.

Yield: *20 servings*

Baba Ghanoush *(Parve)*

1	medium eggplant	½	teaspoon pepper
	(approximately 1 pound)	2	tablespoons tahini or 1 to
2	tablespoons lemon juice		2 tablespoons mayonnaise
1	clove garlic, crushed		Parsley for garnish
½	teaspoon salt		

◆ Preheat oven to 450°. Rinse and dry eggplant. Prick skin with a fork in several places. Place in roasting pan and roast for 40 minutes, turning every 10 minutes so all sides become tender. Remove from oven, cool, slit skin with fork and scoop out flesh into a bowl.

◆ Add lemon juice, garlic, salt and pepper and mash well. Add tahini or mayonnaise and blend well.

◆ Place in serving dish, garnish with parsley and refrigerate until ready to serve. Serve with pita.

Yield: *6 to 8 servings*

Marinated Eggplant *(Parve)*

1	red pepper, cored and seeded	1	tablespoon white wine vinegar
3	medium eggplants		Pinch of salt
	Oil	½	teaspoon sugar, or to taste
15	cloves garlic, minced	1	tablespoon chopped parsley
	Juice of 3 lemons		for garnish
3	tablespoons olive oil		

◆ Cut red pepper and unpeeled eggplants into strips.

◆ Stir-fry eggplant in oil in wok until soft. Stir-fry red pepper.

◆ Mix garlic, lemon juice, olive oil, vinegar, salt, and sugar. Pour over eggplant and pepper mixture and chill.

◆ Garnish with parsley.

Yield: *20 servings*

Stuffed Grape Leaves *(Parve)*

50 grape leaves, fresh or in jar in
    brine
1   tablespoon water
4   medium onions, chopped
1   tablespoon olive oil
⅔   cup uncooked rice, or instant
    rice

Salt and pepper to taste
1   cup fresh parsley or cilantro,
    chopped
    Juice of 1 lemon
1   cup water

◆ Preheat oven to 350°. Wash leaves thoroughly.

◆ For fresh leaves, microwave for 3 minutes on medium with 1
  tablespoon water.

◆ Sauté onions in oil. Mix with rice, salt and pepper, and parsley or
  cilantro.

◆ Put 1 teaspoon of mixture on a leaf and roll, sealing the sides. Place in
  a 9x13-inch shallow oven dish sprayed with vegetable spray. Add
  lemon juice and water. Cover and bake for 1 hour.

Yield: *12 servings*

Note: *This recipe freezes well. Serve hot or cold. For variety you may add
chopped meat to mixture and serve as a main dish.*

Herring with Cranberries *(Dairy)*

Easy and delicious!

1   (12-ounce) jar herring in wine
    sauce
1   cup regular or low-fat sour
    cream

⅓   cup whole cranberry sauce
1   large sweet onion, sliced thin
    and separated

◆ Drain herring. Cut into small pieces. Mix remaining ingredients with
  herring.

◆ Refrigerate for several hours or overnight. Serve with party rye bread.

Yield: *6 servings*

Herring Salad *(Dairy)*

1	cup sour cream	1	(6-ounce) can sliced black olives, drained and rinsed
½	cup mayonnaise		
1	tablespoon celery seed	¾	(5-ounce) jar stuffed olives, sliced and rinsed
2	tablespoons lemon juice		
¼	cup sugar	2	carrots, finely grated
1	large green pepper, sliced thin	1	(22-ounce) jar herring in wine sauce, drained, rinsed and cut in ½-inch pieces
2	onions, sliced thin		

◆ Mix together sour cream, mayonnaise, celery seed, lemon juice and sugar. Add remaining ingredients to dressing and toss. Refrigerate.

Yield: *20 servings*

Note: *Lasts for several weeks.*

Deluxe Herring Appetizer *(Dairy)*

A herring lover's treat!

2	cups marinated herring in wine sauce	¼	small bell pepper, cored, seeded and cut into pieces (optional)
1	small red onion, peeled and sliced thin		
		1	cup sour cream
1	medium red Delicious apple or Granny Smith, unpeeled, cored and cubed	4	tablespoons sugar, or to taste

◆ Drain herring well; rinse with cold water. Discard all peppercorns and onions in herring. Squeeze out all liquid from herring and cut into bite-size pieces.

◆ Add red onion and apple. Add bell pepper.

◆ Mix sour cream and sugar together. Pour over herring mixture. Mix well and refrigerate overnight in a glass container.

Yield: *12 to 14 servings*

Chopped Herring *(Parve)*

1	(12-ounce) jar herring in wine sauce	3	eggs, hard-boiled, divided
1	slice rye bread or challah	2	apples, peeled and cored

◆ Drain herring thoroughly, saving liquid. Rinse herring. Dip bread in wine liquid.

◆ Chop herring, 2 eggs, apples and bread until well mixed. Grate remaining egg over top of herring for garnish.

◆ Serve with cocktail bread or rye crackers.

Yield: *10 to 12 servings*

Brie en Croûte *(Dairy)*

An elegant beginning.

1	(10-ounce) package prepared puff pastry	4	ounces slivered almonds or pecan halves
1	(2-pound) wheel Brie cheese	4	ounces seedless raspberry jam, or apricot jam
2	tablespoons Dijon mustard		
1	egg, beaten		

◆ Divide pastry in half and roll into 2 circles, 1 inch larger than the diameter of the cheese.

◆ Spread Dijon mustard lightly over cheese. Place the cheese on one circle of pastry and cover with the second piece. Seal edges and cut off excess. Brush outside of pastry with egg and decorate with almonds or pecan halves.

◆ Refrigerate for 30 minutes or until ready to bake.

◆ Preheat oven to 425°. Bake on a buttered quiche dish or 10-inch pie plate for 25 to 30 minutes or until puffed and brown. Let set 30 minutes before serving.

◆ Melt jam in a saucepan or in microwave and pour around the perimeter of the cheese.

◆ Serve with water crackers and assorted fruits.

Yield: *20 servings*

Artichoke Dip *(Dairy)*

1 (14-ounce) can quartered artichoke hearts, drained	¾-1 cup shredded Parmesan cheese
1 cup low-fat mayonnaise	1-2 teaspoons lemon juice
	1 clove garlic, minced

- ◆ Preheat oven to 350°. Cut up artichokes. Mix with remaining ingredients.
- ◆ Place in a glass baking dish. Bake for 30 minutes. (This recipe may also be prepared in an electric skillet at 200°.) Serve hot with crackers.

Yield: *8 to 10 servings*

Note: *As a variation, you may eliminate the lemon juice and garlic. Instead, add ½ teaspoon Dijon mustard and ¼ teaspoon grated onion. Layer artichokes in bottom of pan and spread mixture evenly over top. Bake 15 to 20 minutes at 350°.*

Spinach Dip *(Dairy)*

An oldie but a goodie!

2 (10-ounce) packages frozen chopped spinach, thawed and drained	1 (1-ounce) package ranch dressing mix
2 cups light sour cream	4-6 green onions with tops, chopped
1 cup mayonnaise	Garlic powder to taste

- ◆ Combine all ingredients in a bowl. Refrigerate several hours or overnight. Serve with raw vegetables.

Yield: 10 to 15 servings

Spinach Artichoke Dip *(Dairy)*

12	ounces marinated artichoke hearts, drained and chopped	1	cup freshly grated Parmesan
10	ounces frozen chopped spinach, thawed and well drained	1¼	cups coarsely grated Monterey Jack cheese, divided
1	cup mayonnaise	2	medium cloves garlic, crushed

◆ Preheat oven to 350°. Combine all ingredients, reserving ¼ cup Monterey Jack cheese, and place in 1½-quart baking dish. Sprinkle with remaining Monterey Jack.

◆ Bake dip in middle of oven until cheese is melted, about 15 minutes. If you want cheese to brown, broil for a few minutes.

◆ Serve warm with chips or crackers.

Yield: *4 servings*

Note: *Dip may be prepared 1 day ahead and chilled, covered, before baking.*

Taco Dip *(Dairy)*

A sure crowd pleaser.

2	(8-ounce) packages cream cheese, softened	2	green onions with greens, chopped
1	(16-ounce) package creamed cottage cheese	1	medium tomato, chopped
1	(1-ounce) package taco seasoning mix	4	ounces shredded cheddar cheese
½	head iceberg lettuce, shredded		Black olives, sliced (optional)

◆ Mix cream cheese, cottage cheese and taco mix in blender.

◆ Spread on bottom of a 9x13-inch, flat nonmetal baking dish or a quiche dish.

◆ Chill in dish for 1 hour. Top with shredded lettuce, green onion, tomato and cheese. Add olives if desired.

◆ Serve with taco chips.

Yield: *12 servings*

Creamy Salmon Dip *(Dairy)*

½ cup slivered almonds, toasted
2 (8-ounce) packages cream cheese, at room temperature
½ cup sour cream
¼ cup mayonnaise
2 tablespoons white wine or cream
2 tablespoons grated onion
1 tablespoon Dijon mustard
1 teaspoon minced fresh garlic
3 drops hot pepper sauce, or to taste
1 (6½-ounce) can boneless salmon, drained and flaked
½ cup minced fresh parsley, divided
   Paprika

◆ To toast almonds, place in nonstick skillet over medium heat for 2 to 4 minutes, stirring constantly until lightly browned.

◆ Mix cream cheese, sour cream, mayonnaise, wine, onion, mustard, garlic and hot pepper sauce in medium saucepan.

◆ Fold in salmon and ¼ cup parsley. Warm over medium heat, stirring constantly, just until hot; do not boil.

◆ Spoon into warm chafing dish or serving dish; sprinkle with remaining parsley, almonds and paprika.

◆ Serve with crackers.

Yield: *4 cups*

Short-Cut Guacamole *(Parve)*

2 ripe avocados, peeled, pitted and mashed
1-2 tablespoons prepared chunky salsa
2 green onions with tops, chopped
   Salt to taste
1 drop liquid red pepper (optional)
   Garlic powder to taste (optional)

◆ Combine all ingredients. Serve with chips.

Yield: *4 to 6 servings*

Guacamole *(Parve)*

3	ripe avocados, peeled, pitted and mashed	2	green onions with tops, chopped
1	tablespoon lemon juice		Salt to taste
1	small tomato, seeds removed	1-2	drops liquid red pepper (optional)

◆ Blend all ingredients in food processor or mix by hand. If preparing ahead, place avocado pit on top, cover and refrigerate. Remove pit before serving.

◆ Serve with taco chips or pita bread.

Yield: 8 to 10 servings

Tex-Mex Dip *(Dairy)*

2	(11-ounce) cans of corn with red and green peppers, drained	1	(16-ounce) container sour cream
1-2	(4-ounce) cans chopped green chilies	8	ounces shredded Monterey Jack or cheddar cheese
½	(3-ounce) can chopped jalapeños	1	teaspoon chili powder
		1	teaspoon garlic powder
		3	chopped green onions, or to taste

◆ Mix together all ingredients and chill for a few hours. Serve with chips.

Yield: *10 to 12 servings*

Note: *If you use canned whole jalapeños, carefully discard seeds before chopping.*

Tropical Salsa *(Parve)*

This is also great as a relish with meat or poultry.

1	cup chopped fresh pineapple or crushed, drained	¼	cup chopped cilantro, basil or dill
1	cup chopped cantaloupe or mango	¼	cup red wine or balsamic vinegar
½	cup chopped red onion	½-1	teaspoon Tabasco sauce (optional)
1	cup chopped red pepper	1	teaspoon salt
1	tomato, chopped		

◆ Combine all ingredients in a medium bowl. Mix well. Marinate in the refrigerator for several hours before serving.

◆ Serve with tortilla chips.

Yield: *12 to 15 servings*

Note: *May be made a day ahead. Store all ingredients separately in refrigerator and combine several hours before serving. Be sure to drain excess juice before combining.*

Refrigerator Pickles *(Parve)*

1	cup white vinegar	7	cups sliced, unpeeled cucumbers
1	cup sugar		
1	tablespoon salt	1	onion, sliced
1	teaspoon celery seed	2	sweet peppers, sliced
1	teaspoon turmeric		Celery and carrots (optional)

◆ Bring vinegar, sugar, salt, celery seed and turmeric to a boil. Pour the boiling liquid over the remaining ingredients and store in refrigerator in covered container.

Yield: *6 cups*

Note: *They'll keep as long as they're refrigerated.*

Peppers in Oil and Vinegar *(Parve)*

4-5	large red peppers, cored, seeded, cut in half lengthwise	½	cup sugar
		1	teaspoon salt
		¼	cup oil
1	cup white vinegar	2	tablespoons chopped garlic
½	cup cold water		

◆ Preheat broiler. Place peppers, cut side down, on baking sheet. Make small slit in each end of pepper, press flat and broil about 4 inches from heating element until charred.

◆ Place in paper bag to cool, approximately 15 minutes.

◆ Slip skin off peppers. Cut each pepper into 6 julienne pieces.

◆ Mix remaining ingredients.

◆ Place peppers in jar and fill with liquid.

Yield: *12 servings*

Note: *This may be made up to 1 month ahead. Store in refrigerator in tightly covered jar.*

Dill Pickles *(Parve)*

12	(½ gallon) jars with canning lids	60	cloves garlic, peeled
150	large pickling cucumbers	1	cup coarse kosher salt
100	small pickling cucumbers	1	cup pickling spices
24	stalks dill		Water

◆ Scald clean jars.

◆ Fill each jar with 2 stalks dill, 4 to 5 cloves garlic, 4 teaspoons salt and 1 tablespoon spices.

◆ Pack jar with pickles, using small pickles for small spaces, but do not pack too tightly or pickles will become soft.

◆ Fill jars with water, leaving about 1 inch at top. Wet lids in hot water and put on jars. Be sure rims on jars are dry. Tighten rings and turn jars upside down overnight. Tighten any covers that leaked. Store in a cool, dry place.

Yield: *12 jars*

Hot Spiced Cider *(Parve)*

A Committee Favorite!

2	cups apple cider	2	cinnamon sticks
½	lemon, sliced thin	1	can sugar-free ginger ale
½	orange, sliced thin		

- ◆ Combine all ingredients except ginger ale in medium saucepan. Cover and simmer over low heat for 15 minutes.
- ◆ Add ginger ale and heat 5 minutes longer.
- ◆ Remove fruit and cinnamon sticks and serve warm.

Yield: *2 to 3 servings*

Mulled Wine Punch *(Parve)*

1	gallon apple cider	3	slices lemon
1	quart dry red wine	½	cup orange juice
¼	pound brown sugar	1	cup raisins
2	sticks cinnamon	1	cup almonds
6	cloves		

- ◆ Mix all ingredients together in a large pot and let simmer for 30 minutes.

Yield: *20 servings*

Sparkling Fruit Punch *(Parve)*

2	(48-ounce) cans grapefruit juice, chilled	4	liters lemon-lime soda, chilled
1	(48-ounce) can pineapple juice, chilled	1	(12-ounce) can frozen orange juice concentrate, thawed

- ◆ In a large punch bowl, mix all ingredients.

Yield: *25 to 30 servings*

Note: *You may add a decorative ice ring, made in a ring mold with canned fruit and water or sherbet.*

Strawberry-Banana Smoothie *(Parve)*

2	cups strawberries (frozen or fresh)	1½	cups cranberry juice
2	peeled bananas	1	cup crushed ice

◆ Combine first 3 ingredients in blender and blend until smooth.
◆ Add crushed ice and process again.

Yield: *2 servings*

Tropical Paradise *(Parve)*

½	cup pineapple juice	½	peeled kiwi
½	cup orange juice	6	ice cubes, crushed
½	ripe banana		

◆ Combine fruits and juices in blender. Add crushed ice and blend.

Yield: *2 servings*

Orange Freeze *(Dairy)*

1	(6-ounce) can frozen orange juice concentrate, not thawed	2	cups milk
		¼	cup sugar
		8-10	ice cubes

◆ Combine all ingredients in blender and blend at high speed until mixed.
◆ Serve immediately.

Yield: *4 servings*

Quick Fruit Smoothie *(Dairy)*

2   cups orange juice
1½ cups frozen unsweetened fruit
    (any variety)

2   cups nonfat vanilla yogurt

◆ Blend orange juice and fruit in blender until fruit is well chopped, about 8 seconds on liquefy.
◆ Add yogurt and blend until smooth.

Yield: *6 servings*

Sunshine Shake *(Dairy)*

1   cup orange sherbet or frozen
    yogurt
1   cup strawberries
    (fresh or frozen)

1⅓ cups pineapple chunks
1½ cups club soda

◆ Combine first three ingredients in blender and process until smooth.
◆ Add club soda and process again.

Yield: *2 to 3 servings*

Breads

Bread Basics

- 1 ounce compressed cake yeast = 1 envelope active dry yeast or 2¼ to 2½ teaspoons of active dry yeast

- Keep all yeast in the refrigerator to assure freshness.

- Cake yeast takes longer to rise than dry yeast.

- Dry yeast should be dissolved in water at 100° to 115° on a candy or yeast thermometer. Add ¼ teaspoon sugar per package.

- Cake yeast should be dissolved in 80° to 90° water. To determine if yeast is active, add a pinch of sugar once yeast is in water and watch for bubbles.

- Rapid rise yeast rises ⅓ faster than active dry yeast. It may be added directly to the flour rather than to the liquid.

- Dough rises faster in a warm place. Turn oven on to lowest temperature for 1 minute; then turn it off. Cover the dough with a cloth and put it in the oven to rise for about 1 to 1½ hours until doubled. Dough is ready if indentations remain when touched.

- Baking powder can make or break a recipe. To test for freshness of baking powder, put 1 teaspoon in about ½ cup of hot water. If it bubbles vigorously, it is alive and well.

Heavenly Challah *(Parve)*

3	packages dry yeast	½	cup oil
2	cups warm water (100° - 110°)	7-8	cups flour
⅔-¾	cup sugar		Egg glaze (1 egg mixed with
3	eggs		1 teaspoon water)
2	teaspoons salt		

◆ Blend yeast with water; add sugar. Let sit for 10 to 15 minutes until very foamy.

◆ In electric mixer combine eggs, salt and oil with yeast mixture. Blend well. Add 4 cups of flour and mix well again. Switch to the dough hook and slowly add 3 to 4 cups flour. Knead until smooth and elastic, about 3 to 4 minutes. Cover and let rise for 40 minutes.

◆ Punch down and knead for 1 to 2 minutes. Divide into 4 loaves and braid each. Place on lightly greased cookie sheet and cover. Allow to rise for 30 minutes.

◆ Preheat oven to 325°. Brush with egg glaze and sprinkle with sesame or poppy seeds. Bake 20 to 25 minutes.

Yield: *4 loaves*

Eggless Challah *(Parve)*

9	cups flour	1-2	teaspoons salt
3	packages active dry yeast	½	cup oil
½	cup sugar	3½	cups very warm water

◆ Combine 5 cups flour, yeast, sugar and salt; mix in oil and water. Gradually add the remaining flour and mix.

◆ Knead dough on floured board for about 10 minutes, adding flour if necessary. Place dough in greased bowl, turning to grease top. Cover and let rise until doubled.

◆ Knead again. Divide into 4 pieces. Cover and let rise for 10 minutes.

◆ Divide each piece into 3 parts and braid. Place braided loaves on greased baking sheet and let rise for 30 minutes. Brush loaves with water.

◆ Preheat oven to 350°. Bake for 30 to 35 minutes until golden.

Yield: *4 loaves*

Challah *(Parve)*

A delicious and easy recipe — even for a novice bread baker.

1	cup warm water, divided	½	cup oil
1	envelope active dry yeast	2	teaspoons salt
½	cup sugar plus 1 tablespoon, divided	1	egg yolk
4	cups flour, divided	1	teaspoon water
3	eggs		Sesame or poppy seeds (optional)

◆ Rinse bowl with hot water. Put ½ cup warm water in bowl. Sprinkle yeast and 1 tablespoon sugar on top of water. Let sit for 10 minutes.

◆ Add 2 cups flour, eggs, ½ cup sugar, water, oil and salt. Mix well. Add remaining 2 cups flour and mix. Let sit for 10 minutes. Knead for 10 minutes until smooth and elastic, adding flour if needed.

◆ Place dough in greased bowl, turning to grease top. Cover with moist towel or plastic wrap and let rise until doubled (about 1 hour). Punch down, cover and let rise again (1 hour).

◆ Divide dough in half and divide each half into thirds for braiding. Pinch the 3 pieces together and braid normally. Place braided loaves on a greased baking sheet. Cover and let rise again (1 hour) until almost doubled in size.

◆ Mix egg yolk with water and brush over bread. Sprinkle with seeds if desired.

◆ Preheat oven to 350°. Bake for 30 to 35 minutes until golden. Let cool on wire rack.

Yield: *2 loaves*

Raisin Challah *(Parve)*

◆ Using recipe for challah above, add 1 cup golden or dark raisins to second 2 cups of flour before mixing into dough mixture. Follow instructions as above.

◆ To make a round challah for Rosh Hashanah, make a long roll and swirl into a round form ending on top for each loaf. Tuck in the ends.

◆ Bake as above.

Yield: *2 loaves*

Herbed Wheat Germ Bread *(Parve or Dairy)*

5½-6½	cups flour	½	cup water
2	envelopes active dry yeast	½	cup margarine
⅓	cup sugar	2	eggs, room temperature
1	teaspoon salt	1	egg, separated
1	teaspoon thyme	1⅓	cups wheat germ
1	teaspoon marjoram	1	tablespoon wheat germ
1½	cups milk or nondairy creamer		

- ◆ Combine 3 cups flour, yeast, sugar, salt and herbs in large mixing bowl. Mix well.
- ◆ In saucepan, heat milk (or nondairy substitute), water and margarine until warm. Add to flour.
- ◆ Add whole eggs and separated yolk. Blend at slow speed until moistened. Beat for 3 minutes at medium speed.
- ◆ Gradually stir in 1⅓ cups of wheat germ and enough remaining flour to make a soft dough. Knead for approximately 10 minutes.
- ◆ Place in greased bowl and turn to grease top. Cover and let rise until doubled, approximately 1 hour.
- ◆ Punch down. Divide into 2 parts. Roll or pat each part into an 8x12-inch rectangle.
- ◆ Cut each rectangle into two 4-inch strips. Twist 2 strips together and place in a well-greased 4x8½x2⅝-inch pan. Repeat for second rectangle in a second pan. Cover; let rise until doubled, about 30 to 40 minutes.
- ◆ Preheat oven to 350°. Brush with egg white and sprinkle with wheat germ.
- ◆ Bake for 35 to 45 minutes. Cover with foil for last 5 to 10 minutes. Remove from pans and cool on a rack.

Yield: *2 loaves*

Walnut Bread *(Parve)*

3	cups flour	3	tablespoons oil
½	cup whole wheat flour	1¼	cups very warm water
¼	cup brown sugar	1½	cups chopped walnuts
1	envelope rapid-rise dry yeast	1	egg
1	teaspoon salt	½	teaspoon salt

◆ **Traditional Method:** Combine flours, brown sugar, yeast and 1 teaspoon salt. Add oil and water, stirring to combine.

◆ On lightly floured board, knead dough until smooth and elastic. Knead walnuts into dough. Shape dough into a ball.

◆ Put the dough into an oiled bowl and turn to coat. Cover and let rise until doubled (about 1 hour).

◆ Punch down on floured board and shape into round loaf. Place on greased baking sheet. Cover and let rise again until doubled.

◆ Preheat oven to 400°. Slash top with an "X". Mix egg with salt and brush on loaf. Bake for about 35 minutes or until the loaf is brown and sounds hollow when tapped.

◆ **Processor Method:** Mix brown sugar, yeast and water. Combine 2½ cups flour with whole wheat flour, oil and salt in work bowl. With machine running, pour liquid through feed tube and blend for about 40 seconds. Dough should be uniform and elastic. If dough is too wet, add up to ½ cup more flour through feed tube a little at a time. Push dough down onto blade. Add walnuts and mix for 10 seconds; *do not overprocess.*

◆ Press any loose walnuts into dough. Shape dough into ball. Transfer to greased bowl, turning to coat all surfaces.

◆ Cover bowl with damp towel. Let stand in warm draft-free area until doubled in volume, about 1 hour.

◆ Punch dough down. Turn out onto well-floured surface. Shape into smooth ball. Transfer to baking sheet sprayed with vegetable spray. Cover and let stand in warm draft-free area until doubled, 35 to 40 minutes.

◆ Preheat oven to 400°. Slash top with an "X". Mix egg with salt and brush on loaf. Bake until bread is well-browned and sounds hollow when tapped on bottom, about 35 to 40 minutes. Cool on wire rack before slicing.

Yield: *1 loaf*

Refrigerator Yeast Dough *(Dairy)*

5	cups unsifted flour	½	pound melted butter
1	teaspoon salt	2	(1-ounce) cakes of yeast
¾	cup sugar		dissolved in ½ cup cold water
3	eggs or 6 egg yolks		or 2 envelopes active dry
1	cup sour cream		yeast

◆ Mix first 3 dry ingredients together. Make well in center.

◆ Combine all other ingredients, pour entire wet mixture into hole. Mix to make a stiff dough.

◆ Cover tightly and place in refrigerator overnight to rise. Use within 3 to 4 days.

◆ When ready to use, remove from refrigerator and let stand until pliable.

◆ Punch down and roll into ball.

Note: *Use dough for Pecan Rolls or Kuchen.*

Miniature Pecan Rolls *(Dairy)*

1	recipe Refrigerator Yeast Dough	1	cup brown sugar
½	cup butter (1 stick)	½	cup chopped nuts

◆ Follow directions for Kuchen, omitting jam.

◆ In each muffin tin, place ½ teaspoon butter, 1 teaspoon brown sugar and a pinch of chopped nuts.

◆ Slice rolled kuchen dough into 1-inch pieces and place into prepared tins on top of sugar nut mixture.

◆ Preheat oven to 350°. Bake for 15 to 20 minutes or until browned. Turn out of pan immediately after taking from oven.

Yield: *36 regular or 105 miniature rolls*

Kuchen *(Dairy)*

A piece of this delicious coffee cake starts the day off just right.

Pastry

1	recipe Refrigerator Yeast Dough	½	cup raisins
1	cup sour cream	4	ounces raspberry or apricot jam
¾	cup sugar	½	cup chopped nuts
	Sprinkle of cinnamon	½	cup chocolate chips (optional)

Frosting

½	cup powdered sugar	1	teaspoon vanilla
¼	cup milk		

- ◆ Divide dough in half. Roll out dough to ½ inch thickness in rectangular shape on floured board.

- ◆ Spread with sour cream, a fine coating of sugar and a sprinkle of cinnamon. Dot with raisins, a little jam, chopped nuts and, if desired, chocolate chips.

- ◆ Roll like a jellyroll and place in well-greased tube pans. Allow to rise for 3 hours with thin cloth over top.

- ◆ Preheat oven to 350°.

- ◆ Bake for 30 minutes. Mix frosting ingredients and frost while warm.

Yield: *2 kuchens*

Cheddar Biscuits *(Dairy)*

2	cups flour	1½	cups grated extra-sharp cheddar cheese (about 6 ounces)
1	tablespoon baking powder		
½	teaspoon salt	1¼	cups half-and-half

◆ Preheat oven to 425°. In a bowl sift together the flour, baking powder and salt. Add the Cheddar and mix well.

◆ Add the half-and-half and stir the mixture until it just forms a dough. Gather the dough into a ball and knead it gently 6 times on a lightly floured surface.

◆ Roll dough to ½-inch thickness. Cut as many rounds as possible with a 2½-inch cutter dipped in flour. Transfer them to a lightly greased baking sheet.

◆ Gather the scraps, roll the dough again and cut out more rounds.

◆ Bake for 15 to 17 minutes until golden. Cool on rack for 5 minutes.

Yield: *24 biscuits*

Corn Muffins *(Dairy)*

A special breakfast treat.

1¼	cups flour	½	cup oil
¾	cup yellow cornmeal	2	eggs, lightly beaten
¼	cup sugar	2	tablespoons butter, melted and cooled
1	tablespoon baking powder		
½	teaspoon salt	2	tablespoons honey
1	cup milk	1	teaspoon vanilla

◆ Preheat oven to 400°. Line 12 to 18 muffin tins with muffin liners.

◆ Mix first 5 ingredients in a large bowl. In another bowl, combine next 6 ingredients.

◆ Make a well in dry ingredients and add liquid ingredients. Stir just to combine.

◆ Fill muffin cups ¾ full and bake for 15 to 20 minutes, until cake tester comes out clean. Remove muffins to wire rack and cool a few minutes. Serve warm, or cool completely and store in an airtight container.

Yield: *12 to 18 muffins*

Note: *These muffins freeze well.*

Honey Nut Bran Muffins *(Dairy)*

1	cup flour	2	tablespoons oil
1½	cups bran cereal	1½	cups milk
½	teaspoon baking soda	¾	cup chopped walnuts
½	cup honey		

◆ Preheat oven to 400°. Mix dry ingredients. Add remaining ingredients and mix well.

◆ Pour into greased muffin tins. Bake for 25 to 30 minutes.

Yield: *12 muffins*

Bountiful Blueberry Muffins *(Dairy or Parve)*

2	cups flour	½	cup lightly salted butter or
1	cup plus 1 tablespoon sugar		margarine, melted and cooled
2	teaspoons baking powder	1	egg, lightly beaten
½	teaspoon salt	1	teaspoon fresh lemon juice
½	cup milk or nondairy creamer	1	teaspoon vanilla
		2	cups fresh blueberries

◆ Preheat oven to 400°. Grease 12 muffin cups.

◆ In a large bowl stir together flour, 1 cup sugar, baking powder and salt.

◆ In another bowl stir together milk, butter, egg, lemon juice and vanilla until blended.

◆ Make a well in center of dry ingredients. Add milk mixture and stir just to combine.

◆ Mash ¼ cup blueberries and stir into batter with a few quick strokes. Stir in remaining berries.

◆ Spoon batter into prepared muffin cups and sprinkle with remaining 1 tablespoon sugar. Bake for 20 to 25 minutes or until a cake tester comes out clean.

◆ Remove muffin tin to wire rack. Cool for 5 minutes before removing muffins from cups. Serve warm or cool completely and store in airtight container at room temperature.

Yield: *12 muffins*

Note: *To prevent blueberries from bursting, place in freezer for 20 to 30 minutes before adding to batter. These muffins freeze well.*

Banana Apricot Nut Bread *(Dairy)*

¾ cup butter, softened
1⅓ cups sugar
2 eggs
1½ cups mashed ripe bananas
2¾ cups flour
1 teaspoon baking soda

1 teaspoon baking powder
½ teaspoon salt
½ cup sour cream
1 cup chopped walnuts
1½ cups dried apricots, chopped

◆ Preheat oven to 350°. Cream butter and sugar together. Add eggs, one at a time. Beat well. Add mashed bananas.

◆ Sift flour, baking soda, baking powder and salt together. Add sifted ingredients alternately with sour cream.

◆ Stir in walnuts and apricots.

◆ Bake in a 5x9x3-inch loaf pan for 1 hour and 15 minutes.

Yield: *1 loaf*

Note: *This may also be made in 4 mini loaf pans. Shorten baking time to 1 hour.*

Banana Oatmeal Muffins *(Parve)*

A Committee Favorite!

½ cup sugar
½ cup margarine
2 eggs
3 medium overripe bananas, mashed

¾ cup honey
1½ cups flour
1 teaspoon baking soda
1 teaspoon baking powder
1 cup quick rolled oats

◆ Preheat oven to 375°.

◆ In mixer, cream sugar and margarine. Beat in eggs, bananas and honey.

◆ Stir in flour, baking soda and baking powder. Beat until well blended. Stir in oats.

◆ Fill paper-lined muffin cups ¾ full. Bake until golden and a toothpick inserted in center comes out clean, about 20 minutes.

Yield: *12 muffins*

Oven Brown Bread (Dairy)

2	cups milk	2	teaspoons baking soda
2	tablespoons lemon juice	½	teaspoon salt
1	cup flour	¾	cup raisins
1	cup whole wheat flour	¾	cup molasses
1	cup cornmeal		

♦ Preheat oven to 350°. Combine milk and lemon juice and set aside.

♦ Mix dry ingredients. Add raisins and stir in molasses and milk. Pour into 4 well-greased 20-ounce cans with labels and glue removed.

♦ Bake for 30 minutes, until toothpick comes out clean. Cool, slice and spread with butter or margarine.

Yield: *4 loaves*

Chocolate Tea Bread (Parve)

So delicious it could be dessert.

⅓	cup margarine	⅓	cup cocoa
1¼	cups sugar	1	teaspoon baking soda
2	eggs	¾	teaspoon salt
⅓	cup water	¼	teaspoon baking powder
½	cup applesauce	1	cup chocolate chips
1½	cups flour	⅓	cup chopped nuts

Glaze

½	cup powdered sugar	¼	teaspoon vanilla
1-2	tablespoons water		Pinch of salt

♦ Preheat oven to 350°. Cream margarine and sugar in mixer.

♦ Add eggs, water and applesauce and beat on low speed for 1 minute.

♦ Combine dry ingredients and add to wet mixture. Beat on high for 2½ minutes. Fold in chips and nuts.

♦ Pour into greased and floured 5x9x3-inch loaf pan. Bake for 60 to 70 minutes. Cool in pan for 10 minutes before removing to wire rack. Cool completely.

♦ Mix glaze ingredients and drizzle over cool bread.

Yield: *1 loaf*

Note: *Chocolate powdered sugar may be used for glaze if available.*

Chocolate Chip Apple Bread *(Parve)*

1½	cups oil	1	teaspoon cinnamon
1	cup sugar	½	teaspoon vanilla
1	cup brown sugar	3	cups chopped apples
4	eggs	1	cup chopped walnuts
3	cups flour	¾	cup chocolate chips
1	teaspoon baking soda		

- ◆ Preheat oven to 325°. Mix ingredients in order given.
- ◆ Pour batter into 2 greased 5x9x3-inch loaf pans.
- ◆ Bake for 1 hour and 15 minutes.

Yield: *2 loaves*

Cranberry Banana Bread *(Parve)*

2	cups cranberries	2	teaspoons baking powder
1⅔	cups sugar, divided	¼	teaspoon baking soda
1	cup water	1	teaspoon salt
⅓	cup margarine	1	cup mashed bananas
2	eggs	½	cup chopped nuts
1¾	cups flour		

- ◆ Preheat oven to 350°. In a saucepan combine cranberries, 1 cup sugar and water. Cook over medium-high heat for 5 minutes or until berries begin to pop. Drain.
- ◆ Cream the margarine. Gradually add remaining ⅔ cup sugar. Beat until fluffy. Add eggs and mix well.
- ◆ Combine flour, baking powder, baking soda and salt. Add dry ingredients and bananas alternately to the creamed mixture. Add cranberries and chopped nuts.
- ◆ Spread batter in a greased and floured 5x9x3-inch loaf pan. Bake for 60 to 65 minutes.

Yield: *1 loaf*

Pumpkin Bread *(Parve)*

3	cups sugar	1	teaspoon ground cloves
1	cup oil	2	teaspoons baking soda
4-5	eggs	⅔	cup water
1½	teaspoons salt	1	(16-ounce) can pumpkin
1	teaspoon cinnamon	3⅓	cups flour
1	teaspoon nutmeg	1	cup chopped walnuts (optional)

- ◆ Preheat oven to 350°. Combine all ingredients in order listed.
- ◆ Spray 3x5½-inch loaf tins with vegetable spray.
- ◆ Pour batter into loaf tins and bake for 1 hour (without nuts) or 50 minutes (with nuts).

Yield: *7 loaves*

Zucchini Pineapple Bread *(Parve)*

Can't believe it's zucchini!

3	eggs	½	teaspoon baking powder
2	cups sugar	3	cups flour
1	cup oil	2	teaspoons cinnamon
1	teaspoon vanilla	1	(20-ounce) can crushed
2	cups shredded zucchini,		pineapple, drained well
	drained and squeezed dry	½	cup chopped nuts
1	teaspoon salt	½	cup raisins
1	teaspoon baking soda	½	cup chocolate chips (optional)

- ◆ Preheat oven to 350°. Beat eggs until foamy.
- ◆ Beat in sugar, oil and vanilla. Mix well.
- ◆ Beat in zucchini.
- ◆ Sift together dry ingredients and add to egg mixture.
- ◆ Add pineapple, nuts, raisins and optional chocolate chips.
- ◆ Pour batter into 2 greased 5x9x3-inch loaf pans.
- ◆ Bake for 60 to 75 minutes. Remove from pans and cool on rack.

Yield: *2 loaves*

Note: *This bread freezes well.*

Soups

Helpful Soup Suggestions

Chicken Soup:

◆ It is best to make the soup the day before serving.

◆ Chicken may be skinned before cooking. However, the skin gives the soup flavor, so leave some on. Remove excess fat.

◆ Always start soup with cold water.

◆ After soup comes to a boil, reduce to simmer and skim off foam that rises to top. A small, fine strainer works best.

◆ Remove chicken from bones while still warm. It makes great chicken salad.

◆ Remove all the solid fat from the soup after it is refrigerated overnight. A quick blotting with paper towel across the top and around the sides will remove remaining fat. The flavor will still be in the soup.

◆ Chicken soup freezes well and will keep at least a year in the freezer.

◆ Make ice cubes out of clear chicken soup. Store frozen cubes in plastic bags and keep in freezer to use as chicken stock. One cube equals approximately 2 tablespoons.

For All Soups:

◆ If soup is too salty, add a medium peeled raw potato cut in half. Cook until potato is tender. Discard potato.

Chicken Soup ✡ (Meat)

Also known as "Jewish penicillin"!

5-6 pounds chicken parts	1 parsnip, peeled and quartered
4-6 quarts cold water	6 sprigs parsley
3 ribs celery, cleaned and quartered	Salt and white pepper to taste
2 medium onions, whole and scored	2 tablespoons instant chicken-flavored soup mix
1 pound carrots, peeled and cut into chunks	1 tablespoon sugar (optional)

◆ Remove excess fat from chicken. Place chicken in an 8-quart pot and fill with water. Bring to boil; reduce to simmer and skim. Add celery, onions, carrots, parsnips, parsley and seasonings. Cover pot and simmer for 1½ to 2 hours or until chicken is tender.

◆ Taste to see if more seasoning is needed. When chicken is tender, remove pot from heat and cool slightly. Remove chicken and carrots carefully.

◆ Strain remaining soup into another large pot and return carrots (rinsed) to the soup. Mash the remaining vegetables through a strainer to add more flavor to soup. Discard vegetables remaining in strainer.

◆ Cool and refrigerate overnight. Next day, skim off any excess fat that has risen to the surface.

◆ Serve with noodles, matzo balls, rice or kreplach or any combination.

Yield: *12 to 15 servings*

Note: *There are many variations for this traditional soup. Variations include fresh dill, garlic, leek or parsley root. You may make a chicken vegetable soup by adding potatoes, cabbage, peas, barley or any desired combination.*

Knaidlach ✡ *(Parve or Meat)*

Knaidlach *is a Yiddish term for matzo balls or dumplings.*

2	tablespoons oil	2	tablespoons soup stock or
2	eggs, slightly beaten		water
½	cup matzo meal	½	teaspoon chopped fresh
1	teaspoon salt		parsley (optional)

◆ Mix oil and eggs together. Add matzo meal and salt. Mix well; add soup stock or water and parsley.

◆ Cover mixing bowl and place in refrigerator for at least 20 minutes.

◆ To cook, bring 2 to 3 quarts of salted water to a boil. With wet hands, form matzo meal mixture into 1½-inch balls and drop into boiling water. Reduce heat to low boil. Cover pot and cook for 30 to 40 minutes.

◆ With a slotted spoon, place matzo balls into warm soup and simmer for 5 minutes.

Yield: *8 matzo balls*

Note: *You may use chicken bouillon to season boiling water instead of salt.*

Matzo Balls ✡ *(Parve)*

1	cup matzo meal	½	cup club soda or water
¼	teaspoon baking powder	¼	cup oil
1	teaspoon salt	4	eggs, beaten
	Dash of pepper		

◆ Mix dry ingredients together. Add club soda or water, oil and eggs. Mix well.

◆ Refrigerate for 45 minutes.

◆ With wet hands, form matzo balls and add to pot of boiling water. Simmer for 30 to 45 minutes.

◆ Serve in chicken soup.

Yield: *16 matzo balls*

Note: *Passover baking powder is available.*

Kreplach *(Meat)*

2	eggs, beaten slightly	¼	cup water
½	teaspoon salt	½	teaspoon sugar
1⅓	cups flour		Salt and pepper to taste
1	large onion, chopped	1	pound cooked beef or chicken
3	tablespoons margarine		

◆ **For dough:** Combine eggs and salt. Add flour and mix well in processor with metal blade. (Dough should be stiff.) Store in covered container in refrigerator until ready to use.

◆ Place on floured surface and knead for a few minutes. Roll ¼ inch thick and cut into 2x2-inch squares.

◆ **For filling:** Sauté onion in margarine until golden. Add water and steam in covered skillet. Add sugar, salt and pepper.

◆ Combine cooked meat and onion mixture in food processor with metal blade. Process until fine. Place a spoonful of mixture in center of dough square and fold dough to form a triangle. Rub water on edges and press together.

◆ Drop into boiling water and cook for 15 minutes or until kreplach rise to the top. Drain and add to chicken soup.

Yield: *12 kreplach*

Note: *Other fillings include mashed potatoes, kasha or chopped turkey.*

Soup Mandlen *(Parve)*

Mandlen *is a round puffy cracker.*

3	eggs, slightly beaten	1	tablespoon oil
2	cups flour	1	teaspoon salt

◆ Preheat oven to 350°. Combine all ingredients in a large bowl and mix well.

◆ Divide dough in half and roll into 2 rope shapes, about 1 inch in diameter. Cut in ½-inch pieces and place on a greased cookie sheet.

◆ Bake for 5 minutes or until golden brown. Serve in chicken soup.

Yield: *About 60 pieces*

Bubbie's Cabbage Borscht *(Parve or Meat)*

In Russia, borscht was a staple. The amount of meat used was determined by how much the family could afford.

3	pounds chuck with bone in (optional)	1	(6-ounce) can tomato paste
10	cups water	1	teaspoon salt
8	cups cabbage, shredded	1	teaspoon lemon juice
4	carrots, peeled and sliced	1	teaspoon sour salt
1	extra large onion, chopped	¼	teaspoon white pepper
3	(28-ounce) cans tomatoes and juice, chopped	¼	cup ketchup
		¾	cup brown sugar, firmly packed

◆ In an 8-quart pot, bring beef and water to a boil. Skim broth. Turn down heat, cover, and simmer for about 1 hour.

◆ Add remaining ingredients and simmer an additional 1 hour. Remove meat; discard bones.

◆ Cut meat and return to pot.

Yield: *12 to 15 servings*

Variations:

◆ Borscht may be made vegetarian by replacing meat with ⅛ cup parve beef-flavored soup mix and eliminating the first hour of cooking time.

◆ Add to the basic borscht any or all of the following: ⅓ cup raisins, 1 tart apple peeled and grated, 1 cup sliced beets, 1½ cups sliced potatoes.

◆ For a sweeter borscht, add more sugar; for a more tart taste, add more lemon juice or sour salt.

Beet Borscht the Easy Way *(Dairy)*

This shortcut recipe saves time but keeps the traditional taste.

1	(15-ounce) can cut-up beets and juice	1	(15-ounce) can julienne beets, drained
4	tablespoons sugar		Sour cream or plain yogurt
¼	teaspoon salt		Cucumber, diced
3	tablespoons lemon juice		Boiled potato
1	(32-ounce) jar beet borscht		

◆ In a blender purée cut-up beets and juice with sugar, salt and lemon juice. Add beet borscht and purée. Remove from blender and add drained beets.

◆ Serve cold with a dollop of sour cream and diced cucumbers or boiled potato.

Yield: *12 servings*

Spinach Borscht *(Parve or Dairy)*

I can remember my mother serving this delicious cold soup on the hot days of summer.

1	(10-ounce) package frozen chopped spinach	⅓	cup sugar
5	cups water	1	tablespoon lemon juice
¾	teaspoon sour salt	1	egg
1	teaspoon salt		Sour cream or yogurt (optional)
¼	teaspoon lemon pepper	2-3	scallions, chopped

◆ Bring spinach and water to a boil. Add sour salt, salt, pepper, sugar and lemon juice. Simmer for 2 minutes.

◆ In blender or processor, beat egg. Gradually add hot spinach mixture to egg a little at a time and pulse until it becomes foamy. Empty container into bowl and pulse remainder of spinach mixture in batches. Do <u>not</u> purée the spinach.

◆ Mix all together in a bowl and refrigerate for several hours or overnight. Serve with dollop of sour cream (if dairy) and scallions.

Yield: *4 to 6 servings*

Mushroom Barley Soup *(Parve)*

3	tablespoons margarine, or vegetable spray	1	teaspoon salt
1½	cups chopped onions	1	teaspoon pepper
1	cup chopped carrots	¼	teaspoon nutmeg
1	cup chopped celery	1	teaspoon thyme
2	teaspoons minced garlic	1	cup pearl barley
1	pound mushrooms, sliced	2	tablespoons minced fresh dill
3	quarts parve chicken-flavored bouillon	2	tablespoons chopped fresh parsley

◆ In a 6- or 8-quart stockpot, melt margarine or spray with vegetable spray. Add onions, carrots, celery and garlic. Sauté until tender but not browned. Add mushrooms.

◆ Cook until just soft. Add the broth, salt, pepper, nutmeg, thyme and barley. Bring to a boil. Simmer for 2 hours or until barley is tender.

◆ Just before serving, stir in dill and parsley.

Yield: *12 to 15 servings*

Note: *Cut down on the cooking time by soaking the barley for 2 hours before beginning the soup; then it need simmer for only about ½ hour. The soup may be made up to 2 days in advance, refrigerated, and reheated. If it becomes too thick, thin with additional broth.*

Bean Soup *(Parve or Meat)*

Even better the second day!

1	(16-ounce) package dried bean mix	2	(14½-ounce) cans diced tomatoes with juice
1	very large onion, chopped	6	ribs celery, sliced
2	tablespoons fresh chopped garlic	4	carrots, sliced
1	(12-ounce) box mushrooms, sliced	¼	cup barley
1-2	tablespoons oil	¼	cup parve beef-flavored soup mix
2	pounds boneless short ribs (optional)	1	(10-ounce) package frozen chopped spinach
6	quarts water	¼	cup chopped parsley
2	(6-ounce) packages lima bean soup mix with barley, divided	8	ounces spaghetti, broken into thirds
			Pepper, salt, garlic powder and onion powder to taste

◆   Soak beans overnight; drain.

◆   In 8-quart pot sauté onion, chopped garlic and mushrooms in oil and set aside.

◆   Add meat to pot and brown it.

◆   Add water, beans, lima bean soup mix without seasoning, tomatoes, celery, carrots, barley, beef-flavored soup mix, spinach, parsley and sautéed vegetables. Simmer for 2 hours.

◆   Add the lima bean soup mix "seasoning", spaghetti, and seasonings to taste and cook for another 10 minutes.

Yield: *10 to 12 servings*

Cuban Black Bean Soup *(Parve or Dairy)*

1	pound black beans	2	medium onions
2	quarts cold water	1	teaspoon oregano
¼	cup olive oil	1	teaspoon cumin
2	bay leaves	2	teaspoons salt
2	large green peppers, seeded	1	teaspoon white vinegar
2	cloves garlic		

◆ Rinse beans. Soak overnight in 2 quarts cold water. Bring to a boil in the soaking water. Add a few drops of olive oil and bay leaves. Simmer for 1½ hours or until tender. Do not add water.

◆ Chop the peppers, garlic, onions, oregano and cumin. Sauté in olive oil for 15 minutes. When beans are soft, add the sautéed mixture together with salt and cook for an additional 15 minutes.

◆ Add vinegar and check seasonings for taste. If you want it thicker, mash some of the beans.

◆ Serve with a topping of chopped onion. For dairy, serve with sour cream and/or grated cheddar cheese.

Yield: *8 to 10 servings*

Note: *1½ cups cooked rice may be added to soup.*

Split Pea and Barley Soup *(Meat)*

5	quarts water	1	large onion, quartered
3	pounds chuck with bone in	2	large carrots, cut in chunks
½	teaspoon salt	2	packages split pea soup mix
	Pepper		with barley
1	tablespoon sugar	4	hot dogs, cut up (optional)
3	ribs celery		

◆ In a 6-quart pot, bring water to a boil. Add meat, bones, salt, pepper, sugar, celery, onion and carrots and cook about 1 hour or more to make soup stock.

◆ Discard the onion and celery, remove meat from the bones and return to pot. Add the packages of split pea soup mix with barley and allow to cook until the split peas dissolve. Season to taste.

◆ Before serving, add the cut-up hot dogs and allow to cook for another 10 to 15 minutes.

Yield: *12 servings*

Lentil Soup with Garlic (Parve)

Add a crusty bread and serve as a main course.

¼	cup olive oil	¼	cup tomato paste mixed with ½ cup water
4	cloves garlic, minced	1	tablespoon soy sauce
3	large onions, diced		Freshly ground black pepper to taste
7½	cups water	1	vegetable bouillon cube (optional)
1	cup lentils, rinsed		
4	carrots, sliced thin		
3	ribs celery, sliced thin		

◆ Heat olive oil in a large stockpot over medium heat. Add garlic and onions and sauté for 10 minutes, or until onions are very soft and begin to brown. Stir often.

◆ Add all the remaining ingredients except the bouillon cube. Raise the heat and bring the soup to a boil, stirring often. Reduce heat to a simmer and cook for 45 minutes, or until carrots are very tender and soup has thickened. Taste the soup while it is simmering. If soup does not have enough flavor, add bouillon cube.

Yield: *4 servings*

Fat-Free Vegetable Soup (Parve)

4	quarts cold water	¼	teaspoon pepper
5	carrots, sliced	2	teaspoons parve chicken-flavored or vegetable soup mix
4	ribs celery, cut up		
¾	cup dried split peas	1	(12-ounce) package frozen lima beans
½	cup barley		
1	large onion, chopped	1	(10-ounce) package frozen peas
2	potatoes, cut up		
1	clove garlic, minced (optional)	½	cup macaroni (optional)
⅓	cup fresh parsley, chopped		

◆ Place all ingredients except beans, frozen peas and macaroni in a large pot and bring to a boil.

◆ Allow it to simmer for about 30 minutes, stirring frequently. Taste soup occasionally for desired flavor.

◆ Add beans, frozen peas and macaroni and cook for another 30 minutes, or until done.

Yield: *12 servings*

Garden Vegetable Soup *(Parve)*

⅔ cup sliced carrots	1 tablespoon tomato paste
½ cup diced onion	½ teaspoon each, dried basil, dill
2 cloves garlic, minced	weed and parsley
3 cups parve beef, chicken or	¼ teaspoon dried oregano
vegetable-flavored broth	¼ teaspoon salt (optional)
1½ cups diced green cabbage	½ cup diced zucchini
½ cup green beans	

◆ Spray a large saucepan with vegetable spray. Sauté carrots, onion, and garlic over low heat until softened, about 5 minutes.

◆ Add broth, cabbage, beans, tomato paste and herbs. Bring to a boil. Lower heat, simmer covered for about 15 to 20 minutes, or until green beans are tender. Stir in zucchini and heat for 3 to 4 minutes more. Serve hot.

Yield: *3 to 4 servings*

Note: *This soup freezes well. It contains no fat and no salt. Recipe may be doubled and tripled.*

Gezundte Vegetable Soup *(Parve)*

A delightfully thick and gezundte *(hearty) soup.*

1	tablespoon olive oil	1	teaspoon curry powder, or to taste
2	cloves garlic, minced		
1	onion, chopped	1	teaspoon dill weed
2	ribs celery, sliced	1	teaspoon oregano
2	stalks broccoli, cut into chunks	5	tablespoons brown sugar, or to taste
1	head cauliflower, cut into chunks		
		1	(15-ounce) can corn, or frozen
1	red pepper, cut into chunks	1	(16-ounce) can great northern beans, rinsed well to remove starch
1	medium potato, diced		
1	teaspoon tarragon		
1	teaspoon basil	2	(6-ounce) cans tomato paste
1	teaspoon salt	1	(28-ounce) can crushed or diced tomatoes
1	teaspoon black pepper		
1	teaspoon thyme	4	cups water, or to desired thickness

◆ In a 10-quart pot, sauté garlic in olive oil; add cut-up vegetables. Sauté vegetables until they turn bright. Don't overcook.

◆ Add herbs and brown sugar. Add corn, beans, tomato paste, tomatoes, and water. Simmer for 30 minutes or until thoroughly warmed and all ingredients have had a chance to mingle.

Yield: *12 to 14 servings*

Note: *The quantities here are only a starting point. All ingredients may be varied according to taste and desired thickness.*

Southwest Vegetable Soup *(Parve)*

Swiss chard and kale are the surprise ingredients!

1	cup sliced carrots	1½	cups diced cabbage
1	cup sliced celery	½	cup green beans in chunks
½	cup diced onion	8	leaves Swiss chard, coarsely
2	cloves garlic, minced		chopped
1	tablespoon oil	8	leaves kale, coarsely chopped
8	cups parve chicken or	½	teaspoon pepper, or to taste
	vegetable-flavored broth	1	tablespoon dried basil or diced
3	cups water		fresh basil leaves to taste
1	(6-ounce) can tomato paste or		Salt to taste
	1 (16-ounce) can chopped		
	tomatoes with juice		

- ◆ Sauté carrots, celery, diced onion and garlic in oil until soft.
- ◆ Bring broth and water to a boil; add tomato paste, sautéed vegetables and remaining vegetables. Use seasonings to taste. Cook on low simmer for 1½ to 2 hours and adjust seasonings to taste. Add more water if broth becomes too concentrated.

Yield: *8 to 10 servings*

Note: *Canned cannelloni or garbanzo beans, drained and rinsed, or any other chopped vegetables may be added. Soup freezes well.*

Pronto Gazpacho *(Parve)*

1¾	cups tomato juice	1	teaspoon olive oil
2	medium tomatoes, cubed	½	teaspoon dried basil
1	slice red onion, halved	½	teaspoon garlic salt
½	medium green or red pepper,		Dash of hot pepper sauce
	seeded and cubed		Chopped fresh parsley
¼	small cucumber, seeded and		Herbed croutons
	cubed		

- ◆ Place all ingredients except parsley and croutons in blender container. Cover and process 2 to 3 pulses at high speed until vegetables are coarsely chopped. Do not overprocess.
- ◆ Chill at least 1 hour before serving. Garnish each serving with parsley and 3 to 4 croutons.

Yield: *2 to 3 servings*

Tortilla Soup *(Parve or Meat)*

An easy crowd pleaser.

6	cups chicken or vegetable-flavored broth	3	teaspoons cumin
3	cloves garlic, minced	1	tablespoon salt
1	onion, chopped	⅛	teaspoon white pepper
1	tablespoon oil	1	tablespoon chili powder
	Chopped cilantro to taste (optional)	1	(16-ounce) package frozen corn, preferably baby white corn if available, divided
4	large tomatoes, chopped		Tortilla chips
½	cup tomato paste		Chopped avocado

◆ Heat broth. Sauté garlic and onions in oil until soft. Add to broth along with tomatoes, seasonings and half of the corn kernels. Simmer for 1 hour and adjust seasonings to taste. Let soup cool.

◆ Purée soup in food processor in batches to thicken. Reheat and add remaining corn kernels.

◆ Serve soup and top with crushed tortilla chips or chopped avocado. If you use a vegetable broth, shredded cheese may be added on top.

Yield: *6 to 8 servings*

Gazpacho *(Parve)*

4	cups tomato juice	1	teaspoon tarragon
½	cup minced onion	1	teaspoon basil
1	medium clove garlic, minced	¼	teaspoon cumin
1	medium bell pepper, minced	¼	cup freshly minced parsley
1	teaspoon honey (optional)	1-2	tablespoons olive oil
1	medium cucumber, peeled, seeded and minced		Salt, black pepper and cayenne to taste
2	scallions, minced		Dash of hot pepper sauce
	Juice of ½ lemon and 1 lime	¼	cup chopped carrots
2	tablespoons wine vinegar or cider vinegar	¼	cup chopped celery

◆ Combine all ingredients. Some or all may be puréed in blender.

◆ Chill until very cold.

Yield: *6 servings*

Ivory Gazpacho *(Dairy)*

A Brynwood Country Club specialty!

1	quart buttermilk	4	large cucumbers, peeled, seeded and divided
4	tablespoons olive oil	1	large green bell pepper, seeded and divided
¼	cup sugar		
2	teaspoons coarse kosher salt	2	pounds fresh Roma tomatoes, seeded and divided
1	teaspoon white pepper		
½-1	teaspoon Tabasco sauce	1	bunch green onions, divided
2	teaspoons Worcestershire sauce	2	ounces pimientos
2	teaspoons lemon juice	4	ribs celery
½	cup red wine vinegar		

♦ In blender, combine buttermilk, olive oil, sugar, salt, pepper, Tabasco sauce, Worcestershire sauce, lemon juice and red wine vinegar. Remove half the liquid and reserve.

♦ To remaining liquid in blender add cut up chunks of 2 cucumbers, ½ green pepper, 1 pound tomatoes, ½ bunch of green onions and pimiento. Pulse until mixed and coarsely chopped. Combine with reserved liquid. Refrigerate.

♦ With chopping knife, dice remaining cucumbers, green pepper, tomatoes, green onions and celery. Refrigerate diced vegetables in separate containers until ready to serve.

♦ To serve, spoon buttermilk mixture into bowl and top with diced vegetables.

Yield: *8 to 10 servings*

Red Pepper Soup *(Parve or Dairy)*

Delicious served hot or cold.

2	tablespoons oil (olive or vegetable) or butter	2	cloves garlic, peeled and chopped
8	large red or yellow bell peppers, seeded and coarsely cut up	1	ripe pear and/or apple peeled and cut up
3	carrots, peeled and diced to ¼ inch	1	quart parve chicken-flavored broth or water
3	shallots, peeled, or ¾ cup onions, chopped	1	teaspoon salt
		¼	teaspoon cayenne pepper
		¼	cup orange juice (optional)

Garnishes
Sour cream
Yogurt

Chives
Parsley or cilantro

◆ In a pot or large skillet heat oil over medium heat. Add peppers, carrots, shallots or onions, garlic and pear or apple. Cover and cook until soft, not brown. Keep lid ajar. Add broth or water and simmer uncovered for 20 to 30 minutes or until very soft. Remove from stove and cool. Purée in food processor or blender. Season with salt and cayenne pepper.

◆ Orange juice may be added if soup is too thick. Garnish with sour cream, yogurt, chives, parsley or cilantro.

Yield: *4 to 6 servings*

Garden Zucchini Soup *(Dairy)*

2	tablespoons butter	1	teaspoon curry powder
1	pound zucchini, sliced	½	teaspoon salt
2	tablespoons shallots, chopped fine	½	cup skim milk
1	clove garlic, minced	1¾	cups vegetable or parve chicken-flavored broth

◆ In a 4-quart pot heat butter; add zucchini, shallots and garlic. Cover tightly and simmer until tender. Spoon mixture into a blender and add curry powder, salt, milk and broth and blend for 30 seconds.

◆ Serve hot with croutons or cold with chopped chives.

Yield: *4 servings*

Quick Minestrone *(Parve)*

3	(6-ounce) packages minestrone soup mix	12	cups water
1	(12-ounce) can tomato paste	1	cup finely diced celery
1	medium potato, grated	1	cup finely diced carrots
½	teaspoon pepper	½	(16-ounce) can kidney beans
1	teaspoon garlic powder	½	(16-ounce) can garbanzo beans

◆ Combine first 6 ingredients in pot and simmer for 1 hour. Stir frequently. Add celery and carrots. Cook for 1 hour more. Add beans and cook for ½ hour more. Add more water if soup is too thick.

Yield: *12 to 16 servings*

Note: *Be careful not to burn soup.*

Minestrone *(Parve or Dairy)*

2	tablespoons olive oil or vegetable spray	1	small zucchini, diced
2	cups onion, chopped	3-4	cups, or more, water
5	medium cloves garlic, minced	1	(14½-ounce) can tomato purée
1½	teaspoons salt	1-1½	cups cooked, or canned and drained, garbanzo or kidney beans
1	rib celery, minced		
1	medium carrot, diced		
1	cup eggplant, diced (optional)	½-1	cup dry pasta, any shape
1	teaspoon oregano	1-2	medium ripe tomatoes, diced (optional)
	Fresh black pepper, to taste		
1	teaspoon basil	½	cup freshly minced parsley
1	medium bell pepper, diced		Parmesan cheese (optional)

◆ In a kettle or Dutch oven, heat olive oil or spray well with vegetable spray; add onion, garlic and salt. Sauté over medium heat for about 5 minutes. Add celery, carrot, eggplant, oregano, black pepper and basil. Cover and cook over very low heat for about 10 minutes more, stirring occasionally.

◆ Add bell pepper, zucchini, water and tomato purée. Cover and simmer for about 15 minutes. Add beans and simmer for another 5 minutes. Bring soup to a boil; add pasta and cook until tender.

◆ Stir in fresh tomatoes. Garnish with parsley and cheese, if desired, in each bowl and serve immediately.

Yield: *6 to 8 servings*

Baked Potato Soup *(Dairy)*

Another delicious soup from Brynwood Country Club.

1	cup margarine	10	cups water
1	large onion, chopped	4-5	potatoes, baked, cooled,
6-7	ribs celery, chopped		peeled and cut up
1½	cups flour	2	teaspoons salt, or to taste
½	tablespoon dried thyme	⅛	teaspoon white pepper, or to
3½	tablespoons parve chicken-		taste
	flavored soup mix	2	cups light or regular sour
			cream

◆ In a 6-quart pot, melt margarine. Sauté onion and celery until onions are translucent. Remove pot from heat and push vegetables to side.

◆ Add flour to margarine and mix to create a roux (thickener). Add thyme and soup mix. Add water a little at a time, stirring constantly. Bring to a boil, then simmer for 10 minutes. Stir and watch carefully so it does not burn.

◆ Add potatoes, salt and pepper and bring to a simmer. Turn off heat and add sour cream. Add extra seasoning if needed.

Yield: *10 to 12 servings*

Cream of Cauliflower Soup *(Dairy)*

4	cups water	¾	teaspoon salt
1	medium to large cauliflower,		Pepper to taste
	cut up	4	tablespoons butter or
1	large potato, diced		margarine
1	small onion, diced	4	tablespoons flour
2	tablespoons parve chicken-	2	cups milk, heated
	flavored soup mix	3-4	ounces grated cheddar cheese

◆ Cook vegetables in boiling water until soft. Add parve chicken soup mix and seasonings. Cool slightly. Put into a blender and blend until smooth.

◆ In a saucepan, melt butter and stir in flour. Mix with a little of the hot milk until smooth. Add remaining milk. Combine milk-flour mixture with cauliflower soup. Heat to boiling. Add cheese. Stir.

Yield: *6 to 8 servings*

Cream of 7-Root Soup *(Parve or Dairy)*

A great dish for Sukkot, as a bowl of it makes a complete meal.

2	cups chopped onions	½	pound butter or margarine, melted
2	cups diced rutabaga		
2	cups diced parsnips	1	cup flour
2	cups diced sweet potatoes	1	quart half-and-half, soy milk or nondairy creamer
2	cups diced white potatoes		
2	cups diced carrots	¼	tablespoon pepper
2	tablespoons crushed garlic	¼	tablespoon nutmeg
2	tablespoons salt	1	cup fresh chopped parsley
2	quarts cold vegetable or parve chicken-flavored broth	½	cup sherry or white wine

◆ Combine first 9 ingredients in a large soup pot. Cover and bring to a boil. Lower heat and cook until vegetables are tender, about 30 minutes.

◆ Meanwhile, combine butter or margarine and flour. Add to boiling soup, stirring constantly until mixture has reached sauce consistency. Add remaining ingredients. Add an additional 1 to 2 tablespoons salt if necessary.

Yield: *12 to 14 servings*

Cream of Tomato Soup *(Dairy)*

2	(14-ounce) cans chopped tomatoes, drained		Black pepper to taste
		1	(6-ounce) can tomato paste
1	(14-ounce) can crushed tomatoes	¼	teaspoon baking soda
1	cup chopped onion, sautéed	2	tablespoons margarine
2	teaspoons sugar or 1 packet artificial sweetener	2	tablespoons flour
		2	cups skim milk
1	teaspoon dried basil	1	box frozen chopped spinach, squeezed dry (optional)
1	teaspoon dried thyme		

◆ In a medium saucepan, combine tomatoes, crushed tomatoes, sautéed onions, sugar or sweetener, basil, thyme, pepper and tomato paste. Cover and simmer for 10 minutes. Stir in baking soda; set aside.

◆ In a 6-quart pot, melt margarine and stir in flour. Whisk in milk a little at a time and cook 1 minute or until thickened, whisking constantly. Stir in a small amount of tomato soup. Pour entire mixture into prepared tomato soup.

◆ Soup may be prepared with a dollop of fat-free sour cream or with cooked rice.

Yield: *8 servings*

Cold Berry Soup *(Dairy)*

1	quart orange juice	2	tablespoons lemon or lime juice
2	cups plain yogurt		Dash of cinnamon
2	cups buttermilk		Dash of nutmeg
1	tablespoon honey or a bit more	1	pint fresh berries, any kind

♦ Whisk together all ingredients except berries. Chill well.

♦ Put a few washed berries in each bowl. Pour soup over berries.

Yield: *6 servings*

Strawberry Soup *(Dairy)*

1	pint strawberries, washed and hulled	3	cups ice water
¾	cup sugar	¾	cup semisweet wine, red or white
¾	cup sour cream		

♦ In blender, purée fruit, add sugar, sour cream, water and wine. Mix well. Sweeten to taste and chill.

Yield: *12 servings*

Salads,
Fruits
&
Dressings

Salad Secrets

◆ Nuts, poppy seeds and sesame seeds should be refrigerated or frozen to keep them from turning rancid.

◆ To toast nuts or seeds:

A. Stir often in a nonstick skillet over medium heat until light brown.

B. Toss with a small amount of oil and place on a baking sheet. Bake at 325° for 15 minutes. Watch and stir when necessary.

◆ To peel tomatoes, remove core from tomato and cut an 'X' through skin at other end. Submerge tomato in boiling water for about 30 seconds. Plunge into cold water. Remove with slotted spoon and skin will slide off.

◆ To seed tomatoes, cut in half and squeeze out seeds.

◆ To roast peppers, cut in half, seed and core. Place cut side down on baking sheet. Slit ends so pieces lie flat. Broil about 4 inches from heating element until charred. Place in paper bag to cool, approximately 15 minutes. Slip skins off peppers. Roasted peppers may be frozen.

Hearts of Romaine Salad *(Dairy)*

3	tablespoons cider vinegar	4	ounces crumbled blue cheese
2¼	teaspoons Dijon mustard	1	large head romaine lettuce, torn in bite-sized pieces
½	cup olive oil		
3	tablespoons capers, drained		

◆ Mix vinegar and mustard in a covered jar. Gradually add oil and capers.

◆ Sprinkle crumbled blue cheese over romaine in a large bowl and add desired amount of dressing.

Yield: *4 to 6 servings*

Mandarin Orange Salad *(Parve)*

½	cup sliced almonds	1-2	(11-ounce) cans Mandarin orange slices, drained
5	tablespoons sugar		
1½	pounds romaine (or spinach)	2	green onions, chopped

Dressing

½	cup oil	1	teaspoon salt
4	tablespoons balsamic vinegar	1	tablespoon chopped parsley
4	tablespoons sugar		Dash of red pepper (optional)

◆ Place nuts and sugar in skillet over medium-high heat. Stirring constantly, sauté until sugar melts and nuts brown and caramelize. Remove from heat immediately and spread on wax paper to cool. When cool, break into small pieces for salad. If sugar should harden while cooking, place pan back on heat to melt.

◆ Prepare greens in bite-size pieces. Add oranges and onions.

◆ Place all dressing ingredients in spill-proof container and shake vigorously. Pour over greens and add nuts just before serving.

Yield: *8 servings*

Note: *Nuts and dressing may be prepared a day in advance.*

Spinach Salad with Grapefruit and Pears *(Parve)*

1   bunch spinach
1   grapefruit, peeled and sliced horizontally

1   pear, quartered, cored and sliced thin

Vinaigrette

¼   cup freshly squeezed orange juice
1   teaspoon balsamic vinegar
⅛   teaspoon salt

     Pepper
2   tablespoons olive oil
½   cup small Italian olives

♦ Wash the spinach very well and remove the tough stems. Shake dry, tear into bite-sized pieces and chill.

♦ Arrange the grapefruit and pear slices on the side of the plates.

♦ For the dressing, combine the juice, vinegar, salt and pepper. Whisk in the olive oil. Adjust the vinaigrette for more vinegar if necessary.

♦ Dress the olives with about 1 tablespoon of the vinaigrette and scatter them over the grapefruit and pears. Spoon the remaining vinaigrette over the spinach and toss well. Serve cold along with the sliced fruit.

Yield: *4 servings*

White and Green Salad *(Dairy)*

1   large head cauliflower, broken into bite-size pieces
1   bunch broccoli, broken into bite-size pieces
1   medium onion, chopped
1   (8-ounce) can sliced water chestnuts, drained

1   (10-ounce) package frozen peas, thawed
2   cups mayonnaise
1   cup sour cream
¼   cup sugar

♦ Toss all the vegetables together in a bowl.

♦ In small bowl, mix mayonnaise, sour cream and sugar. Combine with vegetables and marinate for at least 2 hours before serving.

Yield: *10 to 12 servings*

Strawberry Spinach Salad *(Parve)*

1 pound fresh spinach	1 (11-ounce) can Mandarin
1 pint strawberries, sliced	oranges, drained
	¼ cup sunflower seeds

Dressing

¼ cup cider vinegar	2 tablespoons sesame seeds
½ cup oil	1½ teaspoons minced onion
½ teaspoon Worcestershire sauce	¼ teaspoon paprika
½ cup sugar	

◆ Wash and dry spinach; discard stems and tear in pieces. Combine spinach, strawberries, oranges and sunflower seeds.

◆ Just before serving, mix all dressing ingredients in blender and drizzle over spinach salad. Be careful to add dressing slowly and toss well. Do not saturate. Refrigerate leftover dressing.

Yield: *8 to 10 servings*

Crunchy Pea Salad *(Parve)*

A great buffet appetizer.

Salad

1 (16-ounce) package frozen peas, thawed and drained	1 (15-ounce) can garbanzo beans, drained
1 small red onion, finely diced	1 red pepper, diced
1 (2-ounce) can sliced black olives, drained	1 cup salted peanuts, cashews or almonds
	2 tablespoons capers (optional)

Dressing

⅓ cup olive oil	2 cloves garlic, minced
3 tablespoons balsamic vinegar	Salt and fresh ground pepper,
1 heaping tablespoon Dijon mustard	to taste

◆ Mix all vegetables together. Add nuts, capers and vinaigrette dressing. Refrigerate until ready to serve.

Yield: *8 servings*

Note: *You may use ⅓ cup raspberry vinaigrette in place of dressing.*

San Diego Bread Salad *(Dairy)*

Salad

4	large sweet red peppers, roasted, skinned and cut into thick slices	3	cups cubed Italian bread
		8	ounces fresh mozzarella cut into cubes
2	zucchini, cut into rounds and broiled until golden		

Dressing

⅓	cup firmly packed fresh basil leaves	4	anchovy fillets
5	tablespoons extra virgin olive oil	2½	tablespoons balsamic vinegar
		2	cloves garlic

◆ To roast peppers, remove seeds and place thick slices on baking sheet, skin side up. Broil about 4 inches from heating element until charred. Place in paper bag and cool for about 15 minutes, then rub off skin.

◆ Combine all dressing ingredients in food processor and purée.

◆ Combine salad ingredients in separate bowl, add dressing and toss to mix. Let stand 20 to 30 minutes for bread to soften.

Yield: *4 servings*

Note: *The mixture may be pressed into a bowl prepared with vegetable spray and unmolded onto a plate for a gourmet presentation. Garnish with greens.*

Santa Fe Salad *(Dairy)*

1	medium sweet onion	½	cup sweet corn kernels
1	medium zucchini	3	ounces Monterey Jack cheese, diced
1	small red pepper		
1	rib celery	1	cup cilantro leaves
1	(15-ounce) can black beans, rinsed and drained	1	ripe avocado
			Red leaf lettuce for serving

Dressing

1	jalapeño or serrano pepper, seeded and minced	2	tablespoons sherry vinegar
6	tablespoons safflower or vegetable oil	1	teaspoon Dijon mustard
		½	teaspoon ground cumin
		¼	teaspoon salt, or more to taste

◆ Dice onion, zucchini, red pepper, and celery into pieces that are roughly the size of beans and corn. Combine in large bowl with beans, corn, cheese and cilantro.

◆ Combine all dressing ingredients and mix well.

◆ Just before serving, peel and dice the avocado and add to the salad along with the dressing. Mix gently and adjust the seasoning. Serve on lettuce leaves.

Yield: *4 servings*

Note: *You may use any combination of veggies in this recipe.*

Layered Winter Salad *(Parve)*

This can sit for hours without wilting.

Basil Vinaigrette

½ cup olive oil	¼ cup chopped fresh parsley
¼ cup white wine vinegar	1 clove garlic, crushed
2 tablespoons dried basil	2 tablespoons lemon juice
(or ¼ cup chopped fresh basil)	4 drops Tabasco sauce

Salad

1 large cucumber, sliced thin	1 medium red onion, sliced thin
½ pound mushrooms, sliced thin	3 medium tomatoes, sliced thin
1 red or green pepper, seeded and sliced in thin strips	

◆ Combine all ingredients for vinaigrette in food processor with metal blade or in a blender. Refrigerate for up to 4 days.

◆ In a large glass salad bowl, layer cucumber, mushrooms, pepper and onion. Sprinkle half the vinaigrette over the vegetables.

◆ Layer the tomato slices on top and pour on the remaining dressing. Cover with plastic wrap and refrigerate for several hours or overnight.

Yield: *4 to 6 servings*

Marinated Cucumbers *(Parve)*

1 teaspoon sugar	4 cucumbers, sliced
Salt and pepper	1 small onion, minced
¾ cup oil	½ red pepper, seeded and cut up
½ cup vinegar	½ bunch fresh dill
1 teaspoon fresh lemon juice	(or 2 teaspoons dried dill)

◆ Blend sugar, salt, pepper, oil, vinegar and lemon juice, stirring until salt and sugar are thoroughly dissolved.

◆ Put cucumbers, onions and pepper in salad bowl. Pour dressing over them and cut in fresh dill, using only the fine leaves. Stir until vegetables are well coated.

◆ Cover and refrigerate until ready to serve.

Yield: *10 to 12 servings*

Picadilly *(Parve)*

Salad

7	cups sliced unwaxed, unpeeled cucumbers	2	green or red peppers, sliced
3	large onions, sliced	5	ribs celery, sliced
		3	carrots, peeled and sliced

Marinade

1½	cups white vinegar	1½	teaspoons celery seed
1½	cups sugar	1	teaspoon mustard seed
1½	tablespoons salt	1½	teaspoons turmeric

◆ Combine salad ingredients in large bowl.

◆ Over medium-high heat, bring marinade ingredients to a boil. Remove from heat. Allow to cool slightly; pour over vegetables. Cover and refrigerate overnight.

Yield: *10 to 12 servings*

Note: *Picadilly may be prepared up to 3 to 5 days ahead.*

Marinated Vegetable Salad *(Parve)*

A colorful addition to a picnic or buffet.

1	bunch broccoli cut into small florets	¾	cup sugar
1	head cauliflower cut into small florets	1	cup red wine vinegar
		½	cup oil
1	large red onion, sliced thin and slices separated	1½	teaspoons salt
		½	teaspoon pepper
		¼	teaspoon dried basil leaves

◆ Toss vegetables together. Place remaining ingredients in covered jar and shake vigorously. Pour dressing over salad and toss.

◆ Refrigerate, covered, for at least 3 hours. Just before serving, toss and drain.

Yield: *10 to 12 servings*

Note: *Any variety of vegetables may be used in this one.*

Farmer's Chop Suey ✡ (Dairy)

This recipe was traditionally made with all sour cream.

2	cups low-fat cottage cheese	2	cups cut up vegetables (carrots,
½	cup sour cream (optional)		cucumbers, radishes, green
2	teaspoons dried dill		onions, tomatoes, celery)
½	teaspoon lemon pepper		Salt and pepper to taste

◆ Mix cottage cheese and sour cream with dill and lemon pepper. Refrigerate while cutting up vegetables.

◆ Combine vegetables with cottage cheese mixture. Add salt and pepper to taste.

Yield: *4 servings*

Note: *Salad may be made a day ahead and refrigerated.*

Date Coleslaw
with Orange-Ginger Vinaigrette (Parve)

1	(16-ounce) package pre-cut coleslaw mix or 7 cups coarsely shredded green and red cabbage	1	cup coarsely shredded carrots
		1	cup thinly sliced green onions (including a few green tops)
		1	cup chopped pitted dates

Dressing

½	tablespoon grated orange rind	1	teaspoon ground ginger
½	cup orange juice	1	teaspoon salt
3	tablespoons white wine or cider vinegar	¼	teaspoon pepper
2	cloves garlic, minced fine	2	tablespoons olive or vegetable oil

◆ Combine salad ingredients.

◆ To make dressing, whisk together first 7 ingredients. Whisk in oil. Toss with vegetables. Adjust salt and pepper to taste.

Yield: *8 servings*

Oriental Coleslaw Delight *(Parve)*

Salad

½	cup margarine
2	tablespoons sugar
½	cup sesame seeds
2	(3-ounce) packages ramen noodles, broken up

¾	cup slivered or sliced almonds
1	large bok choy (or 1 small bok choy and 1 small napa cabbage)
4	green onions, sliced

Dressing

¾	cup canola oil
¼	cup cider or red wine vinegar

½	cup sugar
2	tablespoons soy sauce

◆ In a large skillet melt margarine; add sugar, sesame seeds, noodles and almonds. Sauté and stir until light brown. Drain on paper towel. Cool to room temperature.

◆ Chop bok choy stalk and leaves; combine with onions and refrigerate.

◆ Combine all dressing ingredients until sugar dissolves. Refrigerate ingredients in 3 separate containers in refrigerator until ready to serve.

Yield: *10 to 12 servings*

Note: *Coleslaw may be made a day ahead. You may use pre-packaged cabbage or broccoli slaw.*

Honey Mustard Coleslaw *(Parve)*

6	cups shredded green cabbage	½	cup minced red pepper, seeded
1	cup shredded carrots	1	teaspoon minced jalapeño
½	cup minced green onions		pepper, seeded (optional)

Dressing

4	teaspoons oil	1	tablespoon seasoned rice
1	tablespoon Dijon mustard		vinegar
		1	tablespoon honey

- ◆ In large mixing bowl, combine cabbage, carrots, onions and pepper.
- ◆ In small bowl, combine remaining ingredients, stirring until blended.
- ◆ Pour dressing over cabbage mixture just before serving and toss to coat thoroughly.

Yield: *6 servings*

Potato Salad for a Crowd *(Parve)*

Salad

10	pounds red potatoes, boiled in jackets	1	tablespoon seasoned salt
		1	teaspoon lemon pepper
1	dozen hard-boiled eggs, peeled	1	cup chopped red or green
3	cups diced celery (8 to 10 ribs)		pepper (optional)
2	large carrots, peeled and shredded	1	cup sliced radishes (optional)

Dressing

4	cups mayonnaise-type salad dressing	¼	cup yellow mustard
		2	tablespoons sugar

- ◆ Cut cooked potatoes into 2-inch chunks. Cut up hard-boiled eggs. Add celery, carrots and seasonings.
- ◆ Mix salad dressing ingredients and mix into potato mixture. Garnish with cherry tomatoes, olives, green pepper and paprika if desired.
- ◆ Refrigerate 4 to 6 hours.

Yield: *25 to 30 servings*

Dilled Potato Salad *(Dairy)*

1	pound red potatoes, unpeeled	½	cup peeled, seeded and diced
½	cup mayonnaise		cucumber
½	cup plain yogurt	1	tablespoon scallions, sliced
1	tablespoon lemon juice		⅛-inch thick diagonally
1	tablespoon whole grain	2	tablespoons chopped dry
	prepared mustard		parsley
¼	teaspoon salt	1½	tablespoons chopped fresh dill
		1	tablespoon sunflower seeds

◆ Scrub and cube potatoes; place in boiling water and simmer until tender. Drain and place in container.

◆ Mix mayonnaise, yogurt, lemon juice, mustard and salt together until well blended. Pour mixture over potatoes while they're still warm and toss until potatoes are well coated.

◆ Refrigerate until fully chilled. Toss with cucumber, scallions, parsley, dill and sunflower seeds.

Yield: *3 to 4 servings*

Colorful Wild Rice Salad *(Parve)*

1	cup wild rice	½	teaspoon salt
2	cups shredded carrots	1	cup raisins, craisins, dried
3	green onions, chopped		cherries or blueberries
¼	cup olive oil	1	cup pecans or walnuts
¼	cup red wine vinegar	½	tablespoon honey

◆ Cook rice according to directions. Do not add butter, oil or seasonings. Drain well and refrigerate until completely cooled. When cool, add carrots and onions; mix well.

◆ Mix together oil and vinegar in blender or covered container. Add salt. Pour dressing over rice and mix thoroughly.

◆ Add dried fruit and nuts and combine. Add honey and mix well. Adjust seasonings to taste.

Yield: *8 to 10 servings*

Note: *If you use packaged shredded carrots, cut them into smaller pieces. Plump dried fruit in warm water. Be sure to drain before adding to rice.*

Fruited Couscous Salad *(Parve)*

2	cups parve chicken broth or water	¼	cup chopped pitted dates
		1	cup diced zucchini
3	tablespoons olive oil, divided	½	cup diced carrots
1	teaspoon ground cumin	½	cup diced red onion
	Dash ground cinnamon	2	tablespoons lemon juice
	Dash ground ginger		Salt and pepper to taste
1	cup couscous	¼	cup pine nuts
¼	cup dried currants		

◆ In a heavy pot or Dutch oven, bring parve chicken broth or water, 2 tablespoons olive oil, cumin, cinnamon and ginger to a boil. Stir in couscous and cook according to package directions.

◆ Stir in currants and dates. Cover tightly and let stand for 15 minutes. Add zucchini, carrots and onion.

◆ In a small bowl, combine lemon juice and remaining 1 tablespoon of oil. Pour over couscous and toss to coat thoroughly. Add salt and pepper. Refrigerate overnight, covered, to blend flavors.

◆ To serve, bring to room temperature. Toss with pine nuts.

Yield: *6 servings*

Tabouli *(Parve)*

½	cup cracked wheat (bulgur)	2	ribs celery
½	cup warm water	1	green pepper, seeded
4	large tomatoes	1	bunch scallions
½	cup chopped parsley		Juice of 2 lemons
1	cucumber		Salt and pepper to taste

◆ Put cracked wheat and water in a bowl and let stand for ½ hour while you chop all vegetables.

◆ Pour lemon juice over the chopped vegetables. Add to cracked wheat.

◆ Refrigerate for at least 2 hours. Bring to room temperature before serving.

Yield: *4 servings*

Oriental Pasta Salad *(Parve or Meat)*

1 bunch broccoli, cut up	½-1 teaspoon crushed red pepper
½ cup smooth peanut butter	2 cooked chicken breast halves,
½ cup hot water	skinned, boned and cut up
¼ cup soy sauce	(optional)
2 tablespoons red wine vinegar	8 ounces linguine, cooked and
1 tablespoon sesame oil	drained
2 teaspoons sugar	½ cup chopped scallions
2 cloves garlic, crushed	

◆ Cook broccoli until light green and crisp, approximately 3 minutes.

◆ Combine peanut butter and hot water and mix until smooth. Add soy sauce, vinegar, sesame oil, sugar, garlic and red pepper and blend well. If using chicken, add to peanut sauce and marinate in refrigerator for 2 hours.

◆ In a large bowl, combine linguine with broccoli, sauce and scallions and toss well. Serve slightly chilled.

Yield: *4 to 6 servings*

Tuna Pasta Salad *(Parve)*

¼ cup fresh lemon juice	1 (7-ounce) package linguine or
¼ cup olive or vegetable oil	penne pasta, cooked and
(or less)	drained
¼ cup sliced green onions	2 (6½-ounce) cans tuna, drained
2 teaspoons sugar	1 (10-ounce) package frozen
1 teaspoon Italian seasoning	green peas, thawed
1 teaspoon seasoned salt	2 medium tomatoes, chopped

◆ In large bowl, combine lemon juice, oil, onions and seasonings; mix well.

◆ Add hot pasta and toss together. Add remaining ingredients and mix well. Chill thoroughly.

Yield: *6 servings*

Note: *This may be made a day in advance and refrigerated. You may need to add liquid (lemon juice and/or oil) to refresh before serving.*

Rice Salad
with Artichokes and Olives *(Parve)*

1	(7-ounce) package herb rice (long grain and wild)	2	(6½-ounce) jars marinated artichoke hearts
12	pimiento-stuffed olives	¾	teaspoon curry powder (or to taste)
4	green onions, sliced		
½	green pepper, chopped	½	cup mayonnaise

◆ Cook rice according to package directions. Omit butter.

◆ Put rice in medium bowl and add olives, onions and green pepper.

◆ Drain artichoke hearts, reserving marinade. Cut hearts in half and add to rice.

◆ Combine reserved marinade, curry powder, and mayonnaise. Add to rice mixture and toss well.

◆ Refrigerate for 3 hours. Bring to room temperature before serving.

Yield: *4 servings*

Chicken Salad
with Tomato Cucumber Dressing *(Meat)*

½	cup fresh lemon juice	1	tomato, peeled and diced
6	tablespoons sesame oil	1	large cucumber, peeled, seeded and diced
¼	cup fresh ginger		
2	tablespoons oil	1	small head Boston lettuce
2	tablespoons fresh cilantro	2	pounds cooked chicken breasts, skinless and boneless
2	cloves garlic		

◆ Blend lemon juice, 6 tablespoons sesame oil, ginger, oil, cilantro and garlic in processor or blender until smooth.

◆ Peel tomato by placing in hot water for 1 minute and then slipping off skin. Combine cucumber and tomato in small bowl. Fold in dressing.

◆ Line platter with lettuce leaves. Cut chicken lengthwise into thin strips. Arrange on lettuce leaves. Top with cucumber mixture and serve.

Yield: *6 servings*

Note: *This recipe may be prepared 4 hours ahead; keep dressing separate and refrigerate. Combine when ready to serve.*

Greek Feta Bow Tie Salad (Dairy)

Salad

8	ounces bow tie pasta, cooked, rinsed and drained	1	medium cucumber, halved lengthwise, cored and sliced
1	tablespoon olive oil	1	large red bell pepper, seeded and julienned
2	tablespoons finely chopped fresh parsley	5-6	medium radishes, sliced
2	tablespoons finely chopped fresh dill	8-10	kalamata olives, pitted and chopped
1	teaspoon fresh thyme leaves	2	teaspoons capers
¼	pound feta cheese, cut into ½-inch cubes	1	tablespoon coarsely chopped red onion

Lemon-Dill Dressing

2	tablespoons fresh lemon juice	2	teaspoons minced shallots
1	clove garlic, minced	3	tablespoons chopped fresh dill
¼	cup finely chopped fresh parsley	¼	cup oil
			Freshly ground black pepper

- ◆ Transfer cooled pasta to a serving dish and toss with olive oil. Add the parsley, dill and thyme to the pasta and mix well.

- ◆ Toss remaining salad ingredients with the pasta.

- ◆ In a small bowl, whisk the lemon juice with the garlic, parsley, shallots and dill. Gradually add the oil and mix the dressing well. Add pepper to taste. Whisk again briefly before adding to salad.

Yield: *8 to 10 side dish servings*

Chinese Chicken Salad (Meat)

Peanut butter is the surprise ingredient in the dressing!

⅓ cup toasted almonds, sliced or slivered

1 package ramen noodles (Oriental flavor)

4 cups cubed cooked chicken or turkey

⅓ cup chopped green onions

1 red or green pepper, seeded and cut in rings (optional)

1 (11-ounce) can Mandarin oranges, drained (optional)

Pea pods (optional)

Dressing

3 tablespoons rice vinegar

1 packet Oriental seasoning (from noodles)

2 tablespoons soy sauce

⅓ cup olive oil

1 tablespoon creamy peanut butter

Dash red pepper

◆ Toast almonds in a nonstick skillet over medium heat 3 to 4 minutes until light brown. Stir often; cool completely.

◆ Break up noodles. Add chicken or turkey, almonds and green onions. Add bell pepper, oranges and pea pods if desired.

◆ Mix all dressing ingredients and pour over salad. Serve on a bed of lettuce.

Yield: *8 servings*

Polynesian Chicken Salad (Meat)

Great company dish served in scooped out pineapple halves.

4	boneless, skinless chicken breasts	¼	cup sliced almonds, toasted
¼	teaspoon seasoned salt, or to taste	1	(8-ounce) can sliced water chestnuts, drained
¼	teaspoon garlic powder, or to taste	1	cup fresh pineapple chunks
⅛	teaspoon pepper, or to taste	1	cup mayonnaise (adjust amount according to taste)

◆ Preheat oven to 350°. Season chicken breasts with salt, garlic powder and pepper.

◆ Place in baking dish and sprinkle with water. Cover and bake for 1 hour and 45 minutes. Meanwhile toast almonds in a nonstick skillet over medium heat for 3 to 4 minutes until lightly brown. Stir often; cool completely.

◆ Allow chicken to cool. Shred chicken. Add almonds, water chestnuts and pineapple chunks. Mix in mayonnaise.

Yield: *8 servings*

Note: *Cooked turkey breast may be used.*

Mom's Delicious Cranberry Sauce (Parve)

They'll ask for seconds on this one.

1　cup sugar
1　cup orange juice
3　cups fresh cranberries

2　apples, peeled, cored and cut
　　into small pieces

- ◆ In medium saucepan, bring sugar and orange juice to a boil. Add berries and apples.
- ◆ When berries pop completely, turn heat off and let mixture sit for 10 minutes.
- ◆ Cool and refrigerate.

Yield: *10 to 12 servings*

Cranberry Relish (Parve)

1　(12-ounce) package cranberries
1　large seedless orange with
　　rind, cut into 8 pieces

2　cups sugar

- ◆ In food processor, coarsely chop cranberries and orange. Mix with sugar. Place in refrigerator for 30 minutes until sugar is dissolved.
- ◆ The relish will keep for 1 to 2 weeks in a tightly closed container.

Yield: *8 servings*

Hot Fruit Compote *(Parve)*

Great cold the next day.

1	(15-ounce) can peaches	1	(15-ounce) can pitted plums
1	(14-ounce) can chunk pineapple	1	(7-ounce) package dried apricots
2	(15-ounce) cans Mandarin oranges	1	(18-ounce) package dried prunes
1	(16-ounce) can dark sweet cherries	¾	cup raisins
1	(16-ounce) can Queen Anne cherries	¾	cup raspberry applesauce
1	(15-ounce) can apricot halves	1	heaping tablespoon tapioca
		½	cup sweet wine (any flavor)

- ◆ Preheat oven to 350°. Drain all canned fruits. Add dried fruits and mix. Add applesauce, tapioca and wine and mix well.
- ◆ Bake in a deep covered 3- or 4-quart baking dish for approximately 45 minutes, or until bubbly.

Yield: *12 to 16 servings*

Fresh Fruit with Tangy Dressing *(Parve)*

2	bananas, sliced	½	cup grapes, washed and stemmed
4	cups cubed melon		
2	pears, cored and sliced		

Dressing

⅓	cup sugar	1	teaspoon celery seeds
1	tablespoon oil	1	teaspoon dry mustard
⅓	cup lemon juice	1	teaspoon paprika
¼	cup water	½	teaspoon salt

- ◆ Combine fruit in a large bowl. Put all of the dressing ingredients in a blender; process until well blended.
- ◆ Serve the fruit drizzled with the dressing.

Yield: *6 servings*

Pineapple Cottage Cheese Mold *(Dairy)*

Delicious as a side dish or even as a snack!

1	(20-ounce) can crushed pineapple with juice	1	(8-ounce) carton frozen whipped topping, thawed
1	(6-ounce) package lime gelatin	1	(8-ounce) carton small curd cottage cheese

♦ Heat pineapple and juice to boiling in 2-quart saucepan on stovetop or in microwave.

♦ Dissolve gelatin in boiling pineapple. Remove from heat, cool and refrigerate to egg white consistency.

♦ Whip in topping with wire whisk. Add cottage cheese.

♦ Place in 1½-quart serving bowl. Refrigerate several hours or overnight.

Yield: *6 to 8 servings*

Raspberry Mold *(Dairy or Parve)*

1	(6-ounce) package raspberry gelatin	1	cup low-fat sour cream or 8-ounce container frozen whipped topping, thawed (optional)
2	cups boiling water		
1	(20-ounce) can crushed pineapple with juice	2	bananas, mashed
2	(10-ounce) containers frozen raspberries with juice, thawed		

♦ Dissolve gelatin in boiling water. Add juice from pineapple and raspberries. Mix well.

♦ Whip in sour cream or whipped topping. Add remaining ingredients. Sour cream or whipped topping may be omitted, if desired, for parve mold.

♦ Place in large glass serving bowl and refrigerate until set, about 3 to 4 hours.

Yield: *12 servings*

Sunshine Citrus Mold *(Dairy)*

Each layer by itself makes a great side dish!

Layer 1

1	(3-ounce) package orange gelatin
¾	cup boiling water

3	ounces frozen orange juice concentrate, thawed
4	ounces frozen whipped topping, thawed

Layer 2

1	(3-ounce) package lemon gelatin
¾	cup boiling water

3	ounces frozen lemonade concentrate, thawed
4	ounces frozen whipped topping, thawed

Layer 3

1	(3-ounce) package lime gelatin
¾	cup boiling water
3	ounces frozen limeade concentrate, thawed

4	ounces frozen whipped topping, thawed
4	ounces drained, crushed pineapple (optional)

◆ In a 4-cup measuring cup, dissolve orange gelatin for Layer 1 in boiling water. Stir in orange juice concentrate.

◆ Place in refrigerator and, when partially set, fold in whipped topping. Pour into 8-cup ring mold sprayed with vegetable spray and place in freezer.

◆ When first layer is frozen, prepare second layer same as the first, and follow the same directions for the third layer. Store in freezer until ready to use. Defrost slightly before serving.

Yield: *12 to 15 servings*

Dijon Vinaigrette Salad Dressing *(Parve)*

¼ cup balsamic vinegar
1 tablespoon Dijon mustard
⅔ cup olive oil
¾ teaspoon salt
1 clove garlic, mashed

2 tablespoons maple syrup or raspberry jam
1 tablespoon lemon juice
Orange juice to taste

◆ Mix all ingredients well. Taste for right amount of sweetness.
◆ Store in airtight bottle.

Yield: *1 cup*

Honey Poppy Seed Dressing *(Parve)*

Enjoy over vegetable or chicken salad.

⅓ cup honey
½ cup canola oil
1 teaspoon grated onion
3 tablespoons white wine vinegar

2 tablespoons lemon juice
½ teaspoon dry mustard
½ teaspoon all-purpose seasoning
1 teaspoon poppy seeds

◆ Heat the honey for 3 seconds in microwave in 2-cup measuring cup.
◆ Add remaining ingredients except poppy seeds; mix together in blender or covered container.
◆ Add poppy seeds after the dressing is blended.

Yield: *1½ cups*

Lime Vinaigrette Dressing *(Parve)*

¼ cup sugar
¼ cup honey
1 tablespoon dry mustard
1½ teaspoons ginger

5 tablespoons lime juice
3½ tablespoons water
¾ cup oil

◆ Mix all ingredients well either in food processor or by shaking vigorously in closed container.

Yield: *2 cups*

Note: *You may prefer a bit less sugar.*

Mango Dressing *(Parve)*

1 very ripe mango, peeled
⅓ cup cider or balsamic vinegar
1 tablespoon Dijon mustard
1 tablespoon honey
½ teaspoon curry powder

½ teaspoon salt
¼ teaspoon pepper, freshly
   ground
½ cup extra virgin olive oil

◆ Cut mango into ½-inch chunks. Combine with vinegar, mustard, honey, curry powder, salt and pepper in food processor and process until smooth. Slowly add the oil and process to blend.

◆ Transfer the dressing to a container or bowl and let stand at room temperature for 1 hour or refrigerate overnight. Dressing should be at room temperature before serving over salad greens or fruit.

Yield: *12 servings*

French Dressing *(Parve)*

½	cup sugar	2	tablespoons ketchup
¼	cup cider vinegar	½	cup oil
1	tablespoon lemon juice	1	teaspoon salt
1	small onion	1	teaspoon paprika

◆ Place all ingredients in blender and purée until well blended.

Yield: *1½ cups*

Zero Salad Dressing ✡ *(Parve)*

Great if you're counting calories.

½	cup tomato juice	1	tablespoon finely chopped onion
2	tablespoons lemon juice or vinegar		Salt and pepper to taste
			Sweetener to taste

◆ Mix all ingredients well in blender or covered container.

Yield: *¾ cup*

Note: *Changing the type of vinegar used will give you a different tasting dressing.*

Lunches
&
Brunches

(Blintzes & Quiche)

The Edible Egg

Safe Eggs:

◆ Eggs have a shelf life of approximately one month and should always be refrigerated in the original carton. Do not leave them at room temperature for more than 2 hours. Discard cracked eggs.

◆ To test for freshness, submerge egg in cool, salted water. Egg is fresh if it sinks to the bottom.

◆ To be salmonella-free, eggs must be heated to 160° or maintained at 140° for 3½ minutes. Fully baked goods and hard-cooked eggs reach this temperature easily. Bring eggs to a boil; then turn off heat, cover and let stand for 4 to 5 minutes for soft-cooked eggs.

◆ Poach eggs in simmering water for 3 to 5 minutes or when whites are set and yolks thicken.

◆ Scrambled eggs should be fully cooked.

◆ A meringue of 3 egg whites put on a hot pie filling and baked at 350° should reach 160° in about 15 minutes. Refrigerate meringue pies until ready to serve.

Other Tips:

◆ Break each egg individually into a small glass dish to check for blood spots which make the egg nonkosher. If blood spots appear, dispose of egg.

◆ To prevent eggs from cracking while boiling, add a pinch of salt to the water.

◆ Poke an egg with a small sewing needle before hard boiling. The egg will then peel easily.

◆ You may also use a pasteurized liquid egg product as a substitute for natural eggs.

Lox Spread *(Dairy)*

⅓	pound lox, chopped	1	tablespoon grated onion
8	ounces regular cream cheese, softened	1	tablespoon sour cream
8	ounces Neufchâtel cream cheese, softened		Pinch garlic powder

◆ Mix all ingredients until well blended. Refrigerate.

Yield: *12 or more servings*

Note: *Spread may be made a day ahead.*

"No Blintz" Soufflé *(Dairy)*

Company's coming and no blintzes in the freezer? Try this!

Batter

½	cup butter or margarine	¾	cup milk
½	cup sugar	1	teaspoon baking powder
2	eggs	½	teaspoon salt
1¼	cups flour		

Filling

1	pound cottage cheese	2	tablespoons sugar
1	egg	½	teaspoon vanilla
2	teaspoons butter or margarine, melted	¼	teaspoon lemon juice
		¼	teaspoon cinnamon

◆ Preheat oven to 350°. Beat together margarine, sugar and 2 eggs until fluffy.

◆ Add flour, milk, baking powder and salt. Mix until smooth.

◆ In separate bowl place all ingredients for filling. Beat until smooth.

◆ Pour half the batter into a greased 9x9-inch pan. Spread filling over it and cover with the remaining batter.

◆ Bake for 1 hour. Cut into squares.

Yield: *8 to 10 squares*

Note: *Skim milk may be used.*

Blintz Soufflé *(Dairy)*

A favorite brunch standby!

12	frozen cheese blintzes	1	tablespoon vanilla
½	cup margarine, melted	¼	cup sugar
4	eggs, beaten	1	(3-ounce) package vanilla
1½	cups light sour cream		pudding

◆ Preheat oven to 350°. Put frozen blintzes in 9x13-inch ovenproof dish sprayed with vegetable spray. Mix remaining ingredients and pour over blintzes.

◆ Bake for 45 minutes until golden.

Yield: *8 to 12 servings*

Note: *This soufflé may be assembled the day before, refrigerated and baked just before serving.*

Tuna Blintzes *(Dairy)*

This was a contest winner for our recipe contributor.

Tuna Filling

2	(12-ounce) cans white tuna, rinsed and drained	¾	cup finely chopped walnuts or pecans
1	(4-ounce) can sliced mushrooms	1½	tablespoons sugar
½	small onion, cut up	¼	teaspoon salt
		⅛	teaspoon white pepper
		2	eggs

Cheese Sauce

½	(10¾-ounce) can cream of mushroom soup	¾	cup shredded yellow cheeses
		⅓	cup milk

◆ Use blintz batter instructions from Traditional Blintzes recipe.

◆ With steel blade in food processor, mince tuna and mushrooms. Add onions, nuts, sugar, salt and white pepper. Add eggs one at a time and mix well. Use filling and baking instructions from Traditional Blintzes recipe.

◆ Heat cheese sauce ingredients until cheese is melted. Drizzle over cooked tuna blintzes.

Yield: *30 blintzes*

Traditional Blintzes *(Dairy)*

These are well worth the effort!

Batter

1	cup cornstarch	½	teaspoon salt
2	tablespoons flour	3	tablespoons sugar
4	cups water	¼	cup butter
6	eggs		

Cheese Filling

1	(8-ounce) package cream cheese	2	eggs
1	pound dry cottage cheese or farmer's cheese	3	tablespoons sugar

◆ Combine cornstarch and flour; add water a little at a time until dry ingredients are dissolved. In separate bowl, beat eggs and add salt and sugar. Add to liquid.

◆ Heat 2 or 3 omelet pans on medium to medium-high heat. Lightly grease bottom with butter. Add ¼ cup batter and swirl pan until bottom is covered. Then pour excess batter back into bowl. When edges of blintz begin to curl away from pan, turn pan over on top of a cloth towel and let blintz cool. Continue until all batter is used. If batter begins to thicken, add a little water. If batter is too thin, add a little cornstarch or flour.

◆ Combine remaining ingredients. Preheat oven to 350°. Place 2 tablespoons of filling in middle of blintz and roll up, first from the bottom, then tuck in the sides and continue rolling until blintz is formed.

◆ Place blintzes on greased jellyroll pan and bake for 10 minutes; turn over half way through. Top with sour cream, any fruit pie filling or fresh berries.

Yield: *30 blintzes*

Cottage Cheese Soufflé ✡ (Dairy)

1	pound large curd cottage cheese (regular or low-fat)	3	tablespoons sour cream (regular or light)
3	eggs		Pinch of salt
¾	cup flour (matzo cake flour works well)	¼	cup margarine Cinnamon and sugar
3	tablespoons sugar		

- ◆ Preheat oven to 375°. Place all ingredients, except margarine and topping, into mixing bowl and beat well.
- ◆ Melt margarine in 2-quart casserole. Pour ingredients from mixing bowl into casserole. Sprinkle top with cinnamon and sugar.
- ◆ Bake for 45 minutes.

Yield: *6 servings*

Note: *Soufflé may be served with canned fruit such as cherries or blueberries.*

Southwestern Quiche (Dairy)

5	eggs	2	cups shredded Monterey Jack cheese
2	tablespoons margarine, melted		
¼	cup flour	1	(4-ounce) can green chilies, chopped
½	teaspoon baking powder		
1	(8-ounce) carton cottage cheese	1	tomato, sliced
			Sour cream and salsa

- ◆ Preheat oven to 400°. In mixer, beat eggs lightly. Add margarine, flour and baking powder. Mix well.
- ◆ Add cottage cheese, Monterey Jack and chilies to mixture.
- ◆ Pour into a well-greased 10-inch quiche dish. Bake for 10 minutes.
- ◆ Reduce temperature to 350°. Arrange tomato over top and return to oven. Bake for another 20 minutes.
- ◆ Serve with sour cream and salsa.

Yield: *4 to 6 servings*

Mushroom Quiche *(Dairy)*

Easy to make and delicious to serve!

1	deep-dish pie shell or your favorite pie crust	1	teaspoon lemon juice
4	tablespoons butter, divided	4	eggs
2	tablespoons finely chopped green onion	1	cup low-fat milk
1	pound mushrooms, sliced	¼	teaspoon pepper
½	teaspoon salt	⅛	teaspoon nutmeg
		¾	cup grated Swiss cheese

♦ Preheat oven to 350°. Spray a 10-inch quiche dish or deep pie dish with vegetable spray. Line with pie dough. Bake for 10 minutes before filling.

♦ In a medium skillet, melt 3 tablespoons butter; add green onions and cook for 1 minute. Add mushrooms, salt and lemon juice; cover and simmer for 10 minutes. Uncover and cook for an additional 5 to 10 minutes until liquid is evaporated and mushrooms are cooked, stirring occasionally.

♦ Beat eggs and milk together; add pepper and nutmeg. Stir in mushrooms and green onions. Pour into crust and sprinkle with cheese. Dot with remaining 1 tablespoon butter.

♦ Bake for 35 minutes or until knife inserted in center comes out clean.

Yield: *6 to 8 servings*

Note: *Quiche may be frozen.*

Tuna Quiche *(Dairy)*

Pastry

1½ cups flour	½ teaspoon salt
½ cup margarine	¼ cup water

Filling

2 (6¼-ounce) cans tuna	Ginger to taste
1 zucchini, chopped	½ cup grated cheddar cheese, divided
1 onion, chopped	
2 eggs	¼ cup grated Swiss cheese, divided
½ cup milk	
Salt and pepper to taste	1 tomato, sliced (optional)

◆ Preheat oven to 350°. For pastry crust, blend together flour, margarine and salt with fork; add water to make dough. Press into greased quiche dish or 10-inch pie plate.

◆ Mix together all ingredients for filling except ¼ cup cheese and tomato and pour into the pastry crust.

◆ Add some grated cheese on top and a sliced tomato for decoration if desired.

◆ Bake for approximately 45 minutes. Allow to cool for 10 to 15 minutes before serving.

Yield: *4 to 6 servings*

Spinach Quiche *(Dairy)*

1 (10-ounce) package frozen chopped spinach, thawed and drained	Salt and pepper to taste
	1 cup shredded Swiss cheese
1 9-inch pie shell, unbaked	1 tablespoon flour
2 teaspoons dried tarragon	3 eggs
	1½ cups half-and-half or milk

◆ Preheat oven to 400°. Layer spinach in bottom of pie shell. Season with tarragon, salt and pepper.

◆ Layer cheese over spinach and dust with flour.

◆ Beat eggs, mix with half-and-half and slowly pour mixture into pie shell. (Sometimes there will be leftover egg mixture. Bake without crust in separate dish.)

◆ Bake for 45 minutes.

Yield: *6 to 8 servings*

Spanakopita (Spinach Pie) *(Dairy)*

3	pounds fresh spinach, or 3 (10-ounce) packages frozen chopped spinach	½	pound feta cheese, coarsely crumbled
10	tablespoons margarine, divided	⅓	cup fresh parsley, chopped
1	medium onion, chopped	1	teaspoon salt
4	eggs	¼	teaspoon pepper
		¼	cup oil
		16	sheets phyllo dough

◆ Wash fresh spinach, trim stems and tear leaves. Steam spinach in large covered saucepan for 10 minutes, or until just cooked. To use frozen spinach, cook according to directions. Drain well and squeeze out liquid when cool.

◆ In skillet, heat 2 tablespoons margarine and sauté onion over medium heat, stirring constantly until onion is soft, about 3 minutes.

◆ In large bowl beat eggs; stir in sautéed onion, cheese, parsley, salt and pepper. Gradually mix in drained spinach.

◆ Preheat oven to 350°. Melt ½ cup margarine. Combine with oil. Brush some over bottom and sides of 9x13-inch pan. Using 8 sheets of phyllo dough, line the bottom and sides of pan, brushing each sheet lightly with oil mixture. Add spinach filling and cover with remaining phyllo, brushing each sheet with oil mixture.

◆ Using a sharp knife, score top layers of phyllo into 12 squares. (For appetizers, score into smaller squares.)

◆ Bake for 35 minutes, or until golden brown. Cool slightly; cut into squares and serve warm.

Yield: *6 to 8 servings*

Note: *Recipe may be prepared ahead and refrigerated until ready to bake. Keep covered in refrigerator.*

Cheese Knishes (Dairy)

Dough
2½ cups flour	1 cup margarine
½ teaspoon baking powder	½ pint sour cream
½ teaspoon salt	

Filling
1 small onion, chopped	2-3 eggs
1 tablespoon oil or margarine	1 teaspoon salt
2 pounds dry cottage cheese or farmer's cheese	

- Sift flour, baking powder and salt together. Cut margarine into flour mixture as you would for pie dough.

- Add sour cream to make a soft dough. Form into ball and refrigerate for 3 to 4 hours or overnight.

- Sauté onion in oil or margarine until transparent. Let cool. Mix remaining filling ingredients together with the onion.

- Preheat oven to 350°. Divide dough into 4 parts. On well-floured board, roll 1 part as thin as possible into an approximately 12x16-inch rectangle. Spread ¼ of filling along the 16-inch edge and roll as for a jellyroll.

- Cut pieces 2 inches long. Pinch each piece closed on both sides and place on well-greased cookie sheet. Finish in the same manner with the remaining dough and filling.

- Bake for 40 minutes, or until lightly browned. Serve warm with sour cream on the side.

Yield: *32 pieces*

Note: *Knishes may be made as hors d'oeuvres by cutting pieces smaller. For a sweet rather than savory flavor, eliminate the fried onion and add 1 tablespoon of sugar; serve with strawberry or raspberry sauce.*

Apple Pancake *(Dairy)*

A fabulous Sunday morning treat!

Pancake
1	tablespoon butter
2	eggs
½	cup milk

½	cup flour
¼	teaspoon nutmeg
1	tablespoon sugar

Apple Filling
2	tart apples, peeled and sliced thin
1	tablespoon butter

1	tablespoon sugar
½	teaspoon cinnamon

◆ Preheat oven to 425°. Melt butter in a 10-inch pie plate. In blender, combine remaining pancake ingredients. Pour into pie plate.

◆ Bake for 15 to 20 minutes.

◆ Over medium heat, cook filling ingredients in a skillet until apples are soft. Fill center of prepared pancake and serve.

Yield: *2 servings*

Note: *You may also use prepared apple pie filling or butter and syrup.*

Company French Toast *(Dairy)*

6	eggs
2	cups light cream or whole milk
	Cinnamon to taste
1	tablespoon vanilla

1	loaf raisin bread, sliced
1	(8-ounce) container whipped cream cheese

◆ Beat eggs with cream. Add cinnamon and vanilla.

◆ Spread half of loaf slices with cream cheese. Top with remaining bread slices. Dip sandwiches in egg mixture.

◆ Fry in oil or butter until brown.

Yield: *6 servings*

Swedish Oatmeal Pancakes *(Dairy)*

4	cups rolled oats	2	teaspoons baking powder
1	cup flour	4	cups buttermilk
¼	cup sugar	4	eggs, beaten
2	teaspoons baking soda	½	cup margarine, melted
	Pinch of salt	2	teaspoons vanilla

♦ Combine oats, flour, sugar, baking soda, salt and baking powder in a large bowl. Blend in buttermilk, eggs, margarine and vanilla. Mix well.

♦ Let batter stand for 30 to 45 minutes to thicken. Heat griddle or large skillet over medium heat; butter griddle.

♦ Add batter by spoonfuls and cook, turning once, until pancakes are puffed and browned on both sides. Serve immediately with syrup or honey.

Yield: *8 to 10 servings*

Note: *Raisins or dried cranberries may be added to batter. For thinner pancakes, add more buttermilk.*

Entrées

Fish, Meat, Poultry & Vegetarian

Main Dish Hints

Brisket:

◆ Before slicing chilled meat, discard all visible fat.

◆ Slice the cooked brisket about ¼ inch thick against the grain. The lines are the grain. Cut perpendicular to those lines. Place the meat back in the sauce in the pan, distributing sauce over the meat.

◆ Cover with foil and refrigerate or freeze.

◆ Before serving, bring brisket to room temperature and place in preheated 350° oven for 30 to 40 minutes to reheat, or reheat in the microwave.

◆ Leftover brisket may be used for kreplach, meat blintzes or barbecued beef.

Poultry:

◆ Always use clean cutting boards and utensils. Wash hands thoroughly.

◆ After using containers or utensils that have come in contact with raw poultry, wash thoroughly in hot sudsy water.

◆ Never place cooked poultry back in uncooked marinade.

◆ To skin raw poultry, use paper towels for easy gripping.

Fish:

◆ Fish is fresh when the eyes are clear and flesh is firm. Fresh fish may be kept refrigerated up to 2 days covered with plastic wrap. Fish may be frozen in a freezer storage bag up to 2 months.

◆ Cook fish until flesh flakes easily.

Tofu:

◆ Tofu can be frozen, then defrosted, to make the texture meatier.

◆ All tofu must be drained before use.

Bouillabaisse (*Parve or Dairy*)

An unbelievable kosher adaptation.

2	medium onions, chopped	¼	teaspoon fennel or anise seed
1	green pepper, seeded and chopped	2	medium potatoes, peeled and cut in ½-inch cubes
1	red pepper, seeded and chopped	3	cups water
		1	cup red or white wine
2	cloves garlic, crushed	2	pounds fish fillets (snapper,
2	tablespoons olive oil		cod and/or imitation crab),
1	(28-ounce) can diced tomatoes		cut in chunks
1	small bay leaf	¼	cup minced parsley
¼	teaspoon crushed red pepper, or to taste	½	cup cream or nondairy creamer
		2	teaspoons salt, or to taste
½	teaspoon grated orange peel	¼	teaspoon pepper, or to taste
½	teaspoon dried thyme		

◆ In large pot, sauté onions, peppers and garlic in hot oil until tender. Add tomatoes, bay leaf, crushed pepper, orange peel, thyme and fennel. Bring to boil.

◆ Add potatoes. Cover and simmer for 10 minutes. Add water and wine; bring to boil. Reduce heat and simmer, uncovered, 5 minutes.

◆ Add fish and parsley. Bring to simmer; cover and cook for 2 minutes or until fish flakes easily with fork. DO NOT OVERCOOK.

◆ Remove bay leaf. Stir in cream, salt and pepper. Serve piping hot in warm bowls.

Yield: *6 servings*

Note: *For a spicier taste, add liquid red pepper to individual bowls.*

Mango Salsa Salmon (Parve)

1	large mango, peeled and diced	1	tablespoon chopped cilantro
3	tablespoons minced onion	1½	tablespoons olive oil
3	tablespoons diced green pepper	½	avocado, diced
		1	tablespoon oil
3	tablespoons diced red pepper	2	pounds salmon fillets
2	tablespoons white wine vinegar		Salt and pepper to taste

- ◆ Combine first 8 ingredients for salsa. Cover and refrigerate.
- ◆ Heat oil in a large flat skillet. Season fillets with salt and pepper. Sear salmon on both sides until browned, turning only once.
- ◆ Preheat oven to 350°. Bake seared salmon for approximately 15 minutes, until flaky. Serve with mango salsa.

Yield: *3 servings*

Sweet and Saucy Salmon (Parve)

½	cup orange juice	1	teaspoon garlic powder
¼	cup honey	½	teaspoon ground ginger
¼	cup low-sodium soy sauce		Pinch ground pepper
2	tablespoons lemon juice	1	pound salmon fillets

- ◆ Combine all marinade ingredients. Place fish, skin side down, in 9x13-inch baking dish prepared with vegetable spray and pour marinade over top. Cover and marinate for 1 hour.
- ◆ Preheat broiler. Remove from marinade and broil for 3 to 4 minutes, then bake at 325° until fish flakes easily, approximately 15 minutes.

Yield: *2 servings*

Poached Salmon with Asparagus and Tomatoes *(Parve)*

1	pound salmon steaks	1	bunch (about 2 cups)
4	cups chopped tomatoes		asparagus, trimmed
1	cup thickly sliced onion	½	cup water
¼	cup chopped parsley	1	vegetable bouillon cube
1	teaspoon salt	2	bay leaves
½	teaspoon pepper		

◆ Preheat oven to 375°. Place salmon in a deep baking dish and add remaining ingredients. Cover and bake for 25 to 30 minutes or until liquid simmers and fish flakes easily with a fork.

Yield: *2 servings*

Grilled Salmon in Citrus Herb Marinade *(Parve)*

Dazzle your guests with this special dish.

6	tablespoons olive oil	2	cloves garlic, peeled and sliced
¼	cup fresh orange juice		thin
3	tablespoons fresh lemon juice	1	(½-inch) piece peeled fresh
2	tablespoons low-sodium soy		ginger, sliced thin
	sauce		Leaves from 1 sprig of fresh
1	tablespoon fresh lime juice		thyme
¼	medium fennel bulb, trimmed,	1	bay leaf
	cored and thinly sliced	⅛	teaspoon fresh ground pepper
	crosswise	2	pounds salmon fillets
½	small red onion, sliced thin		

◆ Combine all ingredients, except salmon, in a large bowl. Add the fillets and coat well with the marinade.

◆ Cover and set aside for up to 30 minutes to marinate. Remove salmon from the marinade, scraping off any vegetables that cling.

◆ Grill the salmon on a lightly greased grill, approximately 10 minutes, until it flakes easily, or broil in the oven.

Yield: *4 servings*

Baked Salmon Fillet *(Parve)*

1 tablespoon mayonnaise	2 pounds salmon fillets (not
1 teaspoon soy sauce	salmon steaks)
1 teaspoon Dijon mustard	Lemon pepper to taste
2 cloves garlic, minced	Lemon slices

◆ Preheat broiler. Mix first 4 ingredients.

◆ Place salmon, skin side down, in greased baking dish and spread mixture over salmon. Sprinkle with lemon pepper.

◆ Broil on second rack setting for approximately 5 minutes. Reduce heat to 350° and bake for 15 to 20 minutes until fish flakes easily.

◆ Serve garnished with lemon slices.

Yield: *4 servings*

Teriyaki Ginger Marinade *(Parve)*

1 cup teriyaki sauce	2 cloves garlic, minced
½ cup orange juice	1 tablespoon honey
1-2 teaspoons fresh gingerroot, peeled and grated	

◆ Combine ingredients and pour over grillable fish or chicken breasts. Marinate for at least 30 minutes in refrigerator.

Yield: *Enough marinade for 1 to 2 pounds fish or chicken*

White Wine Marinade *(Parve)*

⅓ cup white wine	2 tablespoons lemon juice
¼ cup soy sauce	2 green onions, sliced

◆ Combine wine, soy sauce, lemon juice and green onions. Pour over fillets and marinate in refrigerator at least 30 minutes.

Yield: *Enough marinade for 2 pounds of fish*

Tuna Teriyaki (Parve)

⅓ cup low-sodium soy sauce
4 teaspoons rice vinegar or distilled vinegar
2 teaspoons chopped garlic
2 teaspoons ground ginger

1 cup apple juice concentrate
⅓ cup chopped green onions
2 pounds tuna or red snapper fillets

◆ Combine first 5 ingredients in blender. Stir in onions.
◆ Place fish in glass baking dish and pour marinade over. Let sit for 1 hour in refrigerator, turning fish occasionally.
◆ Preheat oven to 350°. Bake fish in marinade for 20 minutes, or until fish flakes easily.

Yield: *4 servings*

Note: *You may remove fish from marinade and grill or broil for 8 minutes. Heat marinade to a boil to serve as sauce for fish.*

Balsamic Glazed Tuna (Parve)

A fabulous company dish!

¾ cup vegetable broth or parve chicken-flavored broth
3 tablespoons balsamic vinegar
4 tablespoons brown sugar
3 tablespoons low-sodium soy sauce
1½ teaspoons cornstarch

4 tuna steaks, 6 ounces each, about ¾ inch thick
½-1 teaspoon coarsely ground black pepper or lemon pepper
¼ teaspoon salt
2 tablespoons olive oil or vegetable spray
¾ cup green onion, sliced diagonally

◆ Combine broth, vinegar, sugar and soy sauce in small pan. Bring to a boil and reduce to simmer. Remove ½ cup liquid to a small dish and add cornstarch. Mix until smooth; return to mixture and cook until thickened, stirring constantly. Keep warm on low heat.
◆ Sprinkle pepper or lemon pepper and salt on tuna. Sauté tuna in oil in skillet over medium-high heat for about 3 minutes until medium-rare or to desired doneness. Remove from heat.
◆ Spoon glaze over cooked fish and top with green onion.

Yield: *4 servings*

Note: *The glaze also tastes great on salmon.*

Salmon Patties *(Parve)*

1	pound salmon	2	tablespoons Dijon mustard
2	cups chopped tomato	¼	cup chopped chives
3	eggs	¼	cup chopped parsley
½	cup finely minced shallots or scallions		Salt and pepper to taste
		1	tablespoon dry mustard
3	cups bread crumbs, divided	½	cup oil

◆ Place salmon in a skillet and cover with boiling water. Simmer for approximately 5 minutes, covered, until poached. Let cool. Pat dry and break into medium pieces.

◆ Preheat oven to 450°. In large bowl, mix salmon with tomato, eggs, shallots, 1 cup of bread crumbs, Dijon mustard, chives, and parsley. Season with salt and pepper.

◆ Mix the remaining bread crumbs with the dry mustard. Place in flat dish for dredging.

◆ Form the salmon mixture into approximately 8 patties and dust with bread crumbs on both sides.

◆ Brush the oil onto a baking sheet and heat for a few minutes.

◆ Place the salmon cakes on the sheet and bake for 5 to 7 minutes or until golden. Turn once and continue to bake for 3 to 5 minutes until crispy.

Yield: *4 servings*

Note: *A great way to use leftover cooked salmon and skip the poaching.*

Crispy Whitefish *(Parve)*

1	pound whitefish	Chopped parsley, lemon slices
2	tablespoons melted margarine	or sautéed slivered almonds
	Seasonings of your choice	(optional)
	(garlic powder, basil, lemon pepper, etc.)	

◆ Line a 9x13-inch baking pan with foil. Place fish in pan, brush with melted margarine and sprinkle with seasonings.

◆ Broil for approximately 7 minutes until fish is crisp and flakes with a fork.

Yield: *2 servings*

Sea Bass Italiano *(Dairy)*

1	pound sea bass or other thick white fish such as halibut or cod, cut into 8 pieces	¼	cup grated Parmesan cheese
¼	cup orange juice	¼	cup Italian bread crumbs
2	cloves fresh garlic, crushed		Raspberries or sliced mangoes (optional)

- ◆ Preheat oven to 350°. Layer fish in 8x11-inch pan and cover with orange juice. Sprinkle garlic, cheese and bread crumbs over top. Cover with fruit.
- ◆ Bake for 30 minutes.

Yield: *2 servings*

Baked Fish Salona *(Parve)*

In the Middle East salona *denotes a sweet and sour fish recipe.*

4	tablespoons brown sugar		Oil
¼	teaspoon turmeric	3	large onions, sliced
4	tablespoons flour	2	large tomatoes, sliced ¼-inch thick
¼	teaspoon cumin		
1	teaspoon curry powder	½	cup lemon juice
	Salt and pepper to taste		
2	pounds fish fillets such as tilapia, orange roughy, or any firm white fish		

- ◆ Preheat oven to 350°. In a plastic bag, mix sugar, turmeric, flour, cumin, curry, salt, and pepper. Shake to mix. Place fish in the bag, one piece at a time, and shake to coat with seasonings.
- ◆ Heat oil in skillet and sauté fillets for 2 minutes on each side. Sauté onion slices until transparent but not browned.
- ◆ Place fish in 9x13-inch glass baking dish coated with vegetable spray. Lay onion and tomato slices on top of fish and pour lemon juice over.
- ◆ Bake uncovered for 30 to 45 minutes. Serve with rice or potatoes.

Yield: *4 servings*

Baked Fish Provençal *(Parve)*

1	pound whitefish, cod or halibut fillets	1	cup assorted vegetables, diced, such as green pepper, onion, celery
½	teaspoon salt-free garlic and herb seasoning		
½	teaspoon lemon pepper	1	(14-ounce) can diced or stewed tomatoes

◆ Preheat oven to 350°. Season fish. Place fillets in 9x13-inch baking dish. Top with diced vegetables.

◆ Spread tomatoes evenly over fish. Bake, covered with foil, for 30 minutes. Remove foil and bake for an additional 30 minutes.

Yield: *2 servings*

Marinated Fish *(Dairy)*

1½	cups water	½	cup oil
	Salt		Juice of 2 lemons
1	rib celery		Salt and pepper to taste
1	carrot, sliced		Sprinkle of oregano
1	bay leaf	2	cloves garlic, cut into large pieces
	Milk, as needed		
2	pounds fish fillets (halibut, cod, sole or whitefish)		Parsley for garnish

◆ In a 10-inch skillet place water, salt, celery, carrot and bay leaf. Bring to boil and boil for about 5 minutes. Add a little milk (to keep the fish white).

◆ Add the fish to the water in the skillet and when the water comes to a boil, poach until the fish flakes easily (approximately 9 minutes for frozen fish). Lift the fish gently to a colander to drain.

◆ In small bowl, mix together oil, lemon juice, salt, pepper, oregano and garlic.

◆ Place fish in a glass or ceramic dish. Pour marinade over fish and refrigerate overnight, turning fish a few times. Before serving, drain, remove garlic and garnish with parsley.

Yield: *8 servings*

Note: *The marinated fish will keep for 4 to 5 days in a covered container in the refrigerator.*

Fillet of Sole Dijonnaise *(Parve)*

4-5	potatoes, sliced	1	tablespoon lemon juice
2	green peppers, sliced	½	cup mayonnaise
1	onion, sliced	1	tablespoon Dijon mustard
2	tablespoons margarine		Paprika
1	pound fillet of sole		

◆ Preheat oven to 400°. Arrange vegetables in 9x13-inch baking pan; dot with margarine. Bake for 30 minutes.

◆ Place fish over vegetables in baking dish. In small bowl mix together lemon juice, mayonnaise and mustard. Spread over fish. Sprinkle with paprika.

◆ Bake for an additional 15 to 20 minutes, until fish flakes easily.

Yield: *2 servings*

Homemade Horseradish ✡ *(Parve)*

This "clear your sinuses" recipe will be a big hit.

3	pounds horseradish root, unpeeled and cut in large chunks	16	ounces cider vinegar
		⅛	teaspoon salt
2	beets, boiled in jackets	⅛	cup sugar, or to taste

◆ Soak horseradish root in cold water in refrigerator overnight or for several days. Peel and remove all brown spots.

◆ Cut in small pieces, keeping in a fresh bowl of cold water until ready to process. Grate with fine blade in food processor. Peel and grate the boiled beets.

◆ Mix all ingredients in bowl. There will be a very strong odor when the vinegar mixes with the horseradish. Either wear goggles or cry!

◆ Place in a jar with a tight lid and keep in refrigerator. Serve with gefilte fish or brisket.

Yield: *25 servings*

Note: *This will keep for months in the refrigerator. It will lose a little strength but it will still be good.*

Tuna Gefilte Fish ✡ *(Parve)*

Your guests will never guess it's tuna!

1	(6½-ounce) can tuna in water	1	teaspoon sugar
2	carrots, 1 sliced, 1 grated	2	eggs, separated
2	large onions, 1 sliced, 1 grated	⅓	cup matzo meal
	Salt and pepper to taste		

- ◆ Rinse tuna under cold water and drain.
- ◆ In medium pot combine 4 cups water, 1 sliced carrot, 1 sliced onion, salt, pepper and sugar. Bring to boil, lower heat and simmer for 20 minutes.
- ◆ Put flaked tuna, egg yolks, grated carrot, grated onion and matzo meal in processor. Mix thoroughly.
- ◆ Beat egg whites separately until stiff. Add to mixture.
- ◆ Make 4 oval balls and put in simmering pot. Cover and simmer for 20 minutes. Cool in pot. Remove and garnish with carrots. Refrigerate.

Yield: *4 servings*

Note: *You can double this. Be careful that the mixture does not become too loose.*

Baked Gefilte Fish Loaf ✡ *(Parve)*

2	pounds fish fillets (whitefish and pike), skinned and cut in 2-inch pieces	1	tablespoon sugar, or to taste
		1	teaspoon oil
2	onions, quartered	½	teaspoon salt, or to taste
1	carrot, cut in 2-inch pieces	¼	teaspoon white pepper, or to taste
2	eggs	1	green pepper, seeded and cut into rings
½	cup water		

- ◆ Preheat oven to 350°. Prepare loaf pan with vegetable spray.
- ◆ Place fish in food processor and process for 20 seconds. Add onions and carrot and process for another 25 to 30 seconds.
- ◆ Add eggs, water, sugar, oil, salt and pepper and process again for 15 seconds.
- ◆ Place green pepper on bottom of pan. Spread fish on top. Bake uncovered for 45 to 60 minutes.
- ◆ To serve, remove loaf by turning pan upside down and slice. Serve either hot or cold.

Yield: *8 to 10 servings*

Bubbie's Gefilte Fish ✡ (Parve)

Bubbie *is Yiddish for Grandma.*

2	pounds whole whitefish	1	large carrot, peeled
2	pounds whole lake trout	6	eggs, beaten
1	pound pike	⅓	cup matzo meal
½	pound salmon fillets	3	tablespoons sugar
2	extra large Spanish or	2	tablespoons salt
	Bermuda onions	¼	teaspoon white pepper

Vegetables for 2 Large Pots
2	large onions, sliced	2	ribs celery, cut in pieces
1	pound carrots, peeled and sliced		Sugar, salt and pepper to taste

◆ Have fish market save skin, bones and heads from fish when filleting them and remove all eyes and gills from fish heads. Clean skin, bones and fish heads. Divide into two portions, wrap in cheesecloth and place in the bottom of each pot.

◆ Grind fish or have fish market grind it for you. Grind with onions and finish with a carrot to clean grinder. Add eggs, matzo meal and seasonings.

◆ Place pot vegetables on top of fish bones. Fill pots ⅔ full of water and bring to a boil. Add salt and pepper and a little sugar to make water very tasty.

◆ Make balls of fish with wet hands and drop into boiling water, starting from outer edge of pot. Cover pots and simmer for about 2½ hours. Check liquid levels of pots, adding water if too much boils out, and skim off any foam that forms.

◆ Let cool slightly in pot. Then remove fish balls with slotted spoon to a serving platter. Place a carrot from the broth on top of each piece of fish. Cool, cover and refrigerate.

Yield: *15 servings*

Note: *You can make a sauce for the fish with 3 cups of the broth. Squeeze some of the cooked vegetables from the pot through a strainer into the broth. Cook on high heat until the broth begins to boil and reduces in volume. Refrigerate when cool. Serve fish with a sprig of parsley and horseradish.*

Traditional Brisket (Meat)

Brisket is often served for Jewish holiday and Shabbat meals.

5-7	pounds brisket	1	pound carrots, cut in chunks
1	envelope onion soup mix	3	pounds potatoes, peeled and
1	tablespoon garlic powder		quartered
	(optional)	1	cup water
½	teaspoon pepper	14	ounces ketchup
2	large onions, sliced		

◆ Preheat oven to 350°. In roasting pan, season brisket with onion soup mix, garlic powder and pepper. Add vegetables around the meat. Mix ketchup with water and pour over brisket.

◆ Bake tightly covered for 3 to 3½ hours, or until meat is easily pierced with a fork.

◆ Cool for 30 minutes and place in refrigerator until cold. Remove and discard fat. Slice brisket against the grain and return to gravy.

Yield: *10 to 12 servings*

Sweet and Sour Brisket (Meat)

5-7	pounds brisket	1	(12-ounce) jar apricot
3	medium onions, sliced		preserves
	Garlic powder, salt and pepper	1	(20-ounce) bottle ketchup
	to taste		

◆ Preheat oven to 350°. Place brisket on top of onions in pan. Season brisket as desired.

◆ Mix preserves and ketchup and pour over brisket. Bake, covered tightly with foil, for 3 to 3½ hours. Cool for 30 minutes and place in refrigerator until cold. Remove and discard fat. Slice brisket against the grain and return to gravy.

Yield: *10 to 12 servings*

Beer Brisket *(Meat)*

5-7	pounds brisket	2	ribs celery, chopped
2½	teaspoons seasoned salt	1	(12-ounce) bottle chili sauce
¼	teaspoon pepper	½	cup brown sugar
2	cloves garlic, minced	½	cup water
2	medium red onions, sliced and ringed	1	(12-ounce) can beer

◆ Preheat oven to 350°. Sprinkle seasoned salt, pepper, and garlic on brisket, fat side up. Top with onion and celery.

◆ Combine chili sauce, brown sugar and water, and pour over brisket. Bake uncovered for 1 hour. Baste after 30 minutes.

◆ Pour beer over brisket and cover pan tightly with aluminum foil. Continue baking for an additional 1½ to 2 hours.

◆ Cool for 30 minutes and place in refrigerator until cold. Remove and discard fat. Slice brisket against the grain and return to gravy.

Yield: *10 to 12 servings*

Glazed Corned Beef Brisket *(Meat)*

Our family loves this with sweet potatoes.

3-4	pounds corned beef brisket	⅓	cup Dijon mustard
3	bay leaves	2	tablespoons dark brown sugar
3	cloves garlic	12	whole cloves
1	cup pineapple juice		

◆ In a large stock pot, boil the brisket with bay leaves and garlic in water to cover the meat.

◆ While brisket is cooking, combine juice, mustard and brown sugar. When meat is almost tender, remove from pot and allow to cool.

◆ Preheat oven to 300°. Pierce with whole cloves and spread sauce over top of brisket. Roast, uncovered, for about 1 hour, until the meat is completely tender and glazed. Remove cloves, slice against the grain and serve.

Yield: *10 to 12 servings*

Rib Roast Supreme (Meat)

1	3-4 pound standing rib roast	⅓	cup Dijon mustard
1	envelope onion soup mix	⅓	cup red wine

◆ Place standing rib roast in a baking pan or ovenproof glass dish.

◆ Combine onion soup mix with Dijon mustard and red wine. Pour over roast and rub into meat. Marinate for about 20 minutes before putting in oven, or prepare and marinate in refrigerator overnight.

◆ Preheat oven to 350°. Bake for 27 to 30 minutes per pound for medium. Use a meat thermometer to get accurate temperature. Check periodically to see if roast needs basting with sauce.

Yield: *6 servings*

Ginger Plum Beef Ribs (Meat)

1	(12-ounce) jar plum preserves	2	cloves garlic, minced
1	cup dark corn syrup	2	teaspoons ground ginger
½	cup soy sauce	4	pounds beef ribs
⅔	cup minced green onion		

◆ In saucepan, combine first 6 ingredients. Stirring constantly, bring to boil over medium heat and boil for 5 minutes. Remove 1 cup and set aside.

◆ Place ribs in shallow baking dish. Pour remaining mixture over ribs. Cover and marinate in refrigerator for at least 4 hours.

◆ Preheat oven to 350° or preheat broiler. Place ribs and marinade in covered roaster and bake until tender, about 1½ hours, or place ribs on rack in broiler pan and broil 6 inches from heat, turning and basting frequently with marinade until brown and crispy.

◆ Heat reserved 1 cup syrup mixture and serve with ribs and cooked rice.

Yield: *4 servings*

Barbecued Beef *(Meat)*

Great idea for leftover brisket.

1	(14-ounce) can stewed tomatoes	1	large onion, chopped
2	teaspoons yellow prepared mustard	2	cloves garlic
2	tablespoons fresh lemon juice	2-4	pounds cooked brisket, shredded with a fork
4-6	tablespoons brown sugar to taste	1	(12-ounce) bottle chili sauce

- ◆ Preheat oven to 350°. In a blender, purée together tomatoes, mustard, lemon juice, brown sugar, onion and garlic. Heat mixture and add shredded cooked brisket. Stir well.
- ◆ Add chili sauce, mix well. Bake for 30 minutes.

Yield: *10 to 12 servings*

Note: *Taste improves if barbecued beef sits for a day or two in the refrigerator.*

Best Cholent Ever *(Meat)*

This traditional dish, cooked overnight, is ready for Shabbat lunch.

1	tablespoon olive oil	1½	cups barley, rinsed
1	onion, diced	4	cups boiling water
2	potatoes, cut up	⅓	cup ketchup
1	sweet potato, cut up	⅓	cup honey
	Salt, pepper, garlic powder to taste	½	envelope onion soup mix
1-2	pounds flanken or chuck, cut up	1	small potato kugel, pre-baked (optional)

- ◆ Place a little olive oil on bottom of slow cooker. Place all ingredients into the pot in the above order. Place kugel on top of mixture.
- ◆ Cover and set on medium-low heat for 20 to 24 hours.

Yield: *8 servings*

Note: *Cholent may also be made in a tightly covered Dutch oven. Bake at 275° for 20 to 24 hours.*

Beef Stew *(Meat)*

1	extra large onion, chopped	¼	teaspoon basil
2	teaspoons minced garlic	2	teaspoons salt
1	pound beef stew meat, trimmed of fat and cut into small chunks	¼	teaspoon pepper
		¼	cup barley
		3	small carrots, cut into slices
⅛	cup flour	3	small potatoes, cut into chunks
2	cups hot water	1	cup sliced celery
1	(15-ounce) can tomato sauce		

- ◆ Spray large heavy saucepan or skillet with vegetable spray. Sauté onions. Add garlic.
- ◆ In small bowl, coat beef with flour. Brown beef in skillet with onions and garlic.
- ◆ Stir in water, sauce, seasonings, and barley. Simmer for 1½ hours.
- ◆ Add vegetables. Simmer for another hour.

Yield: *4 servings*

Quick & Easy Chili *(Meat)*

½	pound ground turkey	1	(8-ounce) can tomato sauce
½	pound ground chuck	1	(1¼-ounce) package chili seasoning mix
1	tablespoon margarine		
1	onion, chopped	1	(16-ounce) can vegetarian baked beans
1	(16-ounce) can diced tomatoes		

- ◆ Brown turkey and chuck in margarine. Add remaining ingredients except beans. Bring to a boil, cover, and simmer for about 1 hour.
- ◆ Add beans, heat well and serve.

Yield: *4 to 6 servings*

Note: *You may use all turkey or all beef.*

Zayde's Chili *(Meat)*

Zayde *is Yiddish for Grandpa.*

1	large onion, chopped	1	(16-ounce) can tomato paste
1	tablespoon oil	5	bay leaves
2	pounds chopped meat	2	teaspoons basil
2	(1¼-ounce) packages chili seasoning mix	2	cloves garlic
1	(28-ounce) can tomatoes	1	tablespoon sugar
2	cans water, using tomato can	1	(16-ounce) can kidney beans with liquid
2	(15-ounce) cans tomato sauce	2	cups macaroni

◆ In a 6-quart pot sauté onion in oil until soft. Add chopped meat and brown. Stir in chili mix. Add tomatoes, water, tomato sauce and tomato paste. Add bay leaves, basil, garlic and sugar.

◆ Bring to a boil, then simmer for about 10 minutes; add kidney beans and cook for ½ hour. Add macaroni and cook for another ½ hour. Remove and discard bay leaves before serving.

Yield: *8 servings*

Zesty Meat Loaf *(Meat)*

This is not the meat loaf Momma used to make.

1	pound ground turkey	¼	cup water or apple juice
1	pound ground chuck	2	tablespoons prepared hot horseradish (red or white)
2	eggs or equivalent egg substitute	1	teaspoon dry mustard
1	onion, chopped	2	teaspoons salt
2	cups bread crumbs	1	cup ketchup, divided

◆ Preheat oven to 400°. Mix all ingredients except ½ cup of the ketchup.

◆ Shape into a loaf. Spread remaining ½ cup ketchup over loaf and bake for 1 hour.

Yield: *8 servings*

Sweet and Sour Meatballs ✡ (Meat)

Try this one as an appetizer.

Meatballs

1	pound ground beef	2	eggs
2	pounds ground veal	1	envelope onion soup mix
1	small potato, peeled and grated fine	¼	teaspoon white pepper
1	large onion, chopped fine	¼	cup matzo meal

Sauce

3	(11-ounce) cans tomato-mushroom sauce	½	cup barbecue sauce
1	(20-ounce) can pineapple tidbits with juice	¼	cup brown sugar

♦ Combine meatball ingredients. Form into 1- to 2-inch balls. In large pot combine sauce ingredients and bring to a boil. Drop meatballs into sauce and cook, covered, for 30 to 40 minutes.

Yield: *8 servings as a main course*

Note: *This recipe may also be used for meat loaf.*

Stuffed Cabbage Rolls *(Meat)*

1	medium head cabbage	1	tablespoon oil
1½	pounds ground chuck, veal or	½	cup water
	turkey, or mixture	1	(14-ounce) can diced tomatoes
½	cup cooked rice.	½	cup ketchup
	Salt and pepper to taste	1	tablespoon lemon juice
1	small onion, grated	3	tablespoons brown sugar

- ◆ Pull off the tough outer leaves from cabbage and cut out bottom core of head with paring knife.
- ◆ Cook cabbage in salted water in covered pot for 5 minutes or until leaves separate easily. Invert and drain well.
- ◆ Separate leaves and pat dry with paper towel.
- ◆ Mix ground meat, rice, salt, pepper and onion together.
- ◆ Lay one cabbage leaf curly side up and place 2 to 4 teaspoons filling on thicker edge. Roll leaf up, tucking in sides. Place seam side down in large electric skillet or Dutch oven with oil. Continue until all meat is used up.
- ◆ Combine remaining ingredients; add to pot and simmer for about 1 hour. Add additional sugar or lemon juice and seasonings to taste.

Yield: *12 servings*

Middle Eastern Stuffed Zucchini ✡ *(Meat)*

6	zucchini	1¼	cups water, divided
1	pound ground meat	1	small onion, chopped fine
3	tablespoons matzo meal	1	(8-ounce) can tomato sauce
¼	teaspoon pepper		Juice of 2 lemons
2	tablespoons crushed mint (optional)	1	tablespoon sugar

◆ Preheat oven to 350°. Peel the zucchini and cut into 3½-inch lengths. Hollow out each piece, saving insides.

◆ Mix meat, matzo meal, pepper and mint. Add ¼ cup water and onion. Fill zucchini with meat mixture.

◆ Spray ovenproof dish with vegetable spray. Arrange zucchini in dish.

◆ Use remaining meat mixture to make meatballs and put in dish.

◆ Mix tomato sauce, 1 cup water, lemon juice and sugar, and pour over everything.

◆ Put insides of cored zucchini on top.

◆ Cover with aluminum foil and bake for 1 hour.

Yield: *6 to 8 servings*

Note: *This may also be served as a side dish.*

Marinated Lamb Chops *(Meat)*

1	scant cup Italian salad dressing	3	tablespoons wine
2	tablespoons soy sauce	6	lamb chops
2	tablespoons Worcestershire sauce		

◆ Mix first 4 ingredients. Marinate lamb chops for at least 2 hours or overnight.

◆ Broil until lamb chops are done to your preference.

Yield: *3 to 4 servings*

Note: *Lamb chops may be frozen in marinade, defrosted and grilled.*

Stuffed Peppers *(Meat)*

2	cups white or brown rice	2	(16-ounce) cans tomato sauce, divided
4	cups chicken broth		
2	pounds ground beef, turkey, chicken or veal	1	(14½-ounce) can diced tomatoes
1	onion, diced (optional) Seasoning to taste	6	peppers (red, yellow or green), cored and seeded

◆ Cook rice according to package directions, using broth in place of water.

◆ Preheat oven to 350°. Brown ground meat and onion and pour off extra fat. Add seasoning to taste.

◆ Add 1 can of tomato sauce and 1 can diced tomatoes to seasoned meat. Add rice to meat and tomato mixture.

◆ Place the peppers in a 9x13-inch glass baking dish. Fill each one to the top with the meat mixture. Put remaining filling around peppers. Cover the top of the stuffed peppers with second can of tomato sauce.

◆ Bake uncovered for 1 to 1½ hours until peppers are tender. Red and yellow peppers are sweeter and cook faster.

Yield: *6 servings*

Barbecued Veal Chops *(Meat)*

The chef says it's his favorite way to prepare veal chops.

½	teaspoon crumbled thyme leaves	1	small onion, chopped
½	teaspoon ground cumin	½	cup cider vinegar
½	teaspoon chili powder	¼	cup oil
¼	teaspoon ground dry red pepper	¼	cup ketchup
		1	clove garlic, sliced
1½	teaspoons salt	6	veal chops

◆ Combine the first 10 ingredients to form a sauce. Arrange the veal chops in 1 layer in a large pan and pour the marinade over them.

◆ Marinate for several hours, basting occasionally.

◆ Broil or grill until done, basting with sauce.

Yield: *6 servings*

Bombay Lamb Stew *(Meat)*

This delicious stew is often served in India for Shabbat.

1	bunch cilantro leaves, rinsed and thick stems removed, or 2 teaspoons ground coriander	1	large onion, thinly sliced
		1	large tomato, cut into pieces
		1	teaspoon turmeric
		1	teaspoon pepper
4	cloves garlic, peeled	1	teaspoon cinnamon
1	(1-inch) piece fresh ginger, peeled and cut into small pieces	2	pounds lamb, cut into cubes
			Salt to taste
		1½	cups hot water, divided
2	long green chili peppers, washed, seeded and cut up	2	potatoes, peeled and cut into 1-inch pieces
3	tablespoons oil		

◆ In processor, combine cilantro leaves or coriander, garlic, ginger and green chilies, making a paste.

◆ In large skillet, brown onion in oil. Add prepared paste and tomato; stir and cook for 5 minutes. Add water if needed. Add turmeric, pepper and cinnamon.

◆ Add lamb and mix well. Cook for 5 to 10 minutes. Add salt and 1 cup of hot water. Simmer covered for 1 hour. Add water if needed as it cooks.

◆ About 30 minutes before stew finishes cooking, add potatoes and ½ cup hot water. Cook until potatoes are tender.

Yield: *4 servings*

Note: *The spices have been decreased for Western tastes.*

Marinated Veal Chops *(Meat)*

½	cup wine vinegar	½	teaspoon dried oregano
¼	cup oil	¼	teaspoon salt
1	small onion, minced	¼	teaspoon pepper
½	teaspoon dried basil	4	veal chops

◆ Combine all ingredients except veal chops. Pour mixture over chops.

◆ Cover and refrigerate in marinade for 1 hour, turning occasionally. Remove meat and broil or grill until done.

Yield: *4 servings*

Veal Stew (Meat)

2	onions, cut up	1½	tablespoons potato starch or cornstarch
6	carrots, cut up		
3	ribs celery, cut up	1	cup chicken broth, divided
2	cloves garlic, minced	1	(28-ounce) can tomato purée
3	pounds veal stew meat	1	(28-ounce) can diced tomatoes
4	tablespoons lemon juice, divided	1	tablespoon chopped fresh basil or 1 teaspoon dried basil
1	cup white wine, divided	1	bay leaf
			Salt and pepper to taste

◆ Preheat broiler. Spray bottom of large, deep roasting pan with vegetable spray or brush with oil.

◆ Place vegetables and garlic on the bottom of the pan. Top with veal in a single layer.

◆ Pour 2 tablespoons lemon juice and ¼ cup wine on top.

◆ Broil for 10 minutes or until golden. Turn, pour remaining lemon juice and ¼ cup wine on top. Continue to broil for an additional 10 minutes.

◆ Reduce oven temperature to 325°. Dissolve starch in 3 tablespoons of broth. Add to pan. Add remaining wine, broth, purée, tomatoes and seasonings.

◆ Cover and cook for 1½ to 2 hours or until tender.

Yield: *8 servings*

Note: *Quartered potatoes and/or fresh mushrooms may be added with broth.*

Veal Marsala *(Meat)*

1½	pounds thinly sliced veal		Dash of pepper
1	clove garlic	1	teaspoon lemon juice
	Flour to coat veal	⅓	cup dry vermouth or white
¼	cup margarine		wine
½	pound sliced mushrooms		Snipped parsley
½	teaspoon salt		

- ◆ Flatten veal to ¼ inch thick and rub both sides with garlic. Flour veal.
- ◆ Melt margarine in skillet and sauté veal until golden brown on both sides.
- ◆ Heap mushrooms on top and sprinkle with salt, pepper and lemon juice.
- ◆ Pour on vermouth and cook over low heat, uncovered, for 20 minutes or until veal is tender. Add 1 tablespoon water if needed.
- ◆ Sprinkle with parsley to serve.

Yield: *4 servings*

Note: *For variation you may substitute a drained 3½-ounce jar of capers for the mushrooms.*

Chili Cranberry Chicken *(Meat)*

Colorful, elegant and a snap to make.

½	cup chili sauce	⅛	teaspoon ground allspice
½	cup whole cranberry sauce	4-6	chicken breast halves, skinned
2	tablespoons orange		and boned
	marmalade	2	teaspoons oil

- ◆ Combine chili sauce, cranberry sauce, orange marmalade and allspice in a small bowl and set aside.
- ◆ Brown both sides of chicken breasts in oil.
- ◆ Remove excess oil from pan; pour sauce over chicken breasts and simmer for 8 to 10 minutes or until chicken breasts are tender and sauce is of right consistency, or place chicken breasts in a baking dish, pour sauce over them and bake at 350° for 15 to 20 minutes.

Yield: *4 to 6 servings*

Honey Cranberry Chicken (Meat)

1¾	cups boiling water	½	teaspoon ground pepper,
1	cup dried cranberries		divided
6	chicken breast halves or	5	tablespoons margarine
	cutlets, skinned and boned	⅓	cup chopped shallots or onions
¾	teaspoon salt, divided	3	tablespoons honey

◆ Pour water over dried cranberries and set aside to steep.

◆ Pound chicken breasts slightly to flatten evenly. Season with ¼ teaspoon salt and ¼ teaspoon pepper.

◆ Melt margarine in large skillet; add chicken breasts. Cook over medium-high heat, turning once, until golden brown, about 3 to 5 minutes per side.

◆ Reduce heat to medium-low. Add shallots or onions to pan. Cook, stirring, for 30 seconds. Add cranberries with their soaking liquid, raise heat to high and boil, uncovered, for 2 minutes. Stir in honey. Continue to cook until chicken is white but still moist in center, about 2 minutes longer.

◆ With back of fork, mash some cranberries into the sauce to help thicken. Reduce sauce further if necessary.

◆ Season chicken with remaining salt and pepper. Spoon sauce and cranberries over chicken and serve.

Yield: *6 servings*

Sassy Salsa Chicken *(Meat)*

1	tablespoon olive oil, divided	¼	cup water
¼	cup sliced almonds	2	tablespoons dried currants
2	garlic cloves, minced	1	tablespoon honey
8	chicken breast halves, skinned and boned	¾	teaspoon cumin
1	cup chunk-style salsa	½	teaspoon cinnamon

◆ In a large nonstick skillet, heat ½ tablespoon oil on medium-high heat and cook almonds 1 to 2 minutes until browned. Set almonds aside.

◆ Add remaining oil and garlic to skillet. Sauté for 30 seconds. Add chicken and cook for 4 to 5 minutes or until browned, turning once.

◆ In medium bowl, combine all remaining ingredients. Mix well. Add to chicken. Reduce heat to medium. Cover and cook for an additional 20 minutes or until tender. Stir sauce occasionally. Stir in almonds.

◆ Serve chicken with rice or couscous.

Yield: *4 to 6 servings*

Chicken with Artichokes *(Meat)*

So easy and delicious!

1	(0.6-ounce) package Italian salad dressing mix	¼	cup oil
½	cup flour	1	(14-ounce) can artichoke hearts, drained and cut up
4	chicken breast halves, skinned and boned		

◆ Preheat oven to 350°. Combine salad dressing mix with flour. Coat chicken breasts with mixture.

◆ Heat oil in skillet and brown chicken breasts on both sides. Put breasts in an ovenproof pan.

◆ With juices in skillet, heat artichoke hearts for a few minutes, scraping off browned bits from bottom of pan. Pour over chicken and bake, covered, for 30 minutes.

◆ Uncover and bake for an additional 10 to 15 minutes. Don't allow chicken to dry out.

Yield: *4 servings*

Apricot Chicken *(Meat)*

½	tablespoon Dijon mustard	¼	cup brown sugar
½	tablespoon stone ground mustard	2	tablespoons lemon juice
1	teaspoon Worcestershire sauce	½	cup apricot preserves
1	teaspoon soy sauce	2	chickens, cut up
1	clove garlic, crushed Freshly ground pepper, to taste	1	(15-ounce) can apricots, drained and cut in half

◆ Preheat oven to 350°. In a bowl mix the mustard, Worcestershire sauce, soy sauce, garlic, pepper, brown sugar, lemon juice and apricot preserves.

◆ Coat chicken generously with apricot mixture. Arrange chicken pieces in a roasting pan.

◆ Bake chicken, uncovered, for 1 hour, basting occasionally. Remove from oven and surround chicken with apricot halves. Return to oven and bake for an additional 15 minutes.

◆ Transfer to a platter, spoon the pan juices over chicken, and serve at once.

Yield: *6 to 8 servings*

Note: *The sauce may be prepared up to 4 days in advance and kept refrigerated until needed.*

Lemon Chicken Breasts with Mushrooms ✡ (Meat)

Mushrooms and wine make this an elegant dish.

1 tablespoon margarine	2 green onions, sliced
4 chicken breast halves or	1 lemon, divided
cutlets, skinned and boned	2 tablespoons sherry or white
¼ pound fresh sliced mushrooms	wine

◆ Heat margarine in large skillet over medium heat. Add chicken and cook until browned, approximately 5 minutes per side. Remove chicken from skillet.

◆ Add mushrooms and green onions to skillet and cook until tender.

◆ Cut half of lemon into slices; add to mushroom mixture. Squeeze juice from other lemon half into small bowl. Combine juice and sherry or wine and add to mushroom mixture.

◆ Return chicken to skillet. Cook until juices run clear, approximately 15 to 20 minutes, basting several times. Be careful not to overcook.

Yield: *4 servings*

Honey Lemon Crispy Chicken *(Meat)*

So easy and so good!

2 tablespoons oil	¼ cup lemon juice
1 (3-4 pound) chicken, cut up	1 tablespoon soy sauce, or to
¼ cup flour	taste
⅓ cup honey	

◆ Preheat oven to 400°. Coat baking pan with oil or vegetable spray.

◆ Coat chicken with flour and place skin side down in pan. Bake uncovered for 30 minutes.

◆ Mix honey, lemon juice and soy sauce together in a small bowl and microwave on high power for 20 seconds.

◆ Turn chicken skin side up. Pour sauce over chicken.

◆ Bake at 375° for an additional 30 minutes, basting chicken every 10 minutes.

Yield: *3 to 4 servings*

Shicker Chicken (Meat)

Shicker *is a Yiddish word for drunk.*

1   (4-6 pound) chicken

Dry Rub

1	teaspoon sugar	1	teaspoon paprika
1	teaspoon onion powder	1	teaspoon dry yellow mustard
1	teaspoon garlic powder	1	tablespoon finely ground
1	teaspoon cayenne pepper		kosher salt

Steaming Liquid
1   (12-ounce) can of your favorite
     beer or fruit juice

Basting Spray

1	cup apple cider	1	tablespoon balsamic vinegar

◆   Discard or drink ½ of the can of beer. Rinse and dry chicken. Combine rub ingredients and use to thoroughly season chicken generously inside and out. Work mixture well into skin and under skin as much as possible. Set aside, covered, in refrigerator for 4 to 5 hours.

◆   Light grill. Place ½ can of beer upright on the grill and lower chicken's body cavity onto the can so that the chicken's legs and the can hold the bird upright. This helps drain off fat as the chicken cooks, and the beer steams the inside of the chicken.

◆   Grill with lid down 2 to 2½ hours, spraying with the basting spray every 20 to 30 minutes until chicken is done and internal temperature is 180° F.

◆   Carefully remove chicken, still perched on the can, and place on a serving tray. Carefully remove chicken from the can, which will be very hot, and carve.

Yield: *4 to 6 servings*

Hungarian Chicken Paprikash and Dumplings (Meat)

A classic worth making!

1	large onion, chopped	3	tablespoons paprika, or to taste
1	tablespoon oil		
3-4	pounds chicken parts	1	(32-ounce) can crushed tomatoes
1	teaspoon salt		
½	teaspoon pepper		

Dumplings

3	cups flour	2	eggs, beaten
½	teaspoon salt	¾	cup water

- In a large pot sauté onion in oil until soft. Add chicken pieces, salt, pepper and paprika. Cook uncovered for 15 to 20 minutes. Add tomatoes and cover pot. Cook for about 45 minutes or until chicken is very tender.

- Place flour and salt in a medium bowl. Make a well in the middle, add eggs and mix. Use enough water to make a stringy dough.

- Boil a large pot of salted water.

- Place dough on a flat dinner plate, cut into small pieces and place in boiling water. Boil for 10 minutes. Remove with slotted spoon.

- Serve chicken and gravy over dumplings.

Yield: *4 servings*

Tandoori Chicken *(Meat)*

This delicious Indian dish has been adapted to dietary laws.

1 teaspoon paprika	1 teaspoon garam masala
¼ cup lemon or lime juice	1 tablespoon olive oil
1 clove garlic, peeled	8 chicken thighs and legs,
1 (1-inch) piece fresh ginger, peeled	skinned and fat trimmed

◆ Place all ingredients except chicken in blender or processor and process to a paste. Heat on the stovetop to thin the mixture slightly.

◆ Rub paste on chicken pieces and marinate in refrigerator for 4 hours or overnight.

◆ Preheat oven to 375°. Place a large baking dish with hot water on lower rack of oven. Spray upper rack with vegetable spray and place the chicken pieces directly on the sprayed oven rack; or place chicken on a rack in a baking pan. Bake for 45 minutes.

Yield: *4 servings*

Note: *Garam masala, a blend of cardamom, cinnamon, cloves, black pepper and star anise, may be found in Indian or natural food grocery stores.*

Spicy Lime Chicken *(Meat)*

4 chicken breast halves, skinned and boned	1 tablespoon margarine
½ tablespoon Dijon mustard	½ cup prepared salsa
½ tablespoon stone ground mustard with horseradish	2 tablespoons fresh lime juice
	¼ cup chopped fresh cilantro

◆ Pound each breast half between sheets of waxed paper to a uniform thickness of ½ inch. Spread with mustards.

◆ Melt margarine in a large skillet over medium-high heat. Add chicken and cook for 2 minutes on each side.

◆ Stir salsa and lime juice together; add to skillet. Simmer gently, uncovered, until chicken is cooked through and sauce has thickened, 6 to 8 minutes. Sprinkle with cilantro.

Yield: *4 servings*

Mustard-Glazed Chicken Breasts (Meat)

1½ tablespoons Dijon mustard
1½ tablespoons stone ground
    mustard
1½ teaspoons lemon juice
1 teaspoon Worcestershire sauce
1 teaspoon minced garlic

½ teaspoon freshly ground
    pepper
4 chicken breast halves, skinned
    and boned
3 medium scallions, trimmed

◆ In a medium glass bowl, whisk together mustard, lemon juice, Worcestershire sauce, garlic and pepper.

◆ Place the chicken breasts between sheets of wax paper and pound lightly to a uniform thickness. Add the breast halves one at a time to the mustard mixture and turn to coat well on both sides. Marinate for 30 to 60 minutes.

◆ Light a grill or preheat broiler. Grill or broil the chicken, turning once and brushing occasionally with the mustard mixture, just until firm and opaque throughout, about 4 minutes per side. Meanwhile, grill or broil the scallions, turning once, until slightly charred all over, about 4 minutes.

◆ Arrange chicken breasts on a platter or individual plates, garnish with the grilled scallions and serve at once.

Yield: *4 servings*

Mandarin Chicken Veronique (Meat)

⅓ cup margarine
1 teaspoon salt
½ teaspoon mace
12 chicken breast halves, skinned
1 (10-ounce) jar orange marmalade

2 tablespoons cornstarch
1 (11-ounce) can Mandarin oranges, drained
1 cup seedless green grapes

◆ Preheat oven to 350°. In a 9x13-inch baking dish, melt margarine in oven for 5 minutes.

◆ Remove dish from oven. Add salt and mace. Stir to blend.

◆ Dip chicken pieces into melted margarine mixture and place in same baking dish.

◆ Bake in center of oven for 35 to 40 minutes or until chicken is fork tender.

◆ In small bowl, combine marmalade with cornstarch; blend well.

◆ Spoon marmalade mixture around and over chicken. Return dish to oven. Continue baking for 15 to 18 minutes or until sauce is clear. Stir in oranges and grapes and heat through.

Yield: *6 to 8 servings*

Pineapple Ginger Chicken (Meat)

5 pounds chicken parts
1 teaspoon ground ginger
¼ cup soy sauce
½ cup water

2 tablespoons red wine vinegar
¼ cup brown sugar
1 (20-ounce) can crushed pineapple, drained

◆ Preheat broiler. Brown chicken under broiler, approximately 10 minutes each side.

◆ Combine ginger, soy sauce, water, vinegar and brown sugar. Place chicken in electric skillet or 9x13-inch baking dish and pour sauce over; add pineapple.

◆ Simmer, covered, in skillet at 200° to 225° for 1 hour, or bake covered in oven at 325° for 1 hour. Watch so sauce doesn't burn. Serve with rice.

Yield: *6 servings*

Chicken with
Pea Pods and Water Chestnuts *(Meat)*

2-3 chickens, cut up
2 (10-ounce) jars apricot jam
1 cup barbecue sauce
3 tablespoons soy sauce
2 green peppers, seeded and cubed

1 (8-ounce) can sliced water chestnuts, drained
2 (10-ounce) packages pea pods, defrosted

◆ Preheat oven to 350°. Place chicken in roasting pan.
◆ Combine apricot jam, barbecue sauce and soy sauce in bowl. Pour sauce over chicken.
◆ Bake, uncovered, for 1 hour and 15 minutes, basting every 20 minutes.
◆ Add green pepper, water chestnuts and pea pods.
◆ Baste and bake for an additional 15 minutes.

Yield: *8 to 10 servings*

Oriental Chicken *(Meat)*

¼ cup margarine
1 (3-4 pound) chicken, cut up
1 (11-ounce) can Mandarin oranges, drained, reserving syrup
¼ cup soy sauce
1 tablespoon cornstarch

1 teaspoon prepared mustard
1 tablespoon vinegar
¼ cup pineapple preserves
¼ teaspoon garlic powder
1 tablespoon dehydrated minced onion
½ cup diced green pepper

◆ Melt margarine in skillet. Sauté chicken skin side down.
◆ Stir ½ cup of Mandarin orange juice and soy sauce together with cornstarch. When smooth, add mustard, vinegar, pineapple preserves, garlic powder and onion.
◆ Pour sauce over chicken, cover and simmer for approximately 15 minutes. Add green pepper and oranges and simmer for another 10 minutes.

Yield: *3 to 4 servings*

Saucy Orange Chicken Rolls *(Meat)*

4	chicken breast halves, skinned and boned	1	teaspoon or cube of chicken-flavored bouillon
1	pound asparagus, trimmed	½	teaspoon ground ginger
1	tablespoon oil	½	teaspoon grated orange peel
½	cup orange juice	1	teaspoon cornstarch
½	cup dry white wine	1	tablespoon water

◆ Pound chicken pieces between sheets of waxed paper to ¼-inch thickness.

◆ Cook asparagus in microwave oven on high power for 3 minutes. Arrange ¼ of asparagus stalks on narrow end of each chicken breast. Roll; fasten with toothpicks.

◆ In a 10-inch skillet over medium-high heat, in hot oil, cook chicken rolls until browned.

◆ Combine orange juice and next 4 ingredients. Add to skillet and heat to boiling. Reduce heat to low; cover and simmer for 10 minutes. Baste; continue cooking 10 minutes longer or until tender.

◆ Blend cornstarch and water; gradually stir into skillet. Cook 5 minutes longer or until sauce is slightly thickened, stirring constantly. Remove toothpicks and serve.

Yield: *4 servings*

Microwave Rosemary Chicken (Meat)

A quick dish for unexpected guests.

1	(3-4 pound) chicken, rinsed and dried	2	sprigs fresh rosemary or 1 teaspoon dried, divided
1	lemon, quartered		Salt and pepper, to taste

- ◆ Rub chicken with lemon quarters. Place lemon quarters in cavity along with 2 sprigs fresh rosemary or ½ teaspoon dried rosemary. If you use dried rosemary, sprinkle remaining ½ teaspoon on chicken. Lightly season with salt and pepper.

- ◆ Truss bird by tying its legs together and tying wings to body with kitchen twine.

- ◆ In a 2-quart dish that is microwave and oven safe and sprayed with vegetable spray, place chicken breast side down. Microwave on high power for 10 minutes. Turn bird over. Continue cooking on high until juices run clear when chicken is pierced in thickest part of leg and body, 8 to 10 minutes. Drain excess juice.

- ◆ Preheat oven to 500°. Transfer dish to top third of oven and bake for 5 to 8 minutes to crisp skin. Be sure to check after 5 minutes to prevent burning. Let stand an additional 10 minutes before serving.

Yield: *3 to 4 servings*

Chicken/Turkey Fried Rice (Meat)

An easy way to use leftover turkey.

1	cup rice	1	cup leftover chicken or turkey, cut into small pieces
2	cups chicken broth		
½	cup margarine	1	teaspoon salt
1	egg, slightly beaten	¼	teaspoon pepper
¼	onion, finely chopped	1½	tablespoons soy sauce

- ◆ Cook rice as directed, using chicken broth in place of water, or use leftover rice.

- ◆ Heat margarine in skillet. Add egg and scramble well, breaking it up as it cooks. Add remaining ingredients. Blend well and continue cooking for 10 minutes.

Yield: *3 to 4 servings*

Autumn Harvest Chicken (Meat)

1	pound small red potatoes, unpeeled and cut in half	½	teaspoon coarsely ground black pepper, divided
2	large carrots, cut into thirds	8	pieces chicken, skin removed
1	jumbo onion, cut into 8 wedges	1	medium red pepper, seeded and cut into 6 wedges
12	cloves garlic, unpeeled		
2	tablespoons olive oil	1	medium green pepper, seeded and cut into 6 wedges
1	teaspoon salt, divided		
¾	teaspoon dried rosemary leaves, divided	½	cup hot water

- ◆ Preheat oven to 425°. In a roasting pan, toss potatoes, carrots, onion and garlic with olive oil, ½ teaspoon salt, ½ teaspoon dried crushed rosemary and ¼ teaspoon black pepper. Cover roasting pan and roast vegetables for 20 minutes.

- ◆ Meanwhile, toss chicken with ½ teaspoon salt, ¼ teaspoon dried crushed rosemary and ¼ teaspoon pepper.

- ◆ Remove pan from oven and add seasoned chicken and peppers. Roast, uncovered, for 25 minutes. Stir vegetables and chicken to brown evenly. Roast an additional 25 minutes or until vegetables are golden and juices run clear when chicken is pierced with a knife. Remove chicken and vegetables and keep warm.

- ◆ Add ½ cup hot water to pan, stirring to loosen brown bits from bottom. Spoon sauce over chicken and vegetables to serve. If you like, cut through skin of each roasted garlic clove and spread the garlic over chicken and vegetables.

Yield: *4 servings*

Note: *You can use the roasted garlic as a spread on bread or crackers.*

Chicken Cholent *(Meat)*

A Shabbat specialty.

6	ounces lima beans (soaked according to package directions)	4-5	potatoes, cut in cubes
		½	cup barley
			Seasoned salt, to taste
2	carrots, sliced	10	pieces chicken
2	ribs celery, sliced	½	teaspoon basil
3	onions, sliced	½	cup water

◆ Put first 6 ingredients into a slow cooker in order listed. Sprinkle seasoned salt over vegetables.

◆ Place chicken on top of vegetables. Sprinkle basil on chicken; add water.

◆ Cook on lowest setting for 20 to 22 hours, or at highest low setting for 7 to 8 hours, or on high heat for 3 hours.

Yield: *6 servings*

Note: *Cholent may also be made in a tightly covered Dutch oven. Bake at 275° for 20 to 22 hours. Watch for bones when serving and eating.*

Microwave Turkey Breast *(Meat)*

1	(5-pound) turkey breast	½	cup chopped dried apricots (optional)
1	(12-ounce) jar low-sugar apricot jam		

◆ Season both sides of breast with whatever seasonings you choose. Turn bone-side up and put in a glass baking dish.

◆ For every pound cook breast for approximately 11 minutes at ¾ power or for 7 minutes at high power. Half way through total cooking time turn breast meat-side up and glaze with apricot jam. Dried apricots may be added to the jam.

◆ Put turkey back in the microwave and cook for remaining time. Remove, cover with aluminum foil and let stand for 10 minutes.

Yield: *6 servings*

Chicken Pilaf *(Meat)*

¼	cup flour	1½	cups rice (not instant)
1	teaspoon paprika	1	(16-ounce) can crushed or
1	teaspoon salt		diced tomatoes
1	(3-4 pound) chicken, cut up	1½	cups hot water
¼	cup oil	1	tablespoon chicken stock
½	cup diced onion	¼	cup chopped parsley, divided
1	cup sliced fresh mushrooms		

♦ Combine flour, paprika and salt. Dust flour mixture over chicken pieces. Brown chicken slowly in oil in a large skillet. Remove chicken from skillet and set aside.

♦ Preheat oven to 350°. Add onion and mushrooms to skillet and brown lightly. Add uncooked rice and stir until coated with oil. Add tomatoes, hot water, chicken stock and ½ of parsley. Heat to boil.

♦ Place sauce in a 9x13-inch baking dish and top with chicken pieces. Cover with foil and bake for 45 minutes to 1 hour or until chicken and rice are tender. Sprinkle remaining parsley on top and serve.

Yield: *3 to 4 servings*

Bar-B-Que Sauce *(Parve)*

3	cups assorted bottled barbecue sauce, favorite varieties	1	teaspoon minced dried onion flakes (optional)
1	cup honey		

♦ Mix all ingredients together. Use as basting sauce for grilled chicken. It may be stored in the refrigerator for up to 2 months.

Yield: *4 cups*

Orange Turkey Breast *(Meat)*

1	(5-6 pound) turkey breast	6	ounces dried apricots
⅛	teaspoon garlic powder	¾	cup golden and dark raisins
⅛	teaspoon pepper		(mixed)
	Ground ginger, to taste	2	onions, sliced
1	cup orange marmalade	3	carrots, cut diagonally, or use
1	(6-ounce) can orange juice		whole baby carrots
	concentrate, thawed	1½	cups dry white wine

- ◆ Preheat oven to 350°. Sprinkle seasonings on inside and top of turkey breast. Place turkey in a large roasting pan.

- ◆ Spread top with marmalade and pour orange juice concentrate over turkey. Place apricots, raisins, onions and carrots around turkey. Add wine to pan.

- ◆ Roast turkey, uncovered, for about 1½ hours, basting every 30 minutes. Cook breast until it has an internal temperature of 185°. Put meat thermometer into thickest part of breast. If top gets too brown before it is done, cover loosely with greased foil. Make sure there is liquid on bottom of pan by adding wine if needed.

- ◆ Let turkey stand for about 20 minutes before slicing. To serve, place vegetables around sliced meat. Serve sauce separately.

Yield: *6 to 8 servings*

Honey Mustard Sauce *(Parve)*

½	cup Dijon mustard with seeds or stone ground mustard	½	cup honey

- ◆ Mix ingredients together. Brush over chicken during the last 20 minutes of cooking. Make enough to use as extra sauce at the table.

Yield: *1 cup*

Turkey Burgers *(Meat)*

A healthy alternative.

1¼	pounds ground turkey	¼	teaspoon pepper
¾	cup plus 2 tablespoons chili sauce, divided	2	tablespoons oil
		1	tablespoon brown sugar
1	medium onion, chopped, divided	1	tablespoon prepared mustard
		1	tablespoon lemon juice
1	teaspoon garlic salt	2	tablespoons water

◆ Combine turkey, 2 tablespoons chili sauce, ½ chopped onion, garlic salt and pepper. Using wet hands, form into 4 burgers about 1 inch thick.

◆ Heat oil in large skillet. Add burgers and cook over medium heat until bottoms are just browned, about 2 minutes. Turn and sprinkle remaining chopped onion around patties. Cook, stirring onion occasionally until second side of patties are just browned and onion is softened, about 2 minutes.

◆ Combine remaining ¾ cup chili sauce, brown sugar, mustard, lemon juice and water. Add to pan; bring to a simmer. Reduce heat to low, cover and cook until sauce is thickened and burgers are cooked through with no trace of pink in center, about 15 minutes. Meat should spring back when lightly pressed.

Yield: *4 servings*

Jalapeño Jelly Glaze *(Parve)*

¼	cup jalapeño jelly	1	tablespoon minced cilantro
2	tablespoons lime juice		

◆ In a bowl combine all ingredients. Brush on baked or grilled chicken during the last 20 minutes of cooking.

Yield: *⅓ cup*

Sweet and Sour Turkey Meatballs ✡ (Meat)

1	(22-ounce) can tomato sauce	⅓	cup dried minced onions
1	large onion, diced	¼	teaspoon pepper
½	cup lemon juice	½	cup matzo meal
¾	cup water	2	eggs
1	cup sugar	1	teaspoon salt
2	pounds ground turkey	½	teaspoon garlic powder
½	cup cold water		

♦ Combine tomato sauce, onion, lemon juice, water and sugar in large, deep pot. Bring to a simmer and let cook while preparing meatballs.

♦ Combine ground turkey, cold water, dried onions, pepper, matzo meal, eggs, salt and garlic powder in large bowl. Mix together with wet hands.

♦ Form into walnut-size balls and drop into simmering sauce. Dampen hands with water as you roll the meatballs to keep them from sticking to your hands.

♦ Cover pot and simmer, without stirring, the longer the better. Shake pot occasionally to redistribute the meatballs in the sauce.

♦ Cool before serving, if possible, and skim fat from sauce.

♦ Reheat and serve over noodles.

Yield: *60 to 65 walnut-sized meatballs*

Note: *This recipe freezes well.*

Orange Sauce (Parve)

⅓	cup packed brown sugar	1	tablespoon grated orange rind
⅓	cup sugar		(optional)
1	tablespoon cornstarch	1	cup orange juice
		¼	teaspoon salt

♦ Combine all ingredients in saucepan. Stir over low heat until the sugars dissolve.

♦ Simmer until the sauce is transparent and thickened, about 5 minutes.

♦ Serve on top of chicken or Cornish hens.

Yield: *1½ cups*

Black Bean Sloppy Joes *(Parve)*

1	onion, chopped	1	(8-ounce) can tomato sauce
1	green pepper, seeded and diced	¼	cup quick rolled oats
		1	tablespoon soy sauce
⅓	cup water	½	tablespoon yellow mustard
1	(15-ounce) can black beans, drained and rinsed	1	teaspoon honey
		1	teaspoon chili powder

◆ Place onion and green pepper in saucepan with water. Cook, stirring often, until vegetables soften, about 5 minutes.

◆ Mash the beans with a bean or potato masher (do not use a food processor). Add the beans and remaining ingredients to the onion and pepper mixture.

◆ Cook over low heat until heated through, approximately 5 minutes.

Yield: *4 to 6 servings*

Easy Lean Bean Stew *(Parve)*

1	(28-ounce) can diced tomatoes, with juice	2	medium bell peppers, seeded and chopped (optional)
1	(15½-ounce) can red kidney beans, undrained	2	large ribs celery, sliced
		1	medium zucchini, chopped
1	(15½-ounce) can great northern beans, undrained	1	cup water
		1-2	teaspoons chili powder
1	(15½-ounce) can garbanzo beans, undrained	2	teaspoons basil, crushed
		¼	teaspoon black pepper
3	medium onions, chopped	1	bay leaf
2-3	cloves garlic, crushed	2	tablespoons powdered vegetable bouillon

◆ Put tomatoes into a large (6-quart) pot. Add beans and all other ingredients.

◆ Bring to boil. Reduce heat, cover and simmer for 2 hours. Vegetables will be tender in 1 hour, but it will be tastier after 2 hours of simmering.

Yield: *6 to 8 servings*

Note: *Increase the amount of liquid for a great soup.*

Black Beans and Rice (Parve)

1 green pepper, seeded and chopped	1 (16-ounce) can black beans, undrained
1 medium onion, chopped	½ teaspoon dried oregano
2 tablespoons oil	½ teaspoon garlic powder
1 (14½-ounce) can stewed tomatoes	1½ cups instant brown rice

◆ Sauté onions and green pepper in hot oil.

◆ Add tomatoes, beans, oregano and garlic powder. Bring to a boil.

◆ Stir in rice, return to boil. Reduce heat; cover and simmer for 5 minutes.

◆ Remove from heat. Let stand for 5 minutes before serving.

Yield: *8 servings*

Shul Cholent (Parve)

Shul *means synagogue.*

5 onions, sliced	1 package onion soup mix or 4 teaspoons parve beef-flavored soup mix
16 ounces bean mix (garbanzo, pinto, navy, black, kidney)	
½ (11-ounce) box barley	⅛ cup oil
4 large potatoes, cut up	Water
4 large carrots, cut up	

◆ Cholent requires approximately 20 to 22 hours cooking time. Oil bottom of a slow cooker. Place some of the sliced onions in a layer on the bottom. Add beans, barley, potatoes, carrots and remaining onions.

◆ Add soup mix to taste, ⅛ cup oil and water to cover by 2 inches.

◆ Turn pot to high for 1 hour, then to low for overnight.

Yield: *6 to 8 servings*

Note: *Cholent may also be made in a tightly covered Dutch oven. Bake at 275° for 20 to 24 hours.*

Tortilla Tamale Pie *(Dairy)*

Can't believe it's meatless!

6	(5-inch) flour tortillas	1	red, orange or yellow bell pepper, seeded and cut into ½-inch pieces
2	tablespoons oil		
12-16	ounces soy "meat" crumbles		
3	green onions, chopped	1	(2-3 ounce) can sliced black olives, drained
1	(1-ounce) package taco seasoning		
1	cup warm water, or more as needed	1½-2	cups grated cheese (Jack, colby, cheddar or a blend)
1	(15-ounce) can corn, drained, or 10 ounces frozen corn		Sour cream (optional) Salsa (optional)

◆ Preheat oven to 350°. With oil, brush both sides of tortillas.

◆ Spray a 10-inch deep-dish pie plate with vegetable spray. Place tortillas in an overlapping flower petal fashion to cover plate. Edges of tortillas should extend ½ to ¾ inch above rim.

◆ Sauté crumbles and onion in a large nonstick skillet. Add taco seasoning and ½ cup water and stir until water is absorbed and mixture is of a slightly wet consistency. If mixture seems too dry, add small amounts of water at a time. Remove from heat.

◆ Combine "meat" mixture with corn, pepper and olives. Turn into prepared pie plate and top with cheese. Bake for 25 to 30 minutes. Serve with sour cream and/or salsa.

Yield: *6 to 8 servings*

Black Bean Burritos *(Dairy)*

Great with a salad and side of rice.

Sauce

1	(14-ounce) can diced tomatoes with chilies, drained	¼	cup chopped onion

Burritos

8	(10-inch) flour tortillas	1	cup grated Monterey Jack or cheddar cheese, divided
2	(15-ounce) cans black beans, drained		Sour cream, guacamole, diced avocado or cilantro for garnish (optional)
½	cup finely chopped red onion		

◆ Preheat oven to 350°. To make sauce, purée tomatoes and onion in blender. Set aside.

◆ To assemble burritos, soften tortillas in microwave according to package directions. Top the middle of each tortilla with ¼ cup beans, 1 tablespoon red onion and 1½ tablespoons cheese.

◆ Wrap the tortilla around the filling and place the burritos seam side down, side by side, in a 9x13-inch glass baking dish sprayed with vegetable spray.

◆ Spoon sauce over the burritos and sprinkle with remaining cheese. Bake, uncovered, for 15 minutes or until cheese has melted and burritos are hot. Serve with any or all of the following: avocado, sour cream, guacamole, or a sprinkling of cilantro.

Yield: *6 to 8 servings*

Vegetable Stuffed Cabbage *(Parve)*

1	cup long-grain rice	1	(10-ounce) package frozen chopped spinach, thawed and squeezed dry
1	medium head green cabbage (about 2½ pounds)		
1	(8-ounce) package mushrooms, chopped	1	egg
		¾	teaspoon salt
1	medium onion, chopped	½	teaspoon pepper
4	tablespoons oil, divided	2	(15 to 16-ounce) cans stewed tomatoes
1	small carrot, coarsely shredded		
		1	teaspoon sugar
		2½	cups water

♦ Prepare rice according to package directions.

♦ With knife, remove core from cabbage. Fill 8-quart pot ¾ full of water. Heat to boiling. Place cabbage in water, cut side up.

♦ Using large spoons, gently separate leaves as outer leaves soften slightly. Drain leaves in colander. Continue until 8 large leaves are removed from cabbage. Trim tough ribs of leaves very thin. Coarsely slice remaining cabbage. Set aside.

♦ In large skillet over medium-high heat, cook mushrooms and onion in 2 tablespoons oil until onion is tender. Remove to large bowl. Stir in cooked rice, shredded carrot, spinach, egg, salt and pepper until blended.

♦ Onto center of each cabbage leaf, place ⅛ of rice mixture. Fold 2 sides of leaf toward center. Starting from an unfolded end, roll up cabbage jellyroll fashion. Repeat to make 8 rolls in all.

♦ In same skillet over medium-high heat cook sliced cabbage for 5 minutes in 2 tablespoons hot oil. Stir in stewed tomatoes, sugar and 2½ cups water. Add cabbage rolls seam-side down; over high heat, heat to boiling. Reduce heat to low; cover and simmer for 40 minutes, occasionally spooning sauce over rolls.

Yield: *4 servings*

Vegetarian Chili *(Dairy)*

You'll never miss the meat!

2	tablespoons olive or vegetable oil	1	teaspoon sugar
1½	cups chopped celery	1½	teaspoons dried basil, crushed
1½	cups seeded, chopped green pepper	1½	teaspoons dried oregano, crushed
1	cup chopped onion	1½	teaspoons ground cumin
3	cloves garlic, minced	1	teaspoon ground allspice
2	(28-ounce) cans tomatoes, undrained, cut up	½	teaspoon salt
		¼	teaspoon pepper
3	(15-ounce) cans beans (kidney, black, great northern or pinto), rinsed and drained	¼	teaspoon hot pepper sauce
		1	bay leaf
		1	(12-ounce) can beer or red wine (optional)
½	cup raisins	¾	cup cashews
¼	cup red wine vinegar	1	cup shredded Swiss, mozzarella or cheddar cheese (optional)
3-4	teaspoons chili powder		
1	tablespoon snipped parsley		

◆ Heat oil in 4- to 6-quart pot. Add celery, green pepper, onion and garlic. Cover and cook over medium heat for about 10 minutes until vegetables are tender, stirring occasionally.

◆ Stir in undrained tomatoes, drained beans, raisins, vinegar and seasonings. Bring to boil, reduce heat and simmer, covered, for 1½ hours.

◆ Stir in beer or wine. Return to boiling, then simmer, uncovered, for 30 minutes longer or to desired consistency.

◆ Remove bay leaf and discard. Stir in cashews. Sprinkle cheese over each serving, if desired.

Yield: *8 main dish servings*

Taco Pizza *(Dairy)*

8 (5-inch) flour tortillas	⅓ cup sliced black olives
½ cup taco sauce or salsa	1½ cups shredded and seasoned
½ cup chopped onion	cheese

◆ Preheat oven to 350°. Line greased pizza pan with flour tortillas, overlapping as necessary to cover pan.

◆ Drizzle your favorite taco sauce or salsa over the tortillas. Cover with onion, black olives and cheese.

◆ Bake for approximately 10 minutes, until cheese is melted and bubbly but not browned.

Yield: *4 to 6 servings*

Note: *You can increase "heat" with hot peppers, different hot sauces and cheeses.*

Portobello Steak Sandwich *(Parve)*

4 portobello mushrooms	4 buns
6 medium cloves garlic, crushed	4 teaspoons margarine
1 cup balsamic vinegar	Salt and pepper to taste
1½ medium Vidalia or sweet onions, sliced (3 cups)	1 medium tomato, sliced
Olive oil spray	Lettuce

◆ Wash mushrooms and place in plastic bag or small bowl. Add garlic, balsamic vinegar and onions. Marinate for 20 minutes, turning bag once.

◆ Prepare large nonstick frying pan with olive oil spray and heat on high until very hot, or preheat grill.

◆ Drain mushrooms, onions and garlic very well and discard marinade. Pat mushrooms dry using paper towels and place mushrooms and onions in hot skillet or in heavy foil packet on grill. Cook for 8 minutes, turning half way through.

◆ Toast buns. Remove mushrooms and onions to plate and season to taste. Serve warm on bun with lettuce and tomato.

Yield: *4 servings*

Braised Tofu in Wine and Ginger *(Parve)*

1	pound tofu, sliced ¼ inch thick	3	scallions, chopped
2	tablespoons oil	¼	cup white wine
1	clove garlic, thinly sliced	3	tablespoons soy sauce
½	teaspoon ground ginger or 3 thin slices fresh gingerroot		

◆ Spread sliced tofu on flat surface covered with a towel. Weight the tofu with heavy plate to remove excess water. Allow tofu to stand for at least ½ hour, or use frozen tofu that has been thawed and drained.

◆ Heat oil in a wok or heavy 10-inch skillet. Add garlic and ginger. Place tofu slices in oil and fry over medium heat for 2 minutes on each side.

◆ Sprinkle scallions, wine and soy sauce on top of tofu.

◆ Cover, reduce heat to low and braise the tofu for 15 minutes. Serve immediately.

Yield: *4 side dish servings*

To-Fish Patties *(Dairy)*

1	(12-ounce) can tuna or salmon, drained	3	tablespoons parsley, chopped
1	egg	3	tablespoons shredded cheddar cheese
½	medium onion, chopped	½	teaspoon baking powder
	Pepper to taste		Bread crumbs, matzo meal or flour
	Basil to taste		Oil
2	tablespoons soy sauce		
12	ounces tofu, drained and crumbled		

◆ In a large bowl mash together tuna, egg, onion, pepper, basil, soy sauce, tofu and parsley until well blended.

◆ Mix in cheese and baking powder. Add enough flour, bread crumbs, or matzo meal so that mixture will hold together when shaped into patties.

◆ Let mixture stand approximately 5 minutes. Shape into patties.

◆ Heat enough oil in large skillet to cover the bottom of pan. Cook patties on medium-high heat, approximately 4 minutes each side until golden and slightly dry. Drain on paper towel.

Yield: *4 servings*

Tofu Nut Loaf
with Mushroom Sauce *(Dairy)*

Tofu Loaf

1	cup rolled oats	½	green pepper, seeded and minced
1	cup walnuts	1	teaspoon salt
1	pound tofu	2	teaspoons sage
1	medium onion, grated	2	teaspoons thyme
1	carrot, grated	1	tablespoon oregano

Mushroom Sauce

3	tablespoons margarine	1-1½	cups milk
1	shallot or 2 scallions, minced		Dash garlic salt
½	pound mushrooms, chopped		Few drops hot sauce
3	tablespoons flour		Salt to taste

◆ Preheat oven to 375°. Put the oats into blender or food processor and process to a coarse flour. Put into large mixing bowl.

◆ Put walnuts into blender or food processor and blend coarsely; then add to oat flour in bowl.

◆ Crumble the tofu into the bowl and add all of the remaining ingredients (the vegetables should total 1 cup). Mix well until all ingredients are blended and mixture has a fluffy but firm texture.

◆ Grease a 9x13-inch casserole dish and place mixture into casserole, shaping into an oval or rectangle in the center of the dish. The loaf should be no more than 2 inches high.

◆ Bake for 45 minutes and pour half the mushroom sauce over the loaf during the last 10 minutes. Serve the rest as gravy.

◆ **Mushroom Sauce:** Sauté the shallot (or scallions) and mushrooms in melted margarine in skillet. Add the flour and blend well.

◆ Add the remaining sauce ingredients and bring to a boil, stirring frequently.

Yield: *6 servings*

Cheesy Tofu "Meatballs" (Dairy)

1	(12-ounce) package tofu	1	teaspoon dried basil or
¼	cup Parmesan cheese		1 tablespoon fresh
½	cup bread crumbs	1	teaspoon dried parsley or
½	cup rolled oats		1 tablespoon fresh
2	eggs	¼	cup olive oil
	Salt to taste	1	(25-ounce) jar marinara sauce

- ◆ Crumble tofu and combine with next 7 ingredients. If dry, add a little moisture with milk or water.
- ◆ Shape into balls 1 inch in diameter. Sauté in oil or bake 20 minutes at 350°. Keep turning until golden.
- ◆ Heat balls in sauce.

Yield: *12 "meat"balls*

Tofu Pot Roast (Parve)

1-2	(12-ounce) blocks tofu, sliced	2	teaspoons salt
2	tablespoons olive oil	½	teaspoon paprika
3	onions, sliced or diced	2	large bay leaves
2	cloves garlic, minced	10	peppercorns
1	carrot, shredded	1½	cups tomato or vegetable juice
1	rib celery, diced	2	tablespoons brown sugar
1	green pepper, seeded and julienned		Olive oil to coat bottom of pot
1	small red pepper, seeded and julienned		Sliced portobello mushrooms (optional)

- ◆ Sauté tofu slices in olive oil on each side until golden brown.
- ◆ Place tofu in large oiled pot with remaining ingredients. Cover and simmer for 1½ to 2 hours. Serve with gravy from pot.

Yield: *4 to 6 servings*

Note: *Tofu may be frozen and then defrosted before cooking, giving it a "meatier" texture.*

Stir-Fry Vegetables with Tofu *(Parve)*

1	tablespoon oil	2	cups bean sprouts
2	tablespoons soy sauce	2	cups bok choy (Chinese
2	teaspoons honey		cabbage), sliced diagonally
2	garlic cloves, minced	½	cup green onions, sliced
1	tablespoon gingerroot, grated		lengthwise
2	cups snow pea pods	8	ounces tofu, cut in small cubes

◆ Place the oil, soy sauce, honey, garlic and ginger in heavy skillet or wok. Heat until sizzling.

◆ Add the vegetables and stir-fry, gently mixing over high heat.

◆ Add the tofu; stir-fry until vegetables are cooked and tofu is well seasoned. Serve immediately over rice or Chinese noodles.

Yield: *2 main dish or 4 side dish servings*

Microwave Stir-Fry *(Parve)*

8	ounces toasted pecans, approximately 2 cups	1	(8-ounce) can bamboo shoots, drained
¼	cup oil	½	pound fresh mushrooms, sliced
1	small bunch broccoli, cut into florets	½	pound fresh snow pea pods, ends and strings removed
12	baby carrots, cut in half lengthwise	¼	cup dry white wine or parve chicken-flavored broth
		¼	cup soy sauce

◆ Toast nuts in nonstick skillet over medium heat until lightly browned, approximately 2 to 3 minutes, stirring often, or toss with a small amount of oil and place on baking sheet in 325° oven for 15 minutes.

◆ In microwave-safe 9x13-inch baking dish, microwave oil on high power for 1 minute. Add broccoli, carrots and bamboo shoots. Cover with waxed paper or paper towel and microwave on high for 2 to 3 minutes, stirring every minute.

◆ Add toasted nuts and stir well. Cover and microwave on high for 2 to 3 minutes, stirring after 1½ minutes.

◆ Add mushrooms, pea pods, wine and soy sauce. Stir well, cover, microwave on high for 3 to 5 minutes, stirring every 1½ minutes.

◆ Serve over hot rice.

Yield: *6 servings*

Summer Vegetable Paella *(Parve)*

Serve this in a bowl with crusty bread.

1	(6-ounce) jar marinated artichoke hearts	2	ears corn, husked and cut crosswise into 2-inch pieces
4	cloves garlic, minced	2	medium zucchini, cut into ½-inch slices
1	large onion, cut into wedges		
3½	cups reduced-sodium vegetable broth	1	medium sweet red pepper, seeded and cut into strips
⅓	cup water	½	teaspoon finely shredded lemon peel
½	teaspoon pepper		
¼	teaspoon powdered saffron	1	(15-ounce) can garbanzo beans, drained
1	cup Arborio or long grain rice		
2	cups green beans cut into 1-inch pieces		

◆ Drain marinade from artichokes into large pot; set artichokes aside. Heat marinade over medium heat. Add garlic and onion, stirring frequently for 5 minutes.

◆ Add vegetable broth, water, pepper and saffron. Bring to boil.

◆ Stir in uncooked rice and green beans. Return to boil. Reduce heat and simmer, covered, for 8 minutes.

◆ Add corn, zucchini, red pepper and lemon peel. Cook, covered, for 7 to 8 minutes more or until vegetables and rice are tender.

◆ Stir in garbanzo beans and artichoke hearts; heat through.

Yield: *4 to 6 servings*

Winter Vegetable Pie *(Parve or Dairy)*

½ cup coarsely chopped walnuts, toasted
1 large leek, diced (or 1½ cups diced onion)
1 tablespoon sesame oil
4 cups mixed diced carrots, squash and parsnips
½ teaspoon salt
½ cup water
1 egg
Pepper to taste
1½ teaspoons chopped fresh basil
½ cup soy milk or cream
2 tablespoons tahini
1 (9-inch) pie shell, unbaked

◆ Toast nuts in a nonstick skillet over medium heat until lightly browned, approximately 2 to 3 minutes, stirring often.

◆ Sauté leek in sesame oil over medium heat in skillet for 3 minutes.

◆ Add diced vegetables and continue to sauté for 3 more minutes. Add salt and ½ cup water. Simmer, covered, for 15 minutes over medium-low heat until vegetables are soft. Drain off excess liquid.

◆ Preheat oven to 425°. Place vegetables, egg, pepper, basil, soy milk or cream and tahini in food processor or blender and purée until creamy. Pour into pie crust and top with roasted walnuts.

◆ Bake at 425° for 10 minutes, then reduce heat to 350° and bake for an additional 20 minutes or until center is firm.

Yield: *6 servings*

Garden Pizza *(Dairy)*

1 (8- to 10-inch) prepared pizza shell
¼ cup pizza sauce or olive oil
1 small red or sweet white onion, sliced
1 yellow bell pepper, sliced thin
½ cup broccoli florets, cut up
¼ cup sliced black olives
¼ cup sliced mushrooms
1 cup shredded mozzarella cheese

◆ Preheat oven to 450°. Spread pizza sauce or olive oil evenly over pizza shell.

◆ Place sliced vegetables on top of pizza. Sprinkle with cheese.

◆ Bake for 5 to 8 minutes.

Yield: *2 servings*

Vegetable Strudel *(Dairy)*

3	cups chopped broccoli	2	teaspoons parsley
3	cups chopped cauliflower	1½	teaspoons basil
2½	cups sliced carrots	1	teaspoon tarragon
2	tablespoons margarine	1	pound cheese, grated (any
1	large onion, chopped		kind)
2	cloves garlic, minced	12	sheets phyllo dough
3	eggs	6	tablespoons butter, melted

◆ Steam the broccoli, cauliflower and carrots until tender. Sauté the onion and garlic in margarine.

◆ Combine eggs and seasonings, and add garlic, onion and vegetables. Add grated cheese.

◆ Preheat oven to 350°.

◆ Using 6 sheets of phyllo at a time, brush each sheet of phyllo with butter and stack together. Spread on half of the vegetable mixture and roll phyllo dough like a jellyroll. Brush top with butter. Repeat with remaining ingredients. Place on greased cookie sheet.

◆ Bake for 20 to 30 minutes. Slice each roll into 4 to 6 slices.

Yield: *8 servings*

Lentils and Rice *(Parve)*

This Middle Eastern dish is often served with yogurt, chopped and sautéed garlic or sunny-side up eggs.

1	cup red lentils	1½	teaspoons tomato paste
2	cups rice	1½	teaspoons cumin
2½	cups water	½	cup margarine
	Salt and pepper to taste		

◆ Separately rinse lentils and rice.

◆ In a large pot place water, salt, pepper, tomato paste and cumin. Bring to boil.

◆ Reduce heat, add rice and cover, cooking for 10 minutes. Add the lentils and margarine.

◆ Stir gently and simmer for 1 hour.

Yield: *6 to 8 main dish servings*

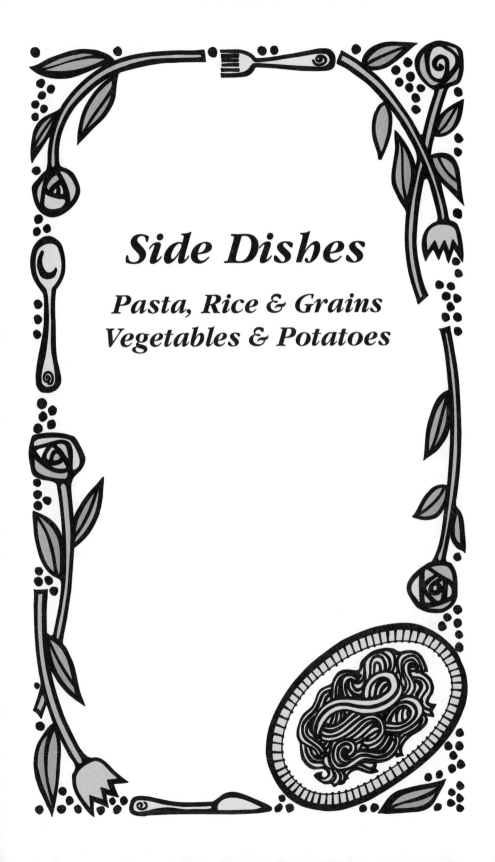

Side Dishes

Pasta, Rice & Grains
Vegetables & Potatoes

Wholesome Foods

Rice & Pasta:

◆ For easy, fluffy rice put 1 cup regular rice and 2 cups water in a 2-quart covered casserole dish. Microwave on high power for 15 to 17 minutes. Let sit for 5 minutes before serving.

◆ Zap garlic cloves in microwave for 15 seconds and the skins slip right off.

Vegetables:

◆ To keep potatoes from sprouting buds, place an apple in the bag.

◆ A pinch of sugar added to boiling water for corn on the cob brings out the corn's natural sweetness.

◆ To cook unhusked corn on the cob, cook 2½ minutes per ear in the microwave on high power. Do not cook more than 6 ears at a time.

Equivalents:

8 ounces uncooked spaghetti = 4 cups cooked

1 cup regular rice = 3 cups cooked

1 cup instant rice = 2 cups cooked

Substitutions:

Garlic	1 clove, minced	=	⅛ teaspoon garlic powder
Fresh Herbs	1 tablespoon	=	1 teaspoon crushed dried or ½ teaspoon ground
Onion	1 small, chopped	=	1 teaspoon onion powder or 1 tablespoon dried minced onion
Prepared Mustard	1 tablespoon	=	½ teaspoon ground mustard + 2 teaspoons vinegar
Tomato Juice	1 cup	=	½ cup tomato sauce + ½ cup water
Tomato Sauce	2 cups	=	¾ cup tomato paste + 1 cup water
Tomatoes, Fresh	3 medium tomatoes, cut up	=	1 (16-ounce) can tomatoes, cut up or 1 (16-ounce) can stewed tomatoes

Kugel is a delicious side dish, best described as a soufflé or casserole. Its versatility is limited only by the imagination of the chef. As part of a holiday menu (including Passover), a dairy brunch or any meal, a good kugel recipe is a necessity in every Jewish kitchen. Whether made sweet or spicy, of noodles, potatoes or vegetables, kugel can be adapted to suit your taste.

Basic Kugel *(Parve)*

Kugel
1 (16-ounce) package medium noodles, cooked and drained	Salt, pepper, paprika to taste
½ cup margarine, melted	⅓-½ cup sugar
⅓-½ cup nondairy creamer	Cinnamon to taste
6 eggs, lightly beaten	Golden raisins

Topping
½ cup brown sugar	1 cup cornflake cereal crumbs
1 teaspoon cinnamon	¼ cup margarine, melted

◆ Preheat oven to 350°. Melt margarine and combine with remaining ingredients. Place in 9x13-inch pan.

◆ Mix together topping ingredients and distribute evenly over kugel. Bake for 1 hour.

Yield: *12 to 15 servings*

Note: Variation 1: *You may top with cherry pie filling during last 10 minutes of baking if desired.* **Variation 2:** *For a basic onion kugel, omit the sugar, cinnamon, raisins and topping. Sauté 1 medium chopped onion in the margarine and combine with noodles, creamer, eggs and seasonings. Bake as directed above.*

Sunshine Kugel *(Parve)*

12	ounces medium egg noodles, cooked and drained	½	cup sugar
		½	teaspoon salt
2	tablespoons margarine, melted	⅓	cup golden raisins or craisins
4	eggs	3	medium tart apples, cored, peeled and grated
2	cups orange juice, including pulp	2	teaspoons lemon juice

- ◆ Preheat oven to 350°. Toss noodles with margarine.
- ◆ Beat eggs. Add orange juice, sugar, salt and raisins. Pour over noodles and mix.
- ◆ Mix apples and lemon juice. Add to noodle mixture.
- ◆ Pour into greased 9x13-inch baking dish and bake for 1 hour.

Yield: *10 to 12 servings*

Fruity Noodle Kugel *(Parve)*

¼	cup margarine	½	teaspoon salt
½	cup light brown sugar	1	teaspoon cinnamon
1	(20-ounce) can pineapple chunks, drained	1	teaspoon lemon juice
		12	ounces medium egg noodles, cooked and drained
2	eggs		
½	cup oil	½	cup raisins
¼	cup sugar		

- ◆ Preheat oven to 350°. Mix all ingredients and place in greased 9x13-inch baking dish.
- ◆ Bake for 35 to 40 minutes or until lightly browned.

Yield: *12 to 15 servings*

Note: *You may add ½ cup chopped nuts or ½ cup of any finely chopped dried fruit instead of raisins or a 20-ounce can of drained fruit cocktail instead of pineapple.*

Jerusalem Kugel *(Parve)*

This spicy kugel combines Ashkenazic and Sephardic cooking.

10	ounces angel hair pasta, cooked and drained	3	eggs, lightly beaten
½	cup oil, divided	1-1½	teaspoons pepper
½	cup sugar		Salt to taste

◆ Preheat oven to 350°. Add ¼ cup oil to pasta and mix thoroughly; set aside.

◆ In medium saucepan, heat remaining ¼ cup oil and add the sugar. Cook over low heat, stirring, for about 5 minutes until sugar dissolves and caramelizes. If sugar hardens, put pot back on low heat and stir until sugar dissolves.

◆ Add the pasta to hot oil and sugar mixture and mix well. Add eggs and seasonings to pasta. Stir well and test to see if more pepper is needed.

◆ Place pasta mixture in a greased tube pan and bake, uncovered, for 45 to 60 minutes until golden brown.

Yield: *6 servings*

Note: *Popular in Jerusalem among Hassidic Jews, this kugel may be baked at 175° overnight and served for the Sabbath meal after morning services.*

Buttermilk Kugel *(Dairy)*

1	(12-ounce) package wide egg noodles, cooked and drained	4	eggs
½	cup margarine	1	quart buttermilk
½	cup sugar	2	cups cornflake cereal crumbs, divided

◆ Preheat oven to 350°. Add margarine to noodles; stir until margarine is melted and add sugar, eggs and buttermilk. Mix well.

◆ Lightly grease a 9x13-inch baking pan and sprinkle bottom with 1 cup of cornflake cereal crumbs. Add noodles to pan, sprinkle with remaining cereal crumbs and bake for 1 hour. Allow to cool for approximately 20 minutes before serving.

Yield: *12 to 15 servings*

Note: *You may also top kugel with mixture of ¼ cup sugar and 1 tablespoon cinnamon.*

Dairy Kugel *(Dairy)*

Kugel

8-10	ounces fine noodles, cooked and drained	1	pint sour cream
¼	cup margarine, melted	1	(3-ounce) package cream cheese
5-6	eggs	¾	cup sugar
1	pound cottage cheese	2	tablespoons lemon juice

Topping

¾	cup graham cracker crumbs	¼	cup margarine, melted
¼	cup brown sugar		

◆ Preheat oven to 350°. Combine all kugel ingredients with hot noodles and place in greased 9x13-inch baking pan.

◆ Mix topping ingredients together and sprinkle on top of noodles. Bake for 45 minutes.

Yield: *15 to 20 servings*

Reduced-Fat Noodle Kugel *(Dairy)*

1	(16-ounce) package wide egg noodles, cooked and drained	2	whole eggs
1	pound low-fat cottage cheese	8	ounces low-fat sour cream
¼	cup margarine, divided	1	cup skim milk
	Egg substitute equivalent to 4 eggs	1	(5½-ounce) can apricot nectar Cornflake cereal crumbs

◆ Preheat oven to 350°. Mix cottage cheese and half of margarine into hot noodles. Add next 5 ingredients and mix well.

◆ Spray a 9x13-inch glass baking dish with vegetable spray. Pour noodle mixture into dish.

◆ Top with cornflake crumbs and bake uncovered for 1 hour.

Yield: *12 to 15 servings*

Swiss Cheese Kugel *(Dairy)*

To use as a main dish, just add a salad!

1	(8-ounce) package medium noodles, cooked and drained	¼	teaspoon pepper
1	tablespoon onion or garlic juice	8	ounces Swiss cheese, grated (about 2 cups)
1	teaspoon Worcestershire sauce	1	pint sour cream (regular or low-fat)
¼	cup margarine, melted	½	cup bread crumbs
½	teaspoon salt (optional)		Melted margarine to drizzle

◆ Preheat oven to 350°. To drained, hot noodles, add onion juice, Worcestershire, margarine, salt, pepper and Swiss cheese. Mix well.

◆ Add sour cream and mix thoroughly.

◆ Pour into ungreased 9x9-inch baking pan and top with bread crumbs. Drizzle melted margarine over crumbs. Bake for 1 hour.

Yield: *6 servings*

Note: *Recipe may be doubled using 9x13-inch pan. It freezes and reheats well.*

Acini de Pepe *(Parve)*

A Rosh Hashanah family favorite!

1 (16-ounce) package acini de pepe or other tiny pasta, cooked and drained	½ pound mushrooms, sliced
	2 teaspoons salt
	½ teaspoon black pepper
¼ cup margarine	1 teaspoon lemon pepper
1 large onion, chopped	

◆ Preheat oven to 350°. Melt margarine in a large skillet and sauté onions and mushrooms until mushrooms are soft and onions translucent.

◆ Add salt, pepper and lemon pepper.

◆ Mix pasta with mushrooms and onions in skillet. Place in a greased 2½-quart casserole.

◆ Bake uncovered until top is brown, approximately 30 minutes.

Yield: *10 servings*

Note: *Recipe may be made ahead and refrigerated before browning.*

Greek Pasta *(Dairy)*

2 tablespoons olive oil	¼ cup chopped, pitted kalamata olives
1 tablespoon balsamic vinegar	
2 medium garlic cloves, crushed	2 tablespoons capers
12 ounces hot cooked penne pasta, cooked and drained	¾ cup (3 ounces) crumbled feta cheese
2 cups chopped fresh spinach	

◆ Combine oil, vinegar and garlic in large bowl.

◆ Add pasta and remaining ingredients and toss well.

Yield: *4 servings*

Lasagna Roll-Ups *(Dairy)*

12 lasagna noodles, cooked, drained and rinsed
1 (10-ounce) package frozen chopped spinach, thawed and drained
1 pound ricotta cheese
2 cups shredded mozzarella cheese
1 (28 to 32-ounce) jar marinara sauce

◆ Preheat oven to 350°. While noodles are cooking, in a small bowl combine chopped spinach, ricotta cheese and 1½ cups of the mozzarella cheese.

◆ After rinsing the noodles, lay 1 flat and spread cheese mixture on the noodle, leaving ¼-inch at each end. Roll up the noodle and place in a 9x13-inch baking dish sprayed with vegetable spray. Repeat with remaining noodles.

◆ Pour the marinara sauce over the top of the prepared noodles and sprinkle with remaining mozzarella cheese.

◆ Bake for 1 hour.

Yield: *4 servings*

Angel Hair Pasta with Artichokes *(Dairy)*

So easy, so fast, so good.

1 teaspoon oil
2 cloves garlic, minced
1 (14-ounce) can diced tomatoes with garlic, undrained
1 (14-ounce) can artichoke hearts, drained and quartered
4 ounces crumbled feta cheese
1 (9-ounce) package angel hair pasta, cooked and drained

◆ Sauté garlic in oil. Add tomatoes and artichokes to garlic and heat.

◆ Add feta to tomatoes and artichokes and toss together. Add tomato mixture to pasta, toss and serve.

Yield: *2 to 3 servings*

Linguine with Roasted Vegetables *(Parve)*

1	cup vegetable soup stock	1	small yellow squash, quartered lengthwise and cut into 2-inch pieces
10	large cloves garlic, peeled and halved		
2	tablespoons balsamic vinegar	1	large red bell pepper, seeded and cut into chunks
1	pound cherry tomatoes, cut in half	8	medium green onions, cut into 2-inch lengths
1	pound asparagus, trimmed and cut into 2-inch lengths	1	tablespoon olive oil
2	small zucchini, quartered lengthwise and cut into 2-inch pieces		Salt and pepper to taste
		1	pound linguine, cooked and drained

◆ In small saucepan, combine stock and garlic. Bring to boil, reduce heat to low and simmer, covered, for 15 to 20 minutes.

◆ Preheat oven to 450°. Purée stock, garlic and vinegar in food processor or blender until smooth; keep warm.

◆ Meanwhile, in large bowl, combine tomatoes, asparagus, zucchini, squash, bell peppers and green onions. Drizzle oil over top, season with salt and pepper and toss to coat.

◆ Place in baking pan and roast, stirring occasionally, for 15 minutes. Place hot linguine in large serving bowl. Toss with the roasted vegetables and stock. Serve immediately.

Yield: *4 servings*

Spinach Mostaccioli *(Dairy)*

8	ounces mostaccioli noodles, cooked and drained
2	tablespoons margarine
1	cup sliced onion
2	tablespoons minced garlic
¼	cup flour
2½	cups milk
1¼	cups grated Parmesan cheese, divided
1½	teaspoons dried Italian seasoning
½	teaspoon pepper
1	(14-ounce) can diced tomatoes with garlic and/or Italian seasonings
1	(10-ounce) package frozen chopped spinach, thawed and drained
¼	cup bread crumbs
2	tablespoons grated Parmesan cheese
1	tablespoon margarine, melted

◆ Preheat oven to 350°. Melt margarine in skillet and sauté onion and garlic for 5 minutes. Add flour and stir.

◆ Gradually add milk, stirring constantly until slightly thickened. Remove from heat and add ¼ cup cheese, Italian seasoning and pepper.

◆ Combine pasta, cheese sauce, 1 cup cheese, tomatoes and spinach in large bowl. Place in 9x13-inch baking dish.

◆ Combine bread crumbs, 2 tablespoons Parmesan and margarine. Sprinkle over pasta. Bake for 30 minutes.

Yield: *8 to 10 servings*

Baked Spaghetti *(Dairy)*

Prepare in advance, then heat and eat.

1 medium onion, minced	Dash garlic salt
3 tablespoons oil	1 tablespoon sugar
3 (8-ounce) cans tomato sauce	½ teaspoon salt
1 cup Burgundy or other dry red wine	¼ teaspoon pepper
¼ teaspoon oregano	½ pound spaghetti, broken in 2-inch pieces, cooked and drained
¼ teaspoon rosemary	1 cup grated cheddar cheese
¼ teaspoon marjoram	
¼ teaspoon basil	

◆ Sauté onions in oil in large pot or Dutch oven. Add tomato sauce, wine and all seasonings. Simmer, covered, for 1 hour, stirring occasionally.

◆ Add spaghetti to sauce with ½ cup of cheese. Place in 3-quart covered casserole and sprinkle with remaining ½ cup cheese. Cool and refrigerate for several hours or overnight.

◆ Remove from refrigerator 30 minutes before baking. Preheat oven to 325°. Bake, covered, for 45 minutes. Uncover and continue to bake for an additional 30 minutes.

Yield: *6 servings*

Note: *Spaghetti freezes well and tastes great the next day.*

Pesto Sauce *(Dairy)*

1 cup fresh basil, shredded	¼ cup pine nuts
½ cup frozen chopped spinach, thawed and drained	2 cloves garlic, minced
¼ cup grated Parmesan cheese	2 tablespoons olive oil

◆ Process all ingredients in food processor and toss with any cooked, hot pasta.

Yield: *2 cups*

Spaghetti Casserole *(Dairy)*

1	pound whole wheat or buckwheat spaghetti	1	green pepper, chopped
2	cups water	6	tomatoes, diced
1	tablespoon oil		Black olives, sliced (optional)
1	large onion, chopped	1	teaspoon salt
1	cup sliced mushrooms	2	tablespoons soy sauce
		2	cups grated cheese

◆ Preheat oven to 350°. Cook spaghetti in 2 cups boiling water until all the liquid is absorbed. Sauté onion in oil until browned.

◆ Mix all ingredients except cheese and place in greased 2-quart casserole dish.

◆ Cover and bake for 30 minutes. Sprinkle cheese on top and bake uncovered for 5 more minutes.

Yield: *5 servings*

Kasha Varnishkas *(Parve)*

A healthy and traditional side dish.

1	cup kasha (buckwheat groats)		Salt and pepper to taste
1	egg	2	cups boiling water or parve bouillon
2	tablespoons oil or margarine, divided	1½	cups bow tie noodles, cooked and drained
2	large onions, chopped		
1	cup chopped mushrooms		

◆ Mix kasha with egg until evenly coated. Sauté in 1 tablespoon oil or margarine until each grain of kasha is dry. Push to the side of the pan.

◆ Sauté onion and mushrooms in 1 tablespoon oil or margarine. Mix with kasha. Add salt and pepper to taste. Add water to cover. Cook over low heat until all liquid is absorbed, about 10 to 12 minutes.

◆ Combine kasha and bow ties.

Yield: *6 to 8 servings*

Super Spaghetti and Meatballs (Meat)

Meatballs also make great hamburgers!

Meatballs

2½-3 pounds lean ground beef	¼ teaspoon pepper
1 medium onion, finely chopped	½ teaspoon garlic powder
2 eggs or equivalent egg substitute	½ teaspoon salt
	1 tablespoon parsley flakes
1½ tablespoons seasoned bread crumbs	

Sauce

2 tablespoons oil	30-36 ounces tomato juice (a 6-pack
1 medium onion, finely chopped	of 5½-ounce cans is perfect)
2 cloves garlic, minced	½ teaspoon salt
3 (12-ounce) cans tomato paste	1 teaspoon Worcestershire sauce
2 tablespoons parsley flakes	¼ teaspoon pepper
1 tablespoon dried basil	½ teaspoon sugar
½ teaspoon baking soda	2 pounds thin spaghetti, cooked and drained

◆ In large bowl, mix together all ingredients for the meatballs by hand and set aside.

◆ In a medium skillet, heat 2 tablespoons oil and lightly sauté the chopped onion and minced garlic for sauce.

◆ Place remaining sauce ingredients into a large pot and heat over medium heat. Stir occasionally, being careful not to let the mixture boil. Add the sautéed onion and garlic to the pot.

◆ Roll the hamburger mixture into small meatballs, approximately 2 inches in diameter. Place directly into the sauce. Continue to cook on medium heat for approximately 75 to 90 minutes, stirring often to avoid burning the bottom. Do not overload the sauce with meatballs, as they will not cook correctly.

◆ Serve over cooked spaghetti.

Yield: *8 servings*

Barley Almond Casserole *(Meat or Parve)*

3½	cups chicken or beef broth or parve beef-flavored bouillon	1	cup quick-cooking barley
6	tablespoons margarine, divided	1	cup chopped onion
		½	teaspoon dried parsley
⅓	cup slivered almonds	½	teaspoon salt
		¼	teaspoon pepper

◆ Preheat oven to 375°. Bring broth to a boil. In large skillet or Dutch oven, melt 2 tablespoons margarine and sauté almonds.

◆ Remove almonds from skillet and melt remaining 4 tablespoons margarine. Add barley and onion and sauté until barley is light brown. Remove skillet from heat.

◆ Stir in almonds, parsley and salt and pepper. Spoon into greased 1½-quart casserole. When broth is boiling, pour over barley mixture. Stir, cover and bake for 1 hour or until liquid is absorbed.

Yield: *8 to 10 servings*

Microwave Barley and Rice Casserole *(Parve)*

½	cup margarine	1	cup barley, uncooked
½	pound mushrooms, sliced	3	teaspoons parve beef-flavored bouillon
2	ribs celery, sliced		
1	medium onion, chopped	2½	cups hot water
1	cup rice, uncooked	1	envelope dry onion soup mix

◆ Put margarine, mushrooms, celery and onion in 3½-quart covered casserole dish. Microwave on high power for 5 minutes. Stir.

◆ Add rice and barley. Microwave on high for 5 minutes.

◆ Dissolve bouillon in hot water. Add onion soup mix, bouillon and water to rice and barley. Microwave on high for 30 minutes.

◆ Let stand for 5 minutes before serving.

Yield: *10 servings*

Note: *You may also cook in microwave for 20 minutes and transfer to 300° oven until liquid is absorbed.*

Middle Eastern Pilaf *(Meat or Parve)*

½ cup chopped onion	1½ teaspoons salt
3 tablespoons margarine	¼ teaspoon pepper
1 tablespoon olive oil	⅓ cup golden raisins
1 cup rice	½ teaspoon dried parsley
½ cup almonds, slivered	1½ teaspoons dried mint leaves
2½ cups chicken broth or parve chicken-flavored bouillon	

◆ Sauté onion in margarine and oil in large skillet until tender, about 5 minutes. Add rice and almonds.

◆ Cook over low heat, stirring constantly, until rice is golden.

◆ Add chicken broth, salt and pepper. Heat to boiling; reduce heat. Cover tightly and simmer for 20 minutes.

◆ Remove from heat and stir in remaining ingredients. Let stand, covered, until all liquid is absorbed, about 5 minutes.

Yield: *6 servings*

Turkish Pilaf *(Meat or Parve)*

2 cups basmati rice	1 cup raisins
4 teaspoons olive oil	1 teaspoon ground nutmeg
1 cup fat-free, low-salt chicken broth or parve chicken-flavored bouillon	1 teaspoon sugar
	4 tablespoons pine nuts
	Salt and pepper

◆ Place rice in strainer and rinse in cold water. Heat oil in nonstick skillet or Dutch oven and add rice. Lower heat; sauté for 2 minutes.

◆ Add chicken broth, raisins, nutmeg and sugar. Bring to a simmer. Lower heat, cover and cook gently for 15 minutes. Liquid will be absorbed and rice tender.

◆ Add pine nuts and toss. Salt and pepper to taste.

Yield: *10 to 12 servings*

Bombay Rice (Parve)

A favorite dish in India!

2	cups basmati rice	1	teaspoon turmeric
3	tablespoons oil		Salt to taste
1	small onion, thinly sliced	½	cup frozen green peas or fresh
3	cloves garlic, minced		green beans or other
4	whole cloves		vegetables
4	whole black peppercorns	½	red bell pepper, seeded and
1	cinnamon stick		finely chopped
2	cardamom pods or ½ teaspoon	3	cups water
	ground cardamom		

♦ Rinse rice. Cover rice with water and soak for ½ hour. Drain water. Let rice stand for 10 minutes.

♦ In large skillet, heat the oil. Sauté the onion, garlic, cloves, peppercorns, cinnamon stick and cardamom pods. Add rice and sauté until golden. Add turmeric, salt, peas, bell pepper and water. Cover and bring to a boil. Lower heat.

♦ When water is absorbed, approximately 10 minutes, stir rice gently, cover and put on lowest heat for 15 minutes. Remove from heat. Do not remove cover for 10 minutes. Remove cardamom pods, cloves, peppercorns and cinnamon stick before serving.

Yield: *6 to 8 servings*

Curried Rice (Parve)

A colorful and tasty side dish.

1	cup rice	2	onions cut into ½-inch pieces
2	medium tomatoes, cut into	4	cups water
	quarters	1	teaspoon curry powder
2	medium green peppers, cut	1	tablespoon salt
	into cubes	¼	pound margarine, cut into pats

♦ Preheat oven to 325°. Mix all ingredients together in covered casserole and bake for 1 hour and 30 minutes.

Yield: *6 servings*

Wild and Brown Rice Pilaf with Cranberries *(Meat)*

A Heartland specialty!

1	(14-ounce) can chicken broth, divided	¾	cup brown rice
1	small onion, minced	¼	cup wild rice
½	cup apple juice or cider, plus a little extra for plumping cranberries	½	cup dried cranberries

- ◆ Heat ¼ cup broth in medium saucepan. Add onion and steam for 5 minutes until onion is tender.
- ◆ Add remaining chicken broth, apple juice and the rices. Bring to boil, reduce to simmer, cover and cook for 40 minutes.
- ◆ Cover the cranberries with additional apple juice and let stand while the rice is cooking.
- ◆ Remove the rice from heat and let stand for 15 minutes. Gently fold the cranberries into the rice and serve.

Yield: *4 to 6 servings*

Micro Farfel Casserole *(Parve)*

8	ounces toasted farfel	½	(8-ounce) can sliced water chestnuts, drained
1	medium onion, chopped		
1	red or green pepper, chopped	2	cups boiling water
4	tablespoons margarine	2	teaspoons parve beef-flavored bouillon
1	envelope dry onion soup mix		
1	rib celery, chopped		Salt and pepper

- ◆ Mix all ingredients together in a 2-quart casserole with cover. Microwave on high power for 12 minutes.

Yield: *4 to 5 servings*

Note: *Farfel is a pebble-shaped wheat product often found in the kosher section of the grocery store.*

Tomato Rice *(Parve)*

2½	tablespoons olive oil	2	tablespoons tomato paste
¼	small onion, diced or		Pepper to taste
	1 teaspoon dehydrated onion	2½	cups boiling water
2	teaspoons salt	2	cups basmati rice, rinsed

◆ Sauté onions in oil. Add salt, tomato paste, pepper and boiling water. Return to boil.

◆ Add rice, stirring once, and cook on medium heat, covered, for 30 minutes.

◆ Remove from heat and place towel under cover of pot to produce a fluffy rice. Let stand for 5 minutes.

Yield: *6 to 8 servings*

Note: *To make dill rice, use 2 tablespoons dried dill or ¼ cup fresh dill in place of the tomato paste.*

Creative Couscous *(Parve)*

For individual tastes!

1	(10-ounce) package couscous	¼	cup slivered almonds (optional)
2	cups boiling water	¼	cup sliced green onions (optional)
½	teaspoon salt (optional)	1	(16-ounce) can black beans
2	tablespoons margarine or oil		or navy beans, drained
½	tablespoon curry powder		(optional)
	(optional)	2	tablespoons lemon or orange
¼	cup currants, raisins or chopped		juice (optional)
	dried apricots (optional)		

◆ Cook couscous according to package directions, adding margarine or oil.

◆ Fluff with a fork and serve plain or with any individual or combination of optional ingredients.

Yield: *5 to 6 servings*

Vegetable Couscous *(Parve)*

2 tablespoons margarine	2 cups boiling water
2 tablespoons oil	1 large bunch broccoli, cut into
1 onion, sliced	small florets
½ cup finely chopped celery	1 large or 3 small zucchini, sliced
2 large carrots, sliced into ⅛-inch	6 small new potatoes, parboiled
rounds	and sliced (optional)
2 cups freshly shelled peas	1 (10-ounce) package couscous
(or frozen)	½ teaspoon thyme
1 large cauliflower, cut into	¼ cup margarine
small florets	1 teaspoon salt
1 vegetable bouillon cube	

◆ In a large saucepan, heat the margarine and oil. Add the onion and celery and sauté over low heat until soft.

◆ Add the carrots and cook for several minutes, stirring often. Add the peas and cauliflower.

◆ Dissolve the bouillon cube in boiling water and pour it over the vegetables. Cover and simmer for 5 minutes over low heat.

◆ Add the broccoli and continue simmering, covered, over low heat for another 5 minutes.

◆ Add the zucchini and potatoes and continue simmering, covered, 5 minutes longer, or until vegetables are tender but not mushy.

◆ Cook couscous according to package directions, adding thyme, margarine and salt.

◆ To serve, combine the couscous with the vegetables.

Yield: *4 to 6 servings*

Roasted Asparagus
with Sesame Vinaigrette *(Parve)*

2	pounds asparagus, rinsed and dried	2	teaspoons extra virgin olive oil
2	teaspoons sesame oil	⅛	teaspoon salt

Vinaigrette

1	tablespoon soy sauce	1½	teaspoons sesame oil
2	tablespoons rice vinegar	1	teaspoon sugar

- ◆ Preheat oven to 400°.
- ◆ Snap ends off asparagus. Place in shallow baking pan in one layer.
- ◆ Combine oils and drizzle over asparagus. Sprinkle with salt.
- ◆ Roast in preheated oven for 10 to 12 minutes, shaking pan once during roasting.
- ◆ In small jar, combine soy sauce, rice vinegar, sesame oil and sugar. Shake well to combine.
- ◆ Serve asparagus warm, at room temperature, or cold with sesame vinaigrette drizzled over top.

Yield: *6 to 8 servings*

Broccoli with
Pine Nuts and Raisins *(Parve)*

1	pound fresh broccoli	½	cup raisins
2	cloves garlic, minced	2	large tomatoes, chopped
¼	cup olive oil		(optional)
½	cup pine nuts		Salt and pepper to taste

- ◆ Cut broccoli into florets. Trim and peel stalks and slice into ⅛-inch pieces.
- ◆ Sauté garlic in hot oil. Add pine nuts and raisins and sauté until pine nuts are toasted.
- ◆ Add broccoli and sauté about 5 minutes. Add tomatoes and heat through. Season with salt and pepper.

Yield: *4 servings*

Sweet Beets ✡ (Parve)

A colorful addition to any plate.

1	bunch beets, unpeeled	1	tablespoon margarine
2	tablespoons brown sugar	1	tablespoon lemon juice
¼	teaspoon salt	1	tablespoon cornstarch or
1	(8-ounce) can pineapple tidbits		potato starch
	or chunks with juice		

- ◆ Cook beets in jackets in boiling water until tender. When beets are cool, remove jackets and slice.
- ◆ In a saucepan, combine brown sugar, salt and pineapple tidbits with juice and cook slowly until thick, about 5 minutes. Add margarine and lemon juice.
- ◆ Remove ¼ cup of pineapple liquid and thicken with cornstarch. Return to pot and add sliced beets. Cook an additional 5 minutes.

Yield: *6 servings*

Note: *You may substitute a 15-ounce can of whole beets for fresh beets.*

Roasted Broccoli and Cauliflower (Parve)

¼	cup olive oil	3	cups cauliflower florets
1	teaspoon minced garlic		Garlic pepper to taste
3	cups broccoli florets		

- ◆ Preheat oven to 425°. Combine olive oil and garlic.
- ◆ Toss vegetables in olive oil and garlic to seal in moisture.
- ◆ Roast florets in single layer on baking pan for 15 minutes, turning once.
- ◆ Serve hot or at room temperature. Vegetables may be arranged on dish and reheated.

Yield: *4 servings*

Note: *For variety, try sliced red and green peppers, or mushrooms.*

Sesame Broccoli *(Parve)*

1 tablespoon sesame seeds	1 tablespoon vinegar
1 pound broccoli, cut up	1 tablespoon soy sauce
1 tablespoon oil	4 teaspoons sugar

◆ Toast sesame seeds in nonstick skillet over medium heat for 4 minutes.

◆ Blanch broccoli in boiling water for several minutes or until done to desired crispness.

◆ In small pan, combine oil, vinegar, soy sauce, sugar, and sesame seeds. Heat to boiling and pour over hot broccoli, turning to coat.

Yield: *4 servings*

Carrots in Orange Sauce ✡ *(Parve)*

2 pounds carrots, peeled and sliced, or whole baby carrots	¼ cup sugar
	3 tablespoons oil
2 cups boiling water	1 tablespoon potato or corn starch
½ teaspoon salt	¼ cup orange juice
½ cup honey	Pinch of ginger

◆ Cook carrots, covered, in salted water until tender, approximately 15 to 20 minutes. Drain carrots, saving ½ cup of liquid.

◆ Stir honey, sugar and oil into reserved liquid.

◆ Dissolve starch in orange juice and add ginger. Add to honey and carrot mixture.

◆ Cook uncovered until thickened, approximately 30 minutes.

Yield: *6 servings*

Mustard-Glazed Carrots *(Parve)*

2	pounds carrots, peeled and sliced, or whole baby carrots	¼	cup packed brown sugar
3	tablespoons margarine		Salt to taste
3	tablespoons Dijon-style mustard		Dried parsley or dill

- ◆ Steam carrots until crisp tender, approximately 10 minutes.
- ◆ Melt margarine in saucepan. Add mustard, brown sugar and salt.
- ◆ Cook for 3 minutes. Add carrots, turning to coat with sauce.
- ◆ Cook for 5 minutes more. Sprinkle with parsley or dill.

Yield: *4 to 6 servings*

Cauliflower Pie *(Parve)*

No one will guess this is cauliflower. So good!

1	large white cauliflower	2	eggs, slightly beaten
4	tablespoons olive oil, divided	2	tablespoons flour
2	cloves garlic, minced	4	tablespoons coarse bread crumbs, divided
	Salt and freshly ground black pepper to taste		

- ◆ Separate florets and discard core of cauliflower. Boil florets in salted water for 10 to 15 minutes, just until tender. Drain and mash.
- ◆ Heat 2 tablespoons of oil in large skillet, add garlic and sauté until golden.
- ◆ Add mashed cauliflower, salt and pepper, and stir over high heat until excess moisture has evaporated. Cool for 10 to 15 minutes.
- ◆ Preheat oven to 450°. Combine eggs and flour with cauliflower mixture. Grease 9-inch pie plate and sprinkle with 2 tablespoons of the bread crumbs. Spread cauliflower mixture in pie plate; top with remaining bread crumbs and drizzle remaining oil over crumbs.
- ◆ Bake for 30 minutes or until top begins to brown.

Yield: *6 to 8 servings*

Honey Carrots with Almonds *(Parve)*

1	pound carrots, sliced thin	1	tablespoon lemon juice
¼	cup golden raisins	¼	teaspoon ground ginger
¼	cup margarine, melted	¼	cup sliced, unpeeled almonds
3	tablespoons honey		

- ◆ Cook carrots, covered, in ½ inch boiling water for about 8 minutes; drain.
- ◆ Stir in raisins, margarine, honey, lemon juice and ginger.
- ◆ Preheat oven to 375°. Turn into a 1-quart baking dish. Bake, uncovered, for 35 minutes; stir occasionally.
- ◆ Transfer to serving bowl and sprinkle with almonds.

Yield: *4 servings*

Stuffed Cauliflower *(Parve)*

1	large head cauliflower	½	teaspoon Worcestershire sauce
1	medium onion, chopped fine		Salt and pepper to taste
½	cup sliced celery	¼	cup water
3	sprigs parsley, chopped fine	½	cup dry bread crumbs
¼	pound fresh mushrooms, sliced	¾	cup blanched almonds, slivered
½	cup margarine, divided		and toasted
1	tablespoon flour		

- ◆ Steam whole cauliflower in 1 inch of boiling salted water for 10 minutes or until barely tender. Drain.
- ◆ Preheat oven to 400°. Cut out center of core. Do not cut through core or cauliflower will not stay intact. Chop core and reserve.
- ◆ Sauté next 4 ingredients in 4 tablespoons of margarine until golden. Stir in flour.
- ◆ Add chopped core, Worcestershire, salt and pepper to taste.
- ◆ Place cauliflower in round casserole, core side up, and stuff with vegetables. Mound the extra stuffing on top. Pour ¼ cup water around cauliflower.
- ◆ Melt remaining margarine and brush over cauliflower. Sprinkle with bread crumbs and almonds.
- ◆ Bake for 15 minutes or until lightly browned.

Yield: *6 to 8 servings*

Scalloped Corn and Tomatoes *(Dairy)*

Vegetables

2 (14-ounce) cans diced tomatoes, drained	2 eggs, slightly beaten (or ½ cup egg substitute)
1 (15-ounce) can corn kernels, drained	¼ cup flour
1 (14-ounce) can cream-style corn	2 teaspoons sugar
	½-1 teaspoon ground pepper

Topping

1 medium onion, chopped	2 cups soft bread crumbs
2 tablespoons margarine	½ cup grated Parmesan cheese (optional)
1-2 cloves garlic, minced	

◆ Preheat oven to 350°. For vegetables: Mix together all casserole ingredients in 2-quart casserole.

◆ For topping: Sauté onions and garlic in margarine until transparent. Do not brown. Remove from heat and stir in bread crumbs and Parmesan cheese.

◆ Sprinkle topping over casserole and bake, uncovered, for 1 hour or until nicely browned. If dish browns too soon, cover lightly with foil.

Yield: *12 side dish servings*

Note: *Vegetables and topping may be prepared 1 day in advance and refrigerated. Bring to room temperature and sprinkle topping on just before baking.*

Safta's Eggplant *(Parve)*

Safta *means grandmother in Hebrew. This recipe comes from Israel.*

3	eggplants, peeled, sliced 1½ inches thick		Flour
1	egg, beaten		Olive oil

Sauce

1	(6-ounce) can tomato paste		Salt, pepper, and oregano to taste
½	cup ketchup		Juice of 1 lemon
½	cup water	2	tablespoons sugar

◆ Dip slices in egg, then flour. Fry lightly in oil and drain on paper towel.

◆ Preheat oven to 350°. For sauce: Mix tomato paste, ketchup and water. Add remaining ingredients and mix.

◆ Place eggplant in 9x13-inch baking pan and cover with sauce. Bake for 20 minutes.

Yield: *6 servings*

Note: *May be served hot or cold.*

Ratatouille Provençale *(Parve)*

⅓ cup olive oil
¾ cup thinly sliced onions
2 cloves garlic, minced
½ cup whole pitted black olives
4 green peppers, cored, seeded and julienned
3 cups zucchini cut into ½-inch slices

1 (14½-ounce) can diced tomatoes, drained
2½ cups diced eggplant
½ teaspoon oregano or 2 teaspoons chopped fresh basil
Salt and pepper to taste

- In a deep skillet, sauté the onions and garlic in olive oil until golden.
- Add the olives, green peppers, zucchini, tomatoes and diced eggplant. Sprinkle with olive oil. Add the oregano (or basil).
- Simmer covered over very low heat for about 45 minutes.
- Uncover and cook an additional 15 minutes to reduce the amount of liquid.
- Salt and pepper to taste.

Yield: *4 to 6 servings*

Note: *Serve hot or cold.*

Green Beans with Lemon Mustard Sauce *(Parve)*

This always adds a tangy taste to our Thanksgiving dinner.

1 pound green beans, fresh or whole frozen
2 teaspoons margarine

1 tablespoon fresh or frozen lemon juice
1½ teaspoons coarse-grained mustard

- Steam beans until barely tender.
- In small saucepan, melt margarine and stir in lemon juice and mustard.
- Toss with green beans and serve.

Yield: *4 servings*

Chinese Green Beans *(Parve)*

2	tablespoons sesame seeds	1	teaspoon mirin or sherry
1	pound green beans, trimmed and sliced lengthwise if necessary	1	clove garlic, minced
		1	teaspoon honey
		⅛	teaspoon cayenne pepper
3	tablespoons rice vinegar	1	tablespoon oil
1	tablespoon minced gingerroot	4	scallions, thinly sliced diagonally
1	tablespoon snipped chives		
2	teaspoons low-sodium soy sauce	1	sweet red or yellow pepper cut into strips

◆ Toast sesame seeds in nonstick skillet over medium heat for 3 to 4 minutes, stirring often, until lightly browned.

◆ Place beans into boiling water for 2 to 3 minutes. Don't overcook. Drain and rinse under cold water.

◆ In small bowl, whisk together vinegar, ginger, chives, soy sauce, mirin, garlic, honey and cayenne. Slowly whisk in oil. Pour 1 tablespoon into a large nonstick skillet and set aside the rest. Heat dressing over medium-high heat.

◆ Add beans and toss to coat. Cover and cook for 3 to 4 minutes, or until crisp-tender; stir occasionally.

◆ Transfer to warmed platter. Top with scallions and peppers.

◆ Whisk dressing again.

◆ Drizzle over beans and sprinkle with sesame seeds.

Yield: *4 servings*

Green Beans with Sunflower Seeds *(Parve)*

¼	cup margarine, softened	⅛	teaspoon thyme
½	teaspoon marjoram	1	small onion, chopped
½	teaspoon basil	1	clove garlic, finely chopped
½	teaspoon chervil (optional)		Boiling water
1	teaspoon chopped parsley	1	pound green beans, trimmed
1	teaspoon chopped chives	¼	cup unsalted sunflower seeds,
⅛	teaspoon savory (optional)		shelled

- ◆ Mix margarine with herbs. Set aside.
- ◆ In a large skillet, place onion and garlic in boiling water. The water should just cover the bottom of the pan. Add beans, cover and cook for about 7 to 10 minutes until crisp-tender. Don't allow beans to burn.
- ◆ Pour off excess liquid. Add herbed margarine and sunflower seed kernels and swirl around to melt margarine. Toss over heat for 1 minute.

Yield: *4 to 6 servings*

Crunchy Green Beans *(Parve)*

1	pound fresh green beans	¼	cup margarine
½	cup cashews or slivered	3	tablespoons honey
	almonds	1	teaspoon lemon juice

- ◆ Cook green beans in boiling water until tender but crisp. Drain and cover to keep warm.
- ◆ Meanwhile, in medium skillet over low heat, sauté almonds or cashews in margarine for about 5 minutes until lightly browned.
- ◆ Add honey and cook, stirring constantly, for 1 minute. Add lemon juice and mix.
- ◆ Pour sauce over beans and toss to coat thoroughly. Serve immediately.

Yield: *4 servings*

Veggie Burger Bean Bake *(Parve)*

Hearty enough for a main dish.

1	tablespoon oil	½	cup brown sugar
1	small onion, chopped	2	(16-ounce) cans vegetarian
3	vegetable burgers, broken up		baked beans
2	tablespoons molasses	1	(16-ounce) can red kidney
¾	cup ketchup		beans, drained
½	teaspoon mustard	1	(16-ounce) can butter or
½	cup white sugar		northern beans, drained

◆ Preheat oven to 350°. Brown onion and burgers in oil.

◆ In a separate bowl, mix together the molasses, ketchup, mustard and sugars. Stir in beans.

◆ Add the onion and burger mixture and place in a 3-quart casserole lightly coated with vegetable spray. Bake, covered, for 1 hour. Remove cover and bake for an additional 30 minutes.

Yield: *12 servings*

Note: *Recipe may be made in a slow cooker.*

Sweet Baby Lima Beans *(Parve)*

1	(16-ounce) package dried baby lima beans	1	cup chopped onion
¼	cup oil	¾	cup honey
		2	teaspoons salt

◆ Soak beans for several hours or overnight. Cover with water and cook over low heat until tender, about 1 hour. Drain.

◆ Preheat oven to 350°. Sauté onion in oil until tender. Stir in honey and salt and add to lima beans.

◆ Bake, covered, in a 2-quart casserole for about 1 hour.

Yield: *12 servings*

Okra with Tomatoes and Onion *(Parve)*

A favorite Middle Eastern vegetable.

2	tablespoons olive oil	1	pound fresh or frozen okra
1	small onion, chopped		(small ones are tender)
2	large tomatoes, chopped		Juice of 1 lemon
1	cup water	1	tablespoon sugar

◆ Sauté onion in oil; add chopped tomatoes and water. Bring to a boil.

◆ Trim top and bottom of okra and add to pan with lemon and sugar.

◆ Cook on low heat for 30 minutes.

◆ Serve as vegetable or over rice.

Yield: *6 to 8 servings*

Pineapple Baked Parsnips *(Parve)*

1½	teaspoons cornstarch	1½	pounds parsnips, peeled and
2	tablespoons packed brown		julienned
	sugar	2	tablespoons margarine
1	(16-ounce) can pineapple chunks,		
	drained, reserving juice		

◆ Preheat oven to 350°. Combine cornstarch, brown sugar and reserved pineapple juice. Stir until smooth.

◆ Place parsnips in ungreased 7½x11½x1½-inch baking dish; pour pineapple juice mixture over parsnips. Dot with margarine and arrange pineapple chunks over top.

◆ Cover with foil and bake for 45 to 60 minutes until parsnips are bubbly and tender.

Yield: *4 to 6 servings*

Yummy Yams ✡ (Parve)

The kids look forward to these every holiday!

5	large yams	1	(20-ounce) can pineapple
¼	teaspoon salt		tidbits, drained
¼	cup brown sugar, packed firm	15	large marshmallows
⅓	cup honey		

- ◆ Preheat oven to 400°. Wrap yams in foil and bake for 1 hour and 30 minutes until pulp is caramelized. Remove from oven and cool.
- ◆ Peel yams and mash pulp. Add salt, brown sugar, honey and drained pineapple.
- ◆ Preheat oven to 350°. Place yam mixture in a 8x11-inch or round casserole dish prepared with vegetable spray. Bake for 30 minutes.
- ◆ Put marshmallows on top and return to oven to brown, about 10 to 20 minutes.

Yield: *10 servings*

Note: *May be prepared a day ahead and refrigerated before baking.*

Sweet Potatoes with Sherry (Parve)

8	sweet potatoes	6	tablespoons margarine
1	cup brown sugar	⅓	cup dry sherry or sweet white
2	tablespoons cornstarch		wine
½	teaspoon salt	¼	cup chopped walnuts
½	teaspoon grated orange rind	½	cup raisins (soak in hot water
2	cups orange juice		and drain)

- ◆ Boil potatoes until almost tender. Peel, cut into circles and place in baking dish.
- ◆ Preheat oven to 325°. In separate pot on top of stove, combine brown sugar, cornstarch and salt. Blend in orange rind and juice. Cook and stir over medium heat until thick and bubbly. Cook 1 minute more.
- ◆ Add margarine, sherry, walnuts and raisins. Allow margarine to melt. Pour over potatoes.
- ◆ Bake for 30 minutes or until potatoes are tender. Baste occasionally or cover while baking.

Yield: *8 servings*

Tzimmes ✡ *(Parve)*

2	pounds sweet potatoes, peeled and cut in chunks	1	teaspoon salt
2	pounds carrots, peeled and cut up	2	tablespoons margarine
¼	cup golden raisins	¾	cup water
½	pound medium dried prunes, pitted	1	(8-ounce) can pineapple tidbits with juice
⅓	cup brown sugar	½	cup honey
		1½	teaspoons cornstarch or potato starch, for thickening

- ◆ Preheat oven to 350°. Combine all ingredients except starch in a 3-quart greased casserole.
- ◆ Bake, covered, for 45 minutes.
- ◆ Remove ⅓ cup of liquid from casserole and combine with starch.
- ◆ Return to casserole and bake, uncovered, for another 45 minutes.

Yield: *12 servings*

Potato Zucchini Casserole *(Parve)*

A great way to use your garden's bounty.

3	pounds small red potatoes, cut in ½-inch slices	¾	cup vegetable broth
3	medium zucchini, sliced	½	(6-ounce) can pitted black olives
3	medium yellow squash, sliced	1	clove garlic, minced
6	tablespoons olive oil	1	teaspoon thyme
			Salt and pepper to taste

- ◆ Preheat oven to 400°. Mix all ingredients together and bake in an ungreased 9x13-inch pan for 1 hour or longer.

Yield: *8 to 10 servings*

Onion Roasted Potatoes *(Parve)*

2-3 pounds unpeeled red potatoes   ⅓   cup olive or vegetable oil
1   envelope dry onion soup mix

- ◆ Preheat oven to 450°.
- ◆ Scrub potatoes and cut into equal chunks.
- ◆ In large plastic bag, combine onion soup mix and oil. Add potatoes and shake until they are evenly coated.
- ◆ Arrange potatoes in a single layer in a 9x13-inch pan. Bake, uncovered, for approximately 40 minutes or until potatoes are tender and golden brown.

Yield: *4 servings*

Fluffy Potato Casserole *(Dairy)*

4½   cups mashed potatoes   2   tablespoons flour
1   (8-ounce) package cream   Salt and pepper to taste
       cheese, room temperature   1   (3½-ounce) container French-
1   small onion, finely chopped   fried onions
2   eggs

- ◆ Preheat oven to 325°. In large bowl of mixer combine potatoes, cream cheese, onion, eggs and flour. Beat at medium speed until blended.
- ◆ Add salt and pepper. Beat at high speed until light and fluffy.
- ◆ Bake, uncovered, in greased 9-inch square dish for 35 minutes.
- ◆ Distribute onions on top during last 5 minutes of baking.

Yield: *8 servings*

Curried Potatoes *(Parve)*

3	cups water, unsalted	4	teaspoons margarine
4	medium potatoes, peeled and cut into 1-inch cubes	1	medium yellow onion, chopped
		1	tablespoon curry powder

♦ In medium saucepan, bring water to boil. Add the potatoes and cook, partially covered, over moderate heat until fork tender, about 15 minutes.

♦ Meanwhile, in heavy skillet, melt margarine over moderate heat. Add onion and cook until soft, about 5 minutes.

♦ Stir in the curry powder and cook 1 minute longer.

♦ As soon as the potatoes are tender, drain, add to the skillet and cook for 1 minute, stirring to coat the potatoes.

Yield: *4 servings*

Potato Kugel ✡ *(Parve)*

6	large red potatoes, peeled	2	teaspoons salt
1	medium onion	¼	teaspoon pepper
½	cup margarine, divided	6	eggs, lightly beaten

♦ Preheat oven to 350°. Grate potatoes and onions with a hand grater or in food processor using grating disc. Drain well.

♦ Melt margarine in 7x11-inch baking pan, swirling around pan to coat it. Add spices and eggs to potatoes and pour in excess melted margarine. Put into prepared pan. Bake for 1 hour and 30 minutes or until brown and crispy.

Yield: *12 servings*

Note: *To increase recipe for larger pan, use one egg for each additional potato.*

Potato Latkes *(Parve)*

5	large red potatoes, peeled	½	teaspoon salt, or to taste
¼	teaspoon lemon juice	¼	teaspoon pepper, or to taste
1	medium onion, peeled	3	tablespoons flour or matzo meal
2-3	eggs		Oil for frying

♦ Grate potatoes; add lemon juice to keep from turning dark. Grate onion and mix with potatoes.

♦ Drain off liquid. Add remaining ingredients.

♦ Form into patties by dropping large spoonfuls into hot oil in skillet. Mixture will darken if not used immediately.

♦ If potatoes fall apart in hot oil, use more flour.

Yield: *10 to 15 pancakes*

Note: *Serve with applesauce or sour cream.*

Short-Cut Potato Latkes *(Parve)*

You'll find these shredded potatoes in the dairy case.

2	medium onions, chopped fine	1-2	teaspoons salt or to taste
1	(16-ounce) package fresh shredded hash brown potatoes	¼	teaspoon pepper
		1	teaspoon sugar (optional)
		¼	cup flour or matzo meal
3	eggs, lightly beaten		Oil for frying

♦ Combine onions and shredded potatoes; add eggs, salt, pepper, sugar and flour. Mix well.

♦ Heat oil in nonstick skillet. Scoop about ¼ cup of potato mixture for each pancake into skillet. Fry on 1 side until edges begin to brown. Turn and fry on other side until done.

♦ Remove to glass dish lined with paper towel to drain off excess oil. Continue adding oil to skillet as needed.

♦ Latkes may be refrigerated until ready to serve. Remove from refrigerator and heat in a 350° oven for 5 to 10 minutes before serving.

Yield: *6 servings*

Squash with Apples (Parve)

1	medium acorn squash	¼	cup sugar
2	medium apples, peeled and cubed	⅛	cup light brown sugar
		1	teaspoon cinnamon
¾	cup water	½	teaspoon salt

♦ Pierce squash with a knife several times and cook in microwave, on paper towel, on high power for 10 minutes or until soft.

♦ Cool, cut in half and discard seeds. Scoop out squash into a bowl.

♦ Meanwhile, in small pot, cook apples with water and sugar until soft.

♦ Mash squash and cooked apples together with the brown sugar, cinnamon and salt.

♦ Put into 2-quart greased casserole and reheat before serving.

Yield: *6 servings*

Note: *You may use 1 cup of prepared applesauce in place of cooked fresh apples.*

Squash Kugel (Parve)

2	(12-ounce) boxes frozen cooked winter squash, defrosted	1	cup flour
		3	eggs, slightly beaten
½	cup margarine, melted	¼	cup nondairy creamer
¾-1	cup sugar		Cinnamon

♦ Preheat oven to 350°. Mix all ingredients together except cinnamon. Pour into 8x8-inch lightly greased pan. Sprinkle cinnamon on top.

♦ Bake for 1 hour.

Yield: *8 servings*

Note: *This recipe is easily doubled and made in a 9x13-inch baking dish.*

Roasted Vegetables *(Parve)*

3	large sweet potatoes, peeled, cut into 2-inch chunks	3	large baking potatoes, peeled, cut into 2-inch chunks
3-4	large zucchini, cut into 2-inch chunks	1	medium butternut squash, peeled, cut into 2-inch chunks
5	large carrots, peeled, cut into 2-inch chunks	1	tablespoon olive oil or vegetable spray
5-6	crooked neck squash, cut into 2-inch chunks		Lemon juice to taste
2	large Spanish onions, cut into 2-inch chunks		Herbs and seasoning to taste (dried oregano, parsley, salt, lemon pepper, dried sage)

◆ Preheat oven to 450°. Combine all ingredients in roasting pan and bake for about 1 hour, stirring every 20 minutes. If vegetables do not taste done, bake a little longer.

Yield: *10 to 12 servings*

Layered Vegetable Casserole *(Parve)*

2	cups sliced carrots	3	tablespoons tapioca
1	onion, chopped	2	tablespoons sugar
2	cups celery, chopped		Salt and pepper to taste
½	green pepper, chopped	⅓	cup cracker crumbs
2	cups green beans	2	tablespoons margarine
1	(14½-ounce) can diced tomatoes, undrained		

◆ Preheat oven to 350°. In a 2-quart casserole dish, layer the carrots, onion, celery, green pepper and green beans.

◆ Heat the tomatoes and juice, tapioca, sugar, salt and pepper and pour over the vegetables.

◆ Mix the cracker crumbs and margarine and spread on top of the tomato mixture.

◆ Bake for 1 hour 30 minutes.

Yield: *8 to 10 servings*

Autumn Vegetable Casserole (Parve)

1	eggplant	¼	pound green beans
2	potatoes	½-1	teaspoon salt
1	large onion	1	(8-ounce) can tomato sauce or
3	carrots, peeled		marinara sauce
4	zucchini or yellow squash	½	cup oil
1	green pepper, seeded		

♦ Preheat oven to 350°. Cut vegetables into medium chunks. Add salt, tomato sauce and oil.

♦ Mix and pour into 1½- to 2-quart casserole dish. Cover and bake for 1 hour.

Yield: *6 servings*

Tangy Vegetable Dressing (Parve)

2	cloves garlic	2	tablespoons Dijon mustard
1	shallot	1	tablespoon sugar
2	tablespoons water or red wine		(or less to taste)
	vinegar	¾	cup oil
1	teaspoon salt	15	fresh basil leaves
⅛	teaspoon fresh ground pepper		Roma tomatoes

♦ Mince garlic and shallot in food processor. Add water or vinegar, salt, pepper, mustard and sugar.

♦ Keep processor running while drizzling in oil. Stop processor, add basil leaves and pulse to coarsely chop.

♦ Refrigerate. Great over green beans or any vegetables that have been thoroughly dried. Garnish with Roma tomatoes. This is also great as a marinade for salmon.

Yield: *1 cup*

Desserts

Cakes, Cookies
Pies & Sweet Treats

Dessert Tips

- ◆ Unless specified, all recipes use large eggs.
- ◆ Peeled bananas may be frozen whole or mashed. Three to four medium-sized bananas equal 2 cups of mashed bananas.
- ◆ When batter does not fill all the muffin cups, fill empty ones with a few tablespoons of water for even baking.
- ◆ To reduce fat content in baked goods, replace half of the oil with applesauce. (Example: ½ cup oil = ¼ cup applesauce + ¼ cup oil.)
- ◆ Brush a slightly beaten egg white on top of unbaked pie crust for a glossy finish.
- ◆ To soften hardened brown sugar, add a slice of bread, close the bag tightly and let sit for a day, or soften in microwave, without bread.
- ◆ Nuts, poppy seeds and sesame seeds should be refrigerated or frozen to keep them from turning rancid.
- ◆ For sour milk or buttermilk, use 1 tablespoon lemon juice or vinegar and enough milk to equal 1 cup. For parve recipes, use nondairy creamer instead of milk.

Common Substitutions

Baking Powder .... 1 teaspoon = ¼ teaspoon baking soda + ½ teaspoon cream of tartar

Light Cream or
  half-and-half .... 1 cup = 1 cup undiluted evaporated milk

Unsweetened Chocolate ...... 1 square = 3 tablespoons cocoa + 1 tablespoon melted butter or vegetable oil

Cornstarch as Thickener .... 1 tablespoon = 2 tablespoons all-purpose flour

Tapioca .... 2 teaspoons = 1 tablespoon all-purpose flour

Cake Flour .... 1 cup = 1 cup all-purpose flour minus 2 tablespoons

Eggs .... 1 egg = 2 egg yolks; 2 eggs = 1 egg + 2 egg whites

Molasses .... 1 cup = 1 cup dark corn syrup or honey

Parve Sour Cream................. 1 cup nondairy creamer + 2 tablespoons baking soda

One-Bowl Apple Cake *(Parve)*

This is great served warm.

4	large or 6 medium apples, peeled and cored	1	cup walnuts, coarsely chopped
2	eggs	½	cup oil
2	cups sugar	1	cup raisins
2	heaping teaspoons cinnamon	2	teaspoons baking soda
		2	cups flour

- ◆ Preheat oven to 350°. Slice apples into large bowl.
- ◆ Add eggs, sugar, cinnamon, nuts, oil and raisins. Mix with fork.
- ◆ Add baking soda and flour. Mix with fork.
- ◆ Grease a 9x13-inch pan; pour batter into pan.
- ◆ Bake for 55 minutes; do not open oven door until done.

Yield: *10 to 12 servings*

Low-Fat Apple Cake *(Parve)*

½	cup chopped nuts, toasted	2	cups flour
1¼	cups sugar	1	teaspoon baking soda
½	cup vegetable oil	½	teaspoon salt
½	cup unsweetened applesauce	½	teaspoon ground cinnamon
5	large egg whites or ⅔ cup liquid egg substitute	4	large apples, peeled, cored, and chopped (3 cups)
1	teaspoon vanilla		

- ◆ Toast nuts in a nonstick skillet over medium heat for 3 to 4 minutes until light brown, stirring often. Cool.
- ◆ Preheat oven to 350°. In a large bowl, combine sugar, oil, applesauce and egg whites. Beat very lightly with a fork. Add vanilla, mix well.
- ◆ In a separate bowl, combine flour, baking soda, salt and cinnamon. Add to sugar mixture. Stir until combined. Stir in apples and nuts.
- ◆ Pour into a 9x13-inch baking pan sprayed with vegetable spray.
- ◆ Bake for 45 to 50 minutes. Test with toothpick.

Yield: *12 to 16 servings*

Banana Cake *(Dairy)*

½ cup butter	1½ cups flour
1¼ cups sugar	¼ teaspoon salt
2 eggs, lightly beaten	1 teaspoon vanilla
1 teaspoon soda	¼ cup chocolate jimmies or chocolate chips (optional)
4 tablespoons reduced-fat sour cream	½ cup chopped nuts (optional)
1 cup mashed bananas (about 3 bananas)	

- ◆ Preheat oven to 350°. Cream butter and sugar. Add eggs.
- ◆ Dissolve soda in sour cream, add to mixture and beat well. Add bananas, flour, salt and vanilla. Mix well. Stir in chocolate chips or jimmies and nuts.
- ◆ Bake in a well-greased and floured 9x13-inch pan or 4 to 5 small loaf pans for 30 to 35 minutes. Make sure cake tester comes out clean.

Yield: *12 to 14 servings*

Note: *For a more dense bread-like cake, use 2 cups flour and bake in greased and floured loaf pans.*

Banana Pineapple Cake *(Parve)*

3   cups flour
2   cups sugar
1   teaspoon salt
1   teaspoon baking soda
3   slightly beaten eggs
1   cup oil

2   cups mashed bananas
    (about 5 bananas)
1½ teaspoons vanilla
1   (8¼-ounce) can of crushed
    pineapple with juice
½   cup chocolate chips

Glaze
2   tablespoons unsweetened
    cocoa powder
2   tablespoons hot water

1   tablespoon oil
½   cup powdered sugar

◆   Preheat oven to 350°. In a bowl mix flour, sugar, salt and baking soda together and make a well.

◆   In another bowl combine eggs, oil, bananas, vanilla and pineapple with juice; mix thoroughly. Pour into the well of the dry ingredients and mix well. Stir in ½ cup chocolate chips.

◆   Pour into a 10-inch greased and floured bundt pan. Bake for 65 to 70 minutes until cake tests done.

◆   Let cool in pan for 10 minutes; turn out onto serving plate.

◆   Combine all glaze ingredients and drizzle over top.

Yield: *12 to 14 servings*

Note: *If glaze is not the consistency you desire, add more water or powdered sugar.*

Carrot Cake (Dairy)

2	cups flour	4	eggs
2	teaspoons baking soda	1	teaspoon vanilla
1	teaspoon salt	3	cups shredded carrots
¼	teaspoon nutmeg	½	cup chopped dates
¼	teaspoon ground cloves	¾	cup flaked coconut
1	teaspoon cinnamon	½	cup golden raisins
1¼	cups oil	1	cup chopped nuts
2	cups sugar		

Frosting

½	cup butter	2½	cups powdered sugar
1	(3-ounce) package cream cheese, softened	½	teaspoon vanilla

◆ Preheat oven to 350°. Sift dry ingredients together.

◆ Place oil in a large mixing bowl. Add sugar and eggs 1 at a time. Add vanilla and beat well. Add dry ingredients; blend in carrots, dates, coconut, raisins and nuts.

◆ Place in a 9x13-inch greased pan and bake 1 hour. Let cake cool.

◆ Mix all frosting ingredients together, blending well. Frost cake.

Yield: *12 servings*

Yummy Cheesecake *(Dairy)*

Crust

2	cups graham cracker crumbs	½	cup butter, melted
⅓	cup sugar		

Filling

4	(8-ounce) packages very soft cream cheese	1	teaspoon vanilla
		2	tablespoons cornstarch
1	cup sugar	1	cup sour cream
2	eggs		

◆ Preheat oven to 450°. In a bowl, mix graham cracker crumbs and sugar. Cut in melted butter with a fork. Press into a 9-inch springform pan, along sides and bottom. Chill in refrigerator.

◆ In mixer, beat cream cheese and sugar until smooth and light. Beat in eggs, vanilla and cornstarch until blended. Stir in sour cream.

◆ Pour mixture into crust and bake for 10 minutes. Reduce oven temperature to 200° and bake for 45 minutes. Turn off oven and open oven door. Cool with door open slightly for 3 hours. Refrigerate.

◆ You may add topping of blueberry or cherry canned pie filling.

Yield: *10 to 12 servings*

Note: *Cheesecake is best served at room temperature. It may be frozen up to 2 months without fruit topping. Thaw in refrigerator overnight. Top before serving.*

Wisconsin Cheesecake *(Dairy)*

You're in for a wonderful surprise!

Crust
2 cups chocolate cookie crumbs   ½ cup butter, melted
3 tablespoons sugar

Filling
4 (8-ounce) packages cream   4 eggs
   cheese, softened   2 egg yolks
1 cup grated cheddar cheese   1¾ cups sugar
¼ teaspoon vanilla   ¼ cup beer
½ teaspoon grated lemon rind   ¼ cup light cream
½ teaspoon grated orange rind

◆ Preheat oven to 500°. In a large bowl, mix together crust ingredients. Press ⅓ of mixture into the bottom and 1 inch up the sides of a 10-inch springform pan prepared with vegetable spray.

◆ Mix cheeses, vanilla and grated rinds together. Add the whole eggs one at a time. Beat well after each addition. Add yolks and sugar and beat well. Stir in beer and cream slowly.

◆ Pour mixture into prepared crust. Bake for 8 minutes; then reduce heat to 250° and bake an additional 1 hour and 45 minutes. Turn off the oven and leave cake in oven for 1 more hour. Refrigerate when cool.

Yield: *12 to 16 servings*

Note: *May be made several days ahead or frozen.*

Lemon Lover's Cake *(Dairy)*

1	cup unsalted butter, softened	1	teaspoon baking powder
2	cups sugar	½	teaspoon baking soda
3	eggs	½	teaspoon salt
3	tablespoons fresh lemon juice	1	cup buttermilk (or 1 cup milk +
1	tablespoon lemon rind		2 tablespoons lemon juice or
3	cups flour		vinegar)

Glaze

½	cup lemon juice	1	teaspoon lemon rind
1	cup powdered sugar		

- ◆ Preheat oven to 350°. In a bowl, cream butter and sugar.
- ◆ Add eggs 1 at a time and beat well. Add lemon juice and lemon rind. Set aside.
- ◆ In another bowl, sift flour, baking powder, baking soda and salt together.
- ◆ Add sifted ingredients alternately with buttermilk to butter and sugar mixture.
- ◆ Place in a 10-inch tube pan that has been prepared with a waxed paper liner on the bottom.
- ◆ Bake for 1 hour and 15 minutes.
- ◆ Remove from oven and cool slightly.
- ◆ Mix lemon juice, powdered sugar and lemon rind together and spread over cake.

Yield: *12 servings*

Lemon Poppy Seed Cake *(Dairy or Parve)*

1 cup sugar	1 teaspoon baking powder
⅓ cup butter or margarine, softened	¼ teaspoon baking soda
	⅛ teaspoon salt
2 egg whites	¾ cup buttermilk
1 egg	(or ½ cup nondairy creamer,
1 tablespoon grated lemon rind	¼ cup water and
1 teaspoon vanilla extract	1 tablespoon vinegar)
1⅔ cups flour	⅔ cup powdered sugar
2 tablespoons poppy seeds	4 teaspoons lemon juice

◆ Preheat oven to 350°. Spray a 4x8x2½-inch loaf pan with vegetable spray and dust with flour.

◆ Beat sugar and margarine in mixer at medium speed for about 4 minutes until well blended. Add egg whites and egg, 1 at a time, beating well after each addition. Beat in lemon rind and vanilla.

◆ Combine flour, poppy seeds, baking powder, baking soda and salt. Add flour mixture to creamed sugar mixture alternating with buttermilk.

◆ Pour batter into prepared pan. Bake for 1 hour, or until done. Cool in pan for 10 minutes before removing from pan.

◆ Combine powdered sugar and lemon juice. Poke holes in top of cake and brush juice mixture over cake while still warm. Cool completely.

Yield: *12 servings*

Note: *Store poppy seeds in the refrigerator or freezer to keep them from becoming rancid.*

Chocolate Zucchini Cake *(Dairy)*

½	cup margarine	1	teaspoon baking soda
½	cup oil	½	teaspoon salt
1¾	cups sugar	4	tablespoons cocoa
2	eggs	1	teaspoon cinnamon
1	teaspoon vanilla	1	teaspoon ginger
½	cup buttermilk (or ½ cup milk with 1 tablespoon lemon juice or 1 tablespoon vinegar)	2	cups grated zucchini, seeds removed
		½	cup chocolate chips
2½	cups flour	½	cup chopped walnuts

- ◆ Preheat oven to 350°. Cream margarine, oil and sugar. Add eggs and vanilla. Mix well.
- ◆ Add buttermilk. Mix well. Stir in flour, baking soda, salt, cocoa, cinnamon, ginger and grated zucchini.
- ◆ Spread in a greased 9x13-inch pan. Top with chocolate chips and walnuts.
- ◆ Bake for 45 to 60 minutes.

Yield: *20 servings*

Note: *Cake will be very moist.*

Flourless Chocolate Cake ✡ *(Parve)*

½ cup plus 2 tablespoons (4 ounces) semisweet chocolate pieces	1 tablespoon orange-flavored liqueur or orange juice
¼ cup margarine	3 eggs, lightly beaten
⅔ cup sugar	1½ cups (6 ounces) finely chopped walnuts
1½ teaspoons grated orange rind	1 cup chopped walnuts for garnish

Chocolate Glaze

6 tablespoons water	⅓ cup sugar
3 ounces semisweet chocolate	3 tablespoons margarine
1 tablespoon orange juice	½ pint fresh raspberries (optional)

◆ Preheat oven to 375°. Grease an 8-inch springform pan. Line bottom of pan with an 8-inch circle of waxed or parchment paper.

◆ In top of double boiler over hot (not boiling) water, melt chocolate and margarine together. Stir until completely melted. Or, microwave in glass bowl on high power for 1 minute. Stir. Microwave for 30 seconds longer if necessary.

◆ Add sugar and grated rind and stir until blended. Transfer to mixing bowl and stir in orange liqueur or juice.

◆ Stir in eggs, then the 1½ cups finely chopped walnuts. Pour into prepared pan.

◆ Bake for 25 to 30 minutes. Do not overbake. Cake will set as it cools.

◆ Transfer pan to rack and cool for 15 minutes. Then carefully run spatula around sides, trying not to break crisp top surface of cake. Release side lock and lift off ring. Turn cake out, upside down, on rack. Remove pan bottom and paper at once. Cool to room temperature. When cake has cooled, prepare chocolate glaze.

◆ Heat water on low. Break chocolate into small pieces and add to warm water. The chocolate should melt gently so it won't scorch or get dry.

◆ Add the orange juice, sugar and margarine to the melted chocolate. Cool for about 4 minutes until the mixture gets thick and even.

◆ Place waxed paper under the cake cooling rack to catch the overflow. Pour the warm glaze over the cake and let it drip down the sides. If glaze is too thick to pour, remove cake to serving plate and spread glaze on top and sides. Garnish top with the 1 cup chopped walnuts.

Yield: *8 to 10 servings*

Note: *This cake is tasty plain or served with a raspberry sauce on top instead of the glaze.* **Raspberry Sauce:** *Combine ½ pint raspberries with a little orange juice and sugar in blender.*

Low-Fat Chocolate Cake *(Parve)*

⅔	cup cocoa	1½	cups water or orange juice
2¼	cups flour	¾	cup unsweetened applesauce
1½	cups sugar	1	cup parve egg substitute or
1½	teaspoons baking soda		3 eggs
1½	teaspoons baking powder	½	cup oil
1½	teaspoons instant coffee powder		
	(decaffeinated may be used)		

◆ Preheat oven to 350°. Prepare a 10-inch tube pan or a 12-cup bundt pan with vegetable spray.

◆ Combine all the dry ingredients in a food processor and process until blended, about 10 seconds.

◆ Add the water or orange juice, applesauce and egg substitute and process again. While processing, add the oil. Continue to process for 45 seconds.

◆ Do not insert the pusher into the feed tube, and do not overprocess.

◆ Pour batter into the greased pan. Bake for 45 to 50 minutes, until cake tests done in center and springs back when pressed lightly.

Yield: *12 servings*

Note: *Don't overbake or cake will dry out. Cool for 20 minutes before removing from pan. This cake is low-fat and parve and freezes well. You can make 24 cupcakes from the same batter. Bake for 18 to 20 minutes at 400° in greased or lined cupcake cups.*

Deep Dark Chocolate Cake *(Parve)*

1¾ cups flour	2 eggs
2 cups sugar	1 cup nondairy creamer
¾ cup dark cocoa	½ cup oil
1½ teaspoons baking soda	2 teaspoons vanilla
1½ teaspoons baking powder	1 cup boiling water

Frosting

⅛ cup (6 teaspoons) margarine, softened	¾ cup dark cocoa
2⅔ cups powdered sugar	⅓-⅔ cup nondairy creamer

◆ Preheat oven to 350°. Combine dry ingredients in a large mixer.

◆ Add eggs, creamer, oil and vanilla. Beat for 2 minutes at medium speed.

◆ Stir in boiling water slowly. Batter will be thin. Pour into 2 greased 8-inch square pans.

◆ Bake for 35 to 40 minutes. Test for doneness. Cool cakes and remove from pans.

◆ Cream margarine. Add sugar and cocoa alternately with nondairy creamer until mixture is rich, smooth and spreadable.

◆ Place one layer on plate, top side down. Spread with generous amount of frosting. Place second layer on top, bottom side down. Frost top and sides with remaining frosting.

Yield: *12 servings*

Note: *This cake freezes well for a long time if wrapped in plastic and aluminum foil. Freeze cake unwrapped first so that frosting will not stick to wrapping.*

Chocolate Fudge Sheet Cake (Dairy)

2	cups flour	1	teaspoon baking soda
2	cups sugar	1	teaspoon vanilla
1	cup water	½	cup buttermilk or ½ cup milk
1	cup butter		with 1 tablespoon lemon
¼	cup cocoa		juice or vinegar
2	eggs		

Frosting

¼	cup cocoa	2½-3	cups powdered sugar
½	cup butter	1	teaspoon vanilla
⅓	cup milk	1	cup chopped nuts

◆ Preheat oven to 400°. Combine flour and sugar and set aside. In a small saucepan, heat the water, butter and cocoa to boiling. Pour hot mixture into sugar and flour. Add eggs, baking soda and vanilla. Then add buttermilk and mix by hand.

◆ Pour into well-greased jellyroll pan and bake for 20 minutes.

◆ During last 5 minutes of baking time, bring to boil on top of stove the cocoa, butter and milk. When mixture is hot, take off stove and add powdered sugar. Mix by hand until smooth and add vanilla and nuts. Spread over hot cake.

Yield: *30 servings*

Two-Step Fudge Cake *(Dairy)*

Step 1

3	(1-ounce) squares unsweetened chocolate	1	egg, well beaten
½	cup milk	⅔	cup sugar

Step 2

½	cup margarine or butter, softened	2	cups cake flour
1	cup sugar	1	teaspoon baking soda
1	teaspoon vanilla	¼	teaspoon salt
2	eggs	⅔	cup milk

◆ In saucepan, cook chocolate, ½ cup milk, 1 egg and ⅔ cup sugar until thick. Cool.

◆ Preheat oven to 350°. Cream margarine or butter in mixer. Gradually add 1 cup sugar and beat until smooth. Add vanilla and 2 eggs, 1 at a time, beating well after each. Combine flour, baking soda and salt. Alternately add the dry mixture and ⅔ cup remaining milk to cake batter. Blend in chocolate mixture.

◆ Bake in 2 greased 8-inch cake pans or a 9x13-inch pan for 25 to 30 minutes. Frost with favorite frosting or chocolate glaze (see the Banana Pineapple Cake recipe).

Yield: *12 servings*

Black Bottom Cake *(Dairy)*

1½	cups flour	1	cup water
1	cup sugar	½	cup oil
¼	cup cocoa	1	tablespoon vinegar
1	teaspoon baking soda	1	teaspoon vanilla
½	teaspoon salt		

Topping

8	ounces cream cheese, softened	1	cup mini chocolate chips (divided)
1	egg		
½	cup sugar	½	cup very finely chopped nuts

- ◆ Preheat oven to 350°. Carefully mix the first 9 ingredients together.
- ◆ Pour into greased and floured 9x13-inch pan.
- ◆ Beat cream cheese until smooth; add egg and sugar. Fold in ½ cup chips. Top cake with cream cheese mixture.
- ◆ Using a knife, cut into cake about 1 inch deep every few inches. Sprinkle with remaining chips and nuts.
- ◆ Bake for 30 to 35 minutes.

Yield: *12 servings*

Sunshine Cake *(Parve)*

A never fail winner!

2	cups flour	¾	cup orange or pineapple juice
1½	cups sugar	½	cup oil
3	teaspoons baking powder	2	teaspoons vanilla
1	teaspoon salt	½	teaspoon cream of tartar
7	eggs, separated		

- ◆ Preheat oven to 325°. Sift flour, sugar, baking powder and salt into a bowl.

- ◆ Make a well in the bowl and add egg yolks, orange or pineapple juice, oil and vanilla.

- ◆ Mix on medium speed for about 1½ minutes.

- ◆ In another bowl, beat egg whites with cream of tartar until they are very stiff and stand in peaks.

- ◆ Fold egg and flour mixture into beaten egg whites very carefully and pour entire mixture into an ungreased tube pan.

- ◆ Bake for 1 hour and 10 minutes.

- ◆ Invert the tube pan onto a bottle and let stand to cool. Remove from pan and sprinkle with powdered sugar, or frost.

Yield: *12 to 16 servings*

Grandma's Fruitcake *(Parve)*

You won't want to give this one away!

½	cup margarine	1	teaspoon cinnamon
1	cup sugar	1	cup applesauce
1	egg	1	cup raisins
2	cups flour	1	cup chopped nuts
1	teaspoon baking soda	1	cup pineapple tidbits, well
¼	teaspoon salt		drained
¼	teaspoon ground cloves	½	cup maraschino cherries,
½	teaspoon nutmeg		drained and cut up

- ◆ Preheat oven to 350°. Cream margarine and sugar. Add egg and beat well.
- ◆ Combine flour, baking soda, salt and spices in a bowl. Add flour mixture and applesauce alternately to creamed mixture. Beat well.
- ◆ In another bowl combine raisins, nuts, pineapple and cherries. Mix into the batter.
- ◆ Pour into greased 5x9-inch loaf pan. Bake for 1 hour and 15 minutes or until brown.

Yield: *8 to 10 servings*

Honey Cake with Cherries *(Parve)*

1	cup chopped dates	1	cup oil
1	(10-ounce) bottle maraschino cherries, drained and chopped	1	cup honey
		4	teaspoons baking powder
		½	teaspoon ground cloves
1	teaspoon baking soda	½	teaspoon ground allspice
1½	cups water	½	teaspoon ground nutmeg
¼	cup margarine	1	teaspoon cinnamon
2½	cups sugar	5	cups flour
5	eggs	1	cup chopped nuts

♦ Preheat oven to 325°. Put chopped dates and cherries in saucepan; add baking soda and water. Cook until hot (do not boil). Remove from heat and let cool.

♦ In large mixing bowl, cream margarine and sugar. Add eggs, oil and honey. Add baking powder, cloves, allspice, nutmeg, cinnamon and flour. Mix well.

♦ Add date and cherry mixture and nuts to batter.

♦ Divide into 3, 5x9-inch greased loaf pans. Bake for 60 to 65 minutes. Test after 60 minutes.

Yield: *18 to 24 servings*

Traditional Honey Cake (Parve)

A light airy cake with lots of flavor!

¾	cup oil	1	teaspoon cinnamon
1	cup sugar		Pinch salt
4	eggs, separated	1	teaspoon baking soda
1	cup honey	½	cup strong coffee, cooled
2½	cups flour	½	cup orange juice
2	teaspoons baking powder	½	cup slivered almonds
1	teaspoon nutmeg		

◆ Preheat oven to 325°. Cream oil, sugar and egg yolks. Add honey.

◆ Sift flour, baking powder, nutmeg, cinnamon, and salt together. Dissolve baking soda in coffee. Combine coffee mixture and orange juice.

◆ Add dry ingredients to egg mixture alternately with coffee and orange juice mixture.

◆ Beat egg whites until peaks form and fold into batter. Pour into greased 9x13-inch pan or 2, 9x5-inch loaf pans, sprinkle almonds on top and bake for 45 to 55 minutes.

Yield: *10 to 12 servings*

Note: *For variety, use 2 tablespoons orange liqueur with ⅓ cup orange juice in place of ½ cup orange juice.*

Cardamom Coffee Cake *(Dairy)*

A traditional coffee cake with a wonderful flavor.

1	cup margarine or butter	2	cups flour
2	cups sugar	¼	teaspoon salt
2	eggs	½	teaspoon cardamom
1	cup sour cream	1	teaspoon baking soda
½	teaspoon vanilla		

Streusel Mix

1	cup chopped nuts	¼	cup flour
2	teaspoons cinnamon	1	tablespoon margarine, melted
½	cup brown sugar		

◆ Preheat oven to 350°. Cream together margarine, sugar and eggs.

◆ Stir in sour cream, vanilla, flour, salt, cardamom and baking soda. Set aside.

◆ In a small bowl combine nuts, cinnamon, brown sugar, flour and margarine.

◆ Pour ⅓ of the cake batter into a greased 10-inch bundt or tube pan and sprinkle with half the streusel topping. Repeat.

◆ Bake for 55 minutes.

Yield: *12 servings*

Sour Cream Coffee Cake *(Dairy)*

1	cup butter	1	teaspoon baking powder
2	cups sugar	¼	teaspoon salt
2	eggs	1	cup chopped pecans
1	cup sour cream	3	tablespoons sugar
½	teaspoon vanilla	1	teaspoon cinnamon
2	cups flour		

◆ Preheat oven to 350°. Cream butter and sugar, beating until light and fluffy. Beat in eggs 1 at a time.

◆ Mix in sour cream and vanilla. Sift flour with baking powder and salt. Fold into creamed mixture.

◆ Combine nuts, sugar and cinnamon.

◆ Place ⅓ of batter in a well-greased and floured 9-inch tube pan. Sprinkle with ¾ of nut mixture. Spoon in remaining batter and sprinkle with remaining nut mixture.

◆ Bake for 1 hour. Remove from pan after 10 minutes and cool on rack.

Yield: *12 servings*

Apple Kuchen *(Dairy)*

1½	cups flour	⅔	cup milk
3	teaspoons baking powder	4	medium apples, peeled, cored and sliced thin
½	cup sugar		
¼	teaspoon salt	¼	cup dark brown sugar
¼	cup butter or margarine	1	teaspoon cinnamon
1	egg, well beaten	1	tablespoon soft butter or margarine
1	teaspoon vanilla		

◆ Preheat oven to 350°. Sift flour, baking powder, sugar and salt together.

◆ Cut in butter or margarine, as for pie crust. Stir in egg, vanilla and milk.

◆ Spread mixture in a greased 8x8-inch pan.

◆ Place apples over batter evenly, overlapping layers. Sprinkle with brown sugar, cinnamon and soft butter or margarine.

◆ Cover pan with foil and bake for 10 minutes.

◆ Remove cover and continue baking for about 30 minutes longer until cake tester comes out dry. Cool in pan.

Yield: *8 servings*

Cherry Kuchen (*Dairy or Parve*)

Dough
½   cup butter or margarine
¼   cup sugar + 1 tablespoon,
     divided
1   egg yolk

1¼ cups flour + 1 tablespoon,
     divided
1   teaspoon salt

Filling
3   tablespoons cornstarch
¼   cup water

1   can sour cherries, drained
     (reserve juice)
½   cup sugar

Topping
2   eggs, beaten
2   tablespoons cream
     (or nondairy creamer)

¾   cup sugar

◆   Preheat oven to 350°. **For Dough:** Cream butter, ¼ cup sugar and egg yolk. Add 1¼ cups flour and salt using a pastry blender to mix.

◆   Pat into a lightly greased 7x11-inch pan, working dough up sides of pan.

◆   Combine 1 tablespoon sugar and 1 tablespoon flour and sprinkle on crust.

◆   **For Filling:** Mix cornstarch with water to dissolve. Mix with juice of cherries and sugar.

◆   Cook until thick. Add cherries. Pour onto crust.

◆   **For Topping:** Combine eggs, cream or nondairy creamer and sugar and mix well. Pour over cherries.

◆   Bake for 20 minutes. Reduce heat to 325° and bake for an additional 30 minutes.

◆   Serve with whipped topping.

Yield: *8 servings*

Triple Chocolate Cookies *(Parve or Dairy)*

These incredible cookies are a special treat.

6	ounces semisweet baking chocolate	2	teaspoons instant coffee powder
2	ounces unsweetened baking chocolate	2	teaspoons vanilla
		¼	teaspoon salt
6	tablespoons unsalted butter or margarine	¼	teaspoon baking powder
		¼	cup flour
2	eggs	1	cup semisweet chocolate chips
¾	cup sugar	1	cup chopped walnuts
		1	cup chopped pecans

◆ Preheat oven to 350°. Microwave both chocolates and the butter in a medium bowl on high power for 1 minute, then stir. Repeat at 30-second intervals until chocolate and butter have melted and mixture is smooth. Let cool slightly.

◆ Meanwhile, using mixer on high speed, beat eggs and add sugar. Add instant coffee, vanilla, salt and baking powder and beat until light in color and bubbly, about 2 minutes. Reduce speed to low and beat in chocolate mixture. Add flour and beat just until blended. Stir in remaining ingredients.

◆ Using a scant ⅛ cup measure and rubber spatula, drop mounds on ungreased cookie sheet, or on cookie sheet lined with parchment paper. Dough will be gooey.

◆ Bake for 13 to 15 minutes. Surface will be dry, shiny and cracked, but inside will be soft.

◆ Cool cookies slightly for 5 minutes on cookie sheet. Remove with spatula to paper towels to cool completely.

Yield: *24 cookies*

Chocolate Chip Tea Cakes *(Dairy)*

A most unusual chocolate chip cookie.

1	cup butter, softened	1	(6-ounce) package chocolate chips
4	tablespoons sugar		Powdered sugar
2	cups flour		
1½	teaspoons vanilla		

- Preheat oven to 325°. Knead first 5 ingredients, adding chips last.
- Shape into small golf sized balls. Place on greased cookie sheet.
- Bake for 25 minutes. Roll in powdered sugar while still warm.

Yield: *24 cookies*

Choco-Cherry Crunch Cookies *(Dairy)*

1½	cups flour	1	teaspoon vanilla
1	teaspoon baking soda	1½	cups oatmeal
1	cup unsalted butter, softened	1	cup dried cherries
¾	cup sugar	1	cup toffee pieces
¾	cup light brown sugar	1	cup semisweet chocolate chips
1	egg		

- Preheat oven to 350°. Sift together flour and baking soda and set aside.
- In mixer, at high speed, cream butter and sugars until light and fluffy, for about 2 to 3 minutes. Scrape down the sides of the bowl once or twice. Add the egg and mix on high to combine. Add vanilla and mix to combine.
- Add flour, baking soda, oats, cherries, toffee pieces and chocolate chips. Scrape down the sides of the bowl.
- Drop by rounded teaspoons onto parchment-lined baking sheets. Dough will be sticky. If you do not have parchment paper, you can grease the cookie sheet.
- Bake until golden brown, 10 to 15 minutes.
- Remove from oven and let sit 1 minute before transferring to paper towel to finish cooling.

Yield: *60 cookies*

Beacon Hill Cookies *(Parve)*

A Brynwood Country Club specialty.

¾	cup semisweet chocolate chips	½	teaspoon vanilla
2	egg whites	½	teaspoon vinegar
½	cup sugar	¾	cup walnut or pecan halves

- ◆ Preheat oven to 350°. Melt chocolate chips in microwave for approximately 90 seconds or in double boiler over hot water. Cool.
- ◆ Beat egg whites until frothy. Gradually add sugar; beat until stiff peaks form.
- ◆ Beat in vanilla and vinegar. Fold in chocolate and nuts.
- ◆ Drop by tablespoons on cookie sheet lined with parchment paper. Bake for 10 minutes.

Yield: *12 cookies*

Cereal Cookies *(Parve or Dairy)*

1	cup butter or margarine	1	teaspoon baking powder
1	cup brown sugar	1	teaspoon baking soda
1	cup sugar	2	cups oatmeal
2	eggs	1	cup cornflake cereal
1	teaspoon vanilla	1	cup crisped rice cereal
2	cups flour	½	cup raisins or chocolate chips
½	teaspoon salt		(optional)

- ◆ Preheat oven to 350°. Cream butter or margarine and sugars. Add eggs and vanilla; mix well.
- ◆ Combine flour, salt, baking powder and soda. Slowly add to creamed mixture.
- ◆ Add oatmeal, cornflake cereal and crisped rice cereal. Mix well; add raisins or chocolate chips.
- ◆ Drop by well-rounded teaspoons on ungreased cookie sheet. Bake for 12 minutes.

Yield: *50 cookies*

Oatmeal Raisin Cookies *(Dairy)*

½ cup butter	2 cups flour
½ cup margarine	1¼ teaspoons salt
¾ cup plus 2 tablespoons sugar	½ teaspoon baking soda
1⅓ cups light brown sugar, packed	2¼ teaspoons baking powder
2 eggs	3¾ cups quick rolled oats
2 tablespoons water	2 cups raisins
1½ teaspoons vanilla	

- ◆ Combine first 4 ingredients and beat well. Add the next 3 ingredients. Mix again. Add remaining ingredients.
- ◆ Chill dough for 15 minutes.
- ◆ Preheat oven to 350°. Drop by tablespoons on foil-lined baking sheet. Bake for 10 to 12 minutes.

Yield: *40 to 50 cookies*

Peanut Butter Kiss Cookies *(Dairy)*

These no-bake cookies are a treat.

1 cup sugar	4 cups cornflake cereal
1 cup light corn syrup	1 bag of chocolate kisses (50)
2 cups crunchy peanut butter	

- ◆ Combine sugar and syrup and boil in a nonstick pot.
- ◆ Remove from heat and quickly add peanut butter and cereal. Mix well with wooden spoon.
- ◆ Make balls out of mixture. Place a kiss into center of each one and press down.
- ◆ Place on a cookie sheet lined with waxed paper. Immediately put into freezer to cool.
- ◆ Eat as they defrost!

Yield: *50 cookies*

Date Nut Crisps *(Dairy)*

They'll ask for an encore!

½ cup butter, softened	1¼ cups flour
½ cup sugar	1 cup chopped dates
¼ cup brown sugar	1 cup chopped walnuts
1 egg	2½ cups sugared cornflake cereal,
½ teaspoon baking soda	slightly crushed
¼ teaspoon salt	

◆ Preheat oven to 375°. Cream butter. Add sugars and cream well; beat in egg.

◆ Combine baking soda, salt and flour. Add to creamed mixture. Add dates and nuts.

◆ Roll a rounded teaspoonful of batter in cornflake cereal. Place on ungreased cookie sheet and bake for 10 to 12 minutes.

Yield: *48 cookies*

Taiglach *(Parve)*

This is a traditional treat served at Rosh Hashanah.

6 eggs	½ cup sugar
6 tablespoons oil	3 tablespoons powdered ginger
2½ cups flour	½ cup chopped nuts
2 cups honey	

◆ Beat eggs until foamy. Add oil and beat again. Add flour, 1 cup at a time, and beat with wooden spoon. Add a bit more flour if too sticky to touch.

◆ Take small portions of the dough at a time, not more than 3 tablespoons, roll out on well-floured board in a rope shape, about 2 inches thick. Cut in 1-inch pieces until all the dough is cut up.

◆ Preheat oven to 375°. Place honey and sugar into an ovenproof 4-quart pot and bring to boiling over medium heat. Add all the pieces of dough; place in oven and bake for 25 to 30 minutes.

◆ Open oven door and stir the mixture; bake for 10 minutes longer. Stir in ginger and nuts; bake for another 10 minutes, or until all honey is absorbed and taiglach acquires desired brownness. Moisten board with cold water; remove taiglach from pot with slotted spoon and turn out on board. Sprinkle generously with more powdered ginger.

Yield: *60 pieces*

Where's the Peanut Butter?
Chocolate Cookies *(Dairy)*

2	cups flour	½	cup sugar
½	cup cocoa	1¼	cups light brown sugar, divided
½	teaspoon baking powder	2	eggs
½	teaspoon baking soda	1	teaspoon vanilla
½	cup unsalted butter, softened	1	cup chocolate chips
½	cup margarine	½	cup peanut butter

◆ Preheat oven to 350°. Sift together flour, cocoa, baking powder and baking soda. Set aside.

◆ In mixer, beat the butter and margarine to combine. Beat in sugar and 1 cup of brown sugar on medium speed until light and fluffy, about 2 minutes.

◆ Add eggs, 1 at a time, mixing well after each. Add vanilla, beating well until creamy.

◆ On low speed, add dry ingredients until well combined. Add chocolate chips until just mixed in. Cover bowl and refrigerate for 1 hour.

◆ In small bowl, combine remaining ¼ cup brown sugar and peanut butter.

◆ Drop refrigerated dough by tablespoons onto parchment-lined or vegetable-sprayed cookie sheet 2 inches apart. Make an indentation with finger in middle of cookie. Fill with 1 teaspoon of peanut butter mixture. Top with a second scoop of dough and mold dough to hide peanut butter filling.

◆ Bake for 12 to 14 minutes until firm. Cool for 5 minutes before removing to cooling rack.

Yield: *24 cookies*

Frosted Chanukah Cookies *(Dairy)*

1	cup butter	½	teaspoon baking soda
1½	cups sugar	½	teaspoon salt
1	egg	½	teaspoon nutmeg
4	cups flour	½	cup sour cream
1	teaspoon baking powder	1	teaspoon vanilla

◆ Cream butter and sugar. Beat in egg. Add remaining ingredients.

◆ Divide into 3 balls and wrap in waxed paper. Chill for several hours or overnight.

◆ Preheat oven to 375°. Roll dough to ¼-inch thick on lightly floured surface. Cut with cookie cutters.

◆ Bake on greased cookie sheet for 8 to 10 minutes. Frost when cool.

Yield: *72 cookies*

Note: *You may decorate with sugar sprinkles before baking if you do not wish to use frosting.*

Frosting for Chanukah Cookies *(Dairy)*

⅓	cup hot milk	3	cups powdered sugar
1	tablespoon butter		Food coloring
1	teaspoon vanilla		

◆ Melt butter in milk. Add vanilla and powdered sugar to make desired consistency.

◆ Mix in food coloring and spread on cooled cookies.

Yield: *2 cups*

Parve Chanukah Cookies *(Parve)*

1	cup margarine	½	teaspoon salt
1	cup sugar	3	cups flour
2	egg yolks	1	teaspoon baking powder
1	teaspoon vanilla	⅓	cup nondairy coffee creamer

- Cream margarine and sugar together. Mix egg yolks and vanilla and add to sugar mixture.

- Sift the dry ingredients. Add alternately with creamer. Chill for several hours or overnight.

- Preheat oven to 375°. Roll out dough to ¼-inch thick on floured surface and cut in desired shapes. Decorate with sugar sprinkles.

- Bake for 8 to 10 minutes.

Yield: *60 to 70 cookies*

Hamantaschen Prune Filling *(Parve)*

1	cup orange juice	2	tablespoons honey
1½	cups (12 ounces) pitted prunes	¼	teaspoon ground cinnamon
2	teaspoons grated orange rind	½	cup chopped nuts
1	orange, peeled and cut into pieces		

- In medium saucepan, combine juice and prunes. Bring to boil, cover and simmer for 10 minutes or until juice is mostly absorbed and prunes are tender. (There will be about 2 tablespoons juice in pan.)

- Pour into blender or food processor. Add rind, orange pieces, honey and cinnamon. Process until mixture is smooth; add nuts and cool.

Yield: *2 cups*

Hamantaschen I (Parve)

A bamantascben is a cookie in the shape of Haman's three-cornered bat.

1	cup unsalted margarine	4	teaspoons vanilla or almond
1⅓	cups sugar		extract
2	eggs		Powdered sugar (optional)
4	cups flour		Canned poppy seed, fruit
½	teaspoon salt		pastry filling or fruit
2	tablespoons orange juice		preserves

◆ Blend margarine and sugar. Add eggs one at a time. Add flour and salt slowly. Add orange juice and extract. Refrigerate for 30 minutes.

◆ Preheat oven to 400°. Roll out to ¼ inch thick on a floured board. Cut out circles 1½ to 2 inches in diameter. Fill as desired and form into triangles.

◆ Bake for 6 minutes on lightly greased cookie sheet. Sprinkle with powdered sugar when serving if desired.

Yield: *75 to 80 hamantaschen*

Hamantaschen II (Parve)

1	cup sugar	1	teaspoon orange juice, lemon
¾	cup oil		juice or vanilla
3	eggs		Canned poppy seed, fruit
3½	cups flour		pastry filling or fruit
3	teaspoons baking powder		preserves
½	teaspoon salt		Chopped nuts (optional)

◆ Preheat oven to 350°. Mix sugar with oil. Add eggs and mix. Add flour and other dry ingredients. Add juice. Chill slightly.

◆ Roll dough out on pastry cloth or floured surface. Cut into circular shapes using the rim of a glass or cookie cutter. Add a dollop of filling and form into triangle.

◆ Bake on lightly greased cookie sheet for 20 minutes or until light brown.

Yield: *85 to 90 small hamantaschen*

Mandelbread *(Parve or Dairy)*

The very best!

½	cup margarine or butter	1	teaspoon baking powder
⅓	cup oil	1	cup golden raisins (optional)
1	cup sugar	1½	cups chocolate chips (optional)
3	teaspoons vanilla or almond extract	½	cup chopped almonds or walnuts (optional)
2	eggs	1	tablespoon cinnamon
3	egg whites	¼	cup sugar
3	cups flour		

◆ Preheat oven to 350°. Mix together margarine or butter, oil and sugar. Add vanilla, eggs and egg whites. Mix for 10 minutes.

◆ Combine flour and baking powder. Add to mixture. Blend in raisins, chocolate chips and nuts.

◆ Divide dough into 4 strips, 2x12-inches, and place on ungreased cookie sheet. Sprinkle cinnamon sugar mix on top of each strip. Bake for 30 minutes.

◆ Remove from oven and cut into 1-inch diagonal slices while warm. Lay each piece on its side on the cookie sheet.

◆ Brush melted margarine on top if desired. Lightly sprinkle with cinnamon sugar and return to the oven at 300° for 30 minutes. Cool.

Yield: *48 slices*

Note: *This freezes well.*

Mandel Crisps *(Parve)*

This wafer-thin version always gets rave reviews!

2	eggs	1	teaspoon almond extract
½	cup sugar	¾	cup sliced almonds
1	cup flour		

- Preheat oven to 350°. Beat eggs in mixer. Add sugar and beat. Add flour and almond extract. Blend well. Add almonds.

- Pour into a well-greased 5x9-inch loaf pan. Bake for 30 to 40 minutes.

- Cool bread in pan, then turn out and wrap in aluminum foil. Let sit overnight.

- Next day, preheat oven to 325°. Remove foil and slice with a very sharp knife into wafer-like slices.

- Place on ungreased cookie sheet and bake for 10 to 12 minutes until lightly browned and crisp.

- Allow to cool. Store in airtight container.

Yield: *36 pieces*

Note: *Vanilla may be used. These will keep 1 to 2 months.*

Easy Kichelach *(Parve)*

Kichel *is an airy, crispy cookie.*

1	(12-ounce) package wonton wrappers	Sugar

- Preheat oven to 450°. Spray a large cookie sheet with vegetable spray.
- Cut wrappers in half diagonally. Set on cookie sheet and spray tops of wrappers with vegetable spray. Sprinkle each wonton with sugar.
- Bake for approximately 3 minutes, checking so that they do not burn. They should be golden brown.
- For a savory rather than sweet taste, eliminate sugar and sprinkle with kosher salt, garlic flakes, cracked pepper, sesame seeds or poppy seeds. Use your imagination.

Yield: *48 pieces*

Note: *For those who cannot have sugar, use a sugar substitute AFTER they come out of the oven.*

Biscotti Chocolata *(Parve)*

¾	cup sugar	2	cups flour
2	eggs	½	teaspoon baking soda
2	tablespoons margarine	¼	teaspoon baking powder
1	teaspoon vanilla	¼	cup cocoa
1	tablespoon orange juice	1	cup chocolate chips
1	tablespoon grated orange rind		

- Preheat oven to 350°. Beat sugar, eggs and margarine. Add vanilla, orange juice and rind. Add remaining ingredients.
- Form into 2 long loaves and place on greased cookie sheet. Bake for 35 minutes or until slightly brown. Cool 10 minutes.
- Cut into 1-inch slices and bake at 300° for 15 minutes.

Yield: *26 pieces*

Low-Fat Almond Biscotti *(Dairy)*

1	cup flour	3	egg whites
1	cup whole wheat flour	1	teaspoon almond extract
⅔	cup sugar	1	teaspoon vanilla extract
2	teaspoons baking powder	1	cup slivered almonds
4	tablespoons light margarine, softened		

- ◆ Preheat oven to 350°. Combine flour, whole wheat flour, sugar and baking powder in mixer.

- ◆ On slowest speed add margarine and mix until mixture resembles coarse meal. Stir in egg whites, almond and vanilla extract. Fold in almonds.

- ◆ Divide into 2 logs, 9x2 inches each, and place on greased cookie sheet.

- ◆ Bake for 25 minutes or until slightly brown.

- ◆ Cool logs to room temperature, about 10 minutes. Slice diagonally into ½-inch slices.

- ◆ Place slices, cut side down, on ungreased cookie sheet and bake for 20 to 30 minutes at 300°. Turn over after 15 minutes and check often to avoid burning.

Yield: *36 pieces*

Note: *You can sprinkle with cinnamon and sugar after baking. Store in an airtight container.*

Irresistible Rugelach *(Dairy)*

A hit at every family simcha *(happy event).*

¼	cup butter	½	pint light cream
¼	cup margarine	1	cup sugar
3	cups flour	1	tablespoon cinnamon
1	package active dry yeast	¼	cup chopped nuts
3	egg yolks		Apricot or raspberry jam
1	teaspoon vanilla		(optional)

♦ Cream butter and margarine. Add flour and yeast. Add egg yolks, vanilla and cream. Mix until well blended.

♦ Make 4 balls; wrap in plastic wrap and refrigerate overnight.

♦ Preheat oven to 350°. Roll out 1 ball at a time into a rectangle and cut into 2-inch squares. Sprinkle with mixture of sugar, cinnamon, nuts and, if desired ¼ to ½ teaspoon jam.

♦ Roll each piece from one corner to opposite corner. Place on ungreased cookie sheet. Bake for 20 to 25 minutes until browned.

Yield: *60 pieces*

Rugelach *(Parve)*

Dough

3	cups flour	2	eggs
3	tablespoons sugar	1	teaspoon vanilla
½	teaspoon salt	1	envelope active dry yeast
1	cup unsalted margarine, melted		dissolved in ¼ cup warm water

Filling

1	cup sugar	Chopped nuts
½	cup brown sugar	Raisins (optional)
2	teaspoons cinnamon	Chocolate chips (optional)
	Apricot or raspberry preserves	

- Mix flour, 3 tablespoons sugar and salt.
- Mix in margarine, eggs, vanilla and dissolved yeast to form dough. Refrigerate 4 hours or overnight.
- Preheat oven to 350°. Combine 1 cup sugar, brown sugar and cinnamon.
- Cut dough into 4 parts and shape into balls. Roll out the first ball on waxed paper that has been coated with ¼ of the sugar mixture. Roll until thin and circular.
- Spread with jelly and nuts (or optional ingredients) up to 1½ inches from edge of circle.
- Cut into 16 wedges. Roll each wedge toward the center. Repeat with remaining 3 balls.
- Bake on greased cookie sheet for 20 minutes.
- Remove to cooling rack while hot.

Yield: *64 pieces*

Strudel (*Parve*)

Filling
1	pound chopped walnuts	3	(20-ounce) cans crushed pineapple, drained, reserving juice
1	pound golden raisins		
1	(16-ounce) jar maraschino cherries, cut fine	½	cup sugar
		½	cup pineapple juice or enough to moisten

Pastry
1	cup lukewarm water	2	tablespoons oil
¼	teaspoon vinegar		Graham cracker crumbs
3	cups flour		Sugar
1	egg		Powdered sugar
¼	teaspoon salt		

- **For Filling:** Prepare filling early so that raisins can "plump" for at least 4 to 6 hours or overnight. Mix all ingredients well.

- **For Pastry:** Combine water and vinegar. Mix by hand with remaining pastry ingredients in a large bowl. Dough will be very sticky.

- Dip hand in oil and divide dough into 4 parts. Brush lightly with oil and let stand 1 hour in warm place, covered tightly.

- Preheat oven to 400°. Use a tablecloth for rolling. Cover cloth with flour generously! Take 1 part dough, place on tablecloth and begin rolling into rectangle until very thin.

- Brush dough lightly with oil. Sprinkle with graham cracker crumbs and a little sugar.

- Along long edge of rolled out dough, spread ¼ of prepared filling. Pick up by the 2 lower corners of the tablecloth and gently allow strudel to roll itself.

- Place strudel on greased cookie sheet or parchment paper and cut ½ way through for each piece *before* baking. You may cut the strudel in order to fit onto the cookie sheet or you may keep the strudel in one piece and place on cookie sheet in horseshoe shape. Repeat with remaining 3 parts.

- Brush with oil and bake for about 20 minutes, or until brown. Cool, then cut pieces through and sprinkle with powdered sugar before serving.

Yield: *125 to 160 pieces, about ½ inch*

Note: *The warmer the kitchen, the farther the dough will stretch.*

Fabulous Brownies *(Dairy or Parve)*

4	eggs	1	cup flour
2	cups sugar	1	teaspoon vanilla
½	cup butter or margarine, melted and cooled	½	cup chopped nuts (optional)
4	ounces unsweetened chocolate, melted	4	ounces semisweet chocolate
		4	tablespoons butter or margarine

- ◆ Preheat oven to 350°. Beat eggs; add sugar and beat again. Beat in butter. Add unsweetened chocolate. Mix in flour and vanilla.
- ◆ Place in greased 9x13-inch baking pan. Pat nuts into top of batter. Bake for 30 minutes.
- ◆ Meanwhile, melt the semisweet chocolate with 4 tablespoons butter or margarine. Drizzle over top of brownies when they come out of the oven. Cool and cut into squares.

Yield: *36 bars*

One-Bowl Brownies *(Parve)*

4	ounces unsweetened chocolate	3	eggs
¾	cup margarine	1	teaspoon vanilla
2	cups sugar	1	cup flour

Topping (optional)

2	cups mini marshmallows	1	cup chocolate chips

- ◆ Preheat oven to 325°. Microwave chocolate and margarine on high power for 2 minutes. Mix well.
- ◆ Add sugar, mixing well. Add eggs and vanilla. Stir in flour.
- ◆ Pour batter into a well-greased 9x13-inch pan and bake for 30 to 35 minutes.
- ◆ Melt marshmallows and chocolate chips in a pan or microwave.
- ◆ Remove from oven and spread melted topping over brownies. Return to oven and bake for 2 more minutes. Remove from oven and swirl topping with knife.

Yield: *36 bars*

Marble Bars *(Parve)*

1	cup margarine	1	teaspoon baking soda
1	cup sugar	1	teaspoon salt
1	cup brown sugar	2½	cups flour
2	eggs	1	(6-ounce) package chocolate chips
1½	teaspoons water		

- ◆ Preheat oven to 350°. Cream margarine and sugars.
- ◆ Add eggs 1 at a time. Add water and dry ingredients.
- ◆ Pour into lightly greased jellyroll pan. Sprinkle chocolate chips on top.
- ◆ Bake for 2 minutes. Remove from oven and swirl chocolate chips into batter. Return batter to oven and bake for an additional 12 minutes.

Yield: *48 bars*

Chocolate Chip Meringue Squares *(Parve)*

½	cup margarine	2	teaspoons baking powder
½	cup sugar	1	teaspoon baking soda
1¼	cups light brown sugar, firmly packed, divided	¼	teaspoon salt
2	eggs, separated	3	tablespoons cold water
1	teaspoon vanilla	1	(10-ounce) package chocolate chips
2	cups flour		

- ◆ Preheat oven to 350°. Cream margarine, adding sugar and ½ cup brown sugar gradually. Mix well. Blend in 2 egg yolks and 1 teaspoon vanilla.
- ◆ Meanwhile, sift together the flour, baking powder, baking soda and salt.
- ◆ Add the cold water alternately with dry ingredients.
- ◆ Press dough into a 9x13-inch greased and floured pan. Sprinkle chocolate chips over dough and gently press in.
- ◆ Beat the 2 egg whites until foamy and gradually add ¾ cup brown sugar. Beat well until mixture stands in peaks.
- ◆ Spread meringue over the chips and bake for 25 to 30 minutes.
- ◆ Cool completely before cutting.

Yield: *24 to 30 bars*

Goldies *(Parve or Dairy)*

1	cup butter or margarine, softened	2	cups flour
2	cups brown sugar	½	teaspoon baking powder
2	eggs	2	cups chocolate chips
2	teaspoons vanilla	1	cup chopped walnuts (optional)

◆ Preheat oven to 350°. Beat butter and sugar until light and fluffy, about 3 minutes. Beat in eggs until thoroughly blended. Beat in the remaining ingredients until blended.

◆ Spread batter evenly into greased 9x13-inch baking pan and bake for about 30 minutes or until a cake tester, inserted in center, comes out clean and top is golden brown. *Do not overbake.*

◆ Allow to cool in pan and then cut into squares or bars. A light sprinkling of powdered sugar is nice.

Yield: *48 bars*

Quick Date Nut Squares *(Parve)*

1	pound pitted dates, cut in half	1½	cups flour
2	tablespoons margarine	1	egg
1	teaspoon baking soda	1	cup chopped nuts
1	cup boiling water		Whipped cream or ice cream (optional)
1	cup sugar		

◆ Preheat oven to 350°. Grease and flour a 9x13-inch baking pan.

◆ Combine dates, margarine, baking soda and boiling water. Let sit for 10 minutes.

◆ Combine sugar, flour, egg and nuts. Stir nut mixture into date mixture until well mixed. Mixture will be thick.

◆ Spread in baking pan and bake 30 minutes. Cool and cut into squares. Sprinkle with powdered sugar. Serve with whipped cream or ice cream if desired.

Yield: *15 bars*

"As You Like It" Oatmeal Squares (Parve)

1½ cups flour	1 teaspoon baking soda
1¾ cups quick oatmeal	1 cup brown sugar
½ teaspoon salt	¾ cup margarine

Date Filling

1 cup dates, pitted and cut up	1 cup water
1 cup sugar	1 cup walnuts, chopped fine

Apricot Filling

1 cup dried apricots, cut up	1 cup water
½ cup sugar	

Rhubarb Filling

2 cups cut up rhubarb	½ cup water
1 cup sugar	1 tablespoon cornstarch

◆ Preheat oven to 375°. Mix dry ingredients together. Work in margarine. Pack ½ of mixture into bottom of a greased 9x13-inch baking pan.

◆ Spread filling over top. Sprinkle on remaining crumb mixture. Press down. Bake for 30 to 35 minutes.

◆ **For Date Filling:** Bring all ingredients except walnuts to boil. Simmer until thick. Cool and add walnuts.

◆ **For Apricot Filling:** Bring apricots, water and sugar to a boil. Simmer for 3 minutes, stirring constantly.

◆ **For Rhubarb Filling:** Place rhubarb and sugar in pot. Mix cornstarch with water and add to pot. Cook until rhubarb sauce is liquid and slightly thick.

Yield: *15 to 20 pieces*

Lemon Bars *(Parve or Dairy)*

Bottom Layer

2¼ cups flour	1 cup butter or margarine
½ cup powdered sugar	

Top Layer

4 eggs	¼ cup flour
2 cups sugar	½ teaspoon baking powder
⅓ cup lemon juice	Powdered sugar

◆ Preheat oven to 350°. For bottom layer, combine flour with powdered sugar. Cut in butter. Press into 9x13-inch lightly greased baking pan and bake for 20 to 25 minutes until lightly brown. Cool slightly.

◆ For top layer, beat eggs. Add sugar and lemon juice. Sift flour with baking powder. Stir into egg mixture. Spread on top of baked bottom layer and return to oven.

◆ Bake 25 minutes longer. Remove from oven and cool. Dust with powdered sugar and cut into squares.

Yield: *12 to 18 bars*

Viennese Raspberry Bars *(Parve)*

1 cup margarine	1 (10- to 12-ounce) jar seedless
1½ cups sugar, divided	raspberry jam
¼ teaspoon salt	1 cup chocolate chips
2 egg yolks	4 egg whites
2 cups flour	2 cups chopped walnuts

◆ Preheat oven to 350°. Grease a 9x13-inch baking pan.

◆ In mixer, cream margarine, ½ cup sugar and salt; add egg yolks and flour.

◆ Pat into bottom of pan and bake for 15 to 20 minutes. Cool slightly and spread jam over crust; add chocolate chips.

◆ Beat egg whites until stiff. Beat in 1 cup sugar. Gently stir in chopped walnuts.

◆ Return to oven and bake an additional 30 minutes. Cut while warm.

Yield: *40 bars*

Chocolate Raspberry Bars *(Dairy)*

Impress your guests with this easy dessert!

1	cup butter or margarine, softened	1	(14-ounce) can sweetened, condensed milk
½	cup light brown sugar	½	cup chopped nuts (optional)
¼	teaspoon salt	⅓	cup seedless raspberry preserves
2	cups flour		
2	cups chocolate chips, divided		

◆ Preheat oven to 350°. Beat butter or margarine until creamy. Beat in brown sugar, then add salt and flour; mix well.

◆ Press 1¼ cups of crumb mixture into the bottom of a 9x13-inch greased baking dish. Reserve remaining mixture for topping.

◆ Bake for 10 to 12 minutes or until edges are golden brown.

◆ Combine 1 cup chocolate chips and condensed milk in a saucepan or 4-cup glass measuring cup. Melt over low heat, stirring until smooth, or place in microwave for 2 minutes on high power, then stir until chocolate is melted. Spread over hot crust.

◆ Stir nuts into remaining crumb batter and sprinkle over chocolate filling. Drop teaspoonfuls of raspberry preserves over crumb mixture. Sprinkle with remaining chocolate chips.

◆ Continue baking for 25 to 35 minutes, or until center is set. Cut when cool.

Yield: *36 bars*

Rocky Road Fudge Bars *(Dairy)*

Well worth the fuss!

Bottom Layer

½	cup butter	1	teaspoon baking powder
1	ounce unsweetened chocolate	2	eggs
1	cup sugar	1	teaspoon vanilla
1	cup flour	½-1	cup chopped walnuts

Filling

6	ounces cream cheese, softened	2	tablespoons flour
¼	cup butter, softened	½	teaspoon vanilla
½	cup sugar	¼	cup chopped walnuts
1	egg	1	cup chocolate chips (optional)

Frosting

2	cups miniature marshmallows	¼	cup milk
¼	cup butter	3	cups powdered sugar
1	ounce unsweetened chocolate	1	teaspoon vanilla
2	ounces cream cheese, softened		

◆ Preheat oven to 350°. Grease and flour a 9x13-inch baking pan.

◆ **For Bottom Layer:** Melt butter and chocolate over low heat. Add remaining bottom layer ingredients in order listed. Mix well and spread in pan.

◆ **For Filling:** Combine cream cheese with butter and sugar and beat with electric mixer until fluffy. Add egg, flour, vanilla and walnuts. Spread over bottom layer. Sprinkle chocolate chips over all. Bake for 30 to 35 minutes until done.

◆ **For Frosting:** Sprinkle marshmallows over top and return to oven for an additional 2 minutes. In saucepan, over low heat, combine butter, chocolate, cream cheese and milk until smooth. Pour over marshmallows. Cut when cool.

Yield: *35 bars*

Never-Fail Pie Dough *(Parve or Dairy)*

2	cups flour	1	cup shortening, margarine or butter
1	teaspoon salt		
1	tablespoon sugar	¼-½	cup cold orange juice or ice water

♦ Mix dry ingredients in bowl. Cut in shortening with fork until crumbly.

♦ Add juice until crust reaches correct consistency for rolling.

♦ Roll out on floured waxed paper or pastry board to correct size for pie plate.

Yield: *2, 9- to 10-inch pie shells or 1 top and 1 bottom for double crust pie.*

Processor Pie Dough *(Parve or Dairy)*

♦ Using Never-Fail Pie Dough recipe, put dry ingredients in food processor bowl with metal blade. Add margarine or butter and process for about 8 seconds until mixture is like coarse meal.

♦ Add juice or ice water and pulse until dough begins to clump together and form a ball.

♦ Divide into 2 to 3 equal parts and put each part in a plastic bag. Work through bags to form into ball. Flatten into a circle. Refrigerate for about 1 hour.

♦ Roll each circle of dough on a lightly floured surface into a circle about ⅛-inch thick. Place in pie plate.

Yield: *3, 9-inch pie shells or 2, 10-inch pie shells*

Apple Crunch Pie *(Parve)*

Topping
1	cup flour	1	teaspoon ground cinnamon
½	cup light brown sugar	½	cup margarine, cut in small
½	cup sugar		pieces

Filling
7	medium tart apples	½	teaspoon cinnamon
1	tablespoon lemon juice	½	teaspoon nutmeg
½	cup sugar	1	(10-inch) pie shell, unbaked
3	tablespoons flour		

♦ Place oven rack in lowest position and preheat oven to 450°. Mix flour, sugars and cinnamon in medium bowl. Cut in margarine until mixture forms moist, coarse crumbs that clump together easily. Set aside.

♦ Peel, halve and core apples. Cut in ⅛-inch slices and put in large bowl. Toss with lemon juice to coat.

♦ Mix sugar, flour and spices in small bowl. Sprinkle over apples. Toss until evenly coated.

♦ Layer slices in pie shell, mounding them higher in center. Pat topping evenly over apples to form top crust.

♦ Place pie on cookie sheet. Bake for 15 minutes at 450°. Reduce oven to 350° and bake for 45 minutes longer or until a skewer meets some resistance when center of pie is pierced and topping is golden. Cool on wire rack before serving.

Yield: *8 servings*

Sugar-Free Apple Pie *(Parve or Dairy)*

1 (9-inch) pie shell, unbaked	2½ tablespoons quick tapioca
5-6 cups sliced apples (about 7 large apples)	½ teaspoon cinnamon
1 (6-ounce) can unsweetened apple juice concentrate	1 tablespoon margarine (optional)

◆ Preheat oven to 400°. Combine apples and apple juice in a saucepan and bring to a simmer for a few minutes. Stir in tapioca.

◆ Fill pie shell and sprinkle cinnamon over mixture. Dot with margarine.

◆ Bake for 10 minutes. Reduce heat to 350° and continue baking for 20 minutes.

Yield: *8 servings*

Pear Pie *(Parve)*

1 cup flour	2 tablespoons margarine, melted
½ cup packed brown sugar	½ cup dark corn syrup
1 teaspoon powdered ginger, divided	½ teaspoon grated lemon rind
½ cup margarine	1 teaspoon lemon juice
½ cup chopped nuts	4 medium fresh pears, peeled and diced
3 tablespoons cornstarch	1 (9-inch) pie shell, unbaked
⅛ teaspoon salt	

◆ Preheat oven to 400°. Mix together flour, brown sugar and ½ teaspoon ginger. Cut in ½ cup margarine until coarse crumbs form. Stir in nuts and set aside.

◆ In a large bowl, stir together cornstarch, salt and remaining ½ teaspoon ginger. Stir in melted margarine, corn syrup, lemon rind and juice until smooth. Add pears, tossing until well coated with corn syrup mixture.

◆ Turn pears into pie shell. Sprinkle flour and brown sugar mixture over unbaked pie. Bake for 15 minutes; reduce heat to 350° and continue baking for 30 minutes or until topping and crust are browned.

Yield: *8 servings*

Lime Sour Cream Pie *(Dairy)*

¾	cup sugar	¼	cup butter or margarine
3	tablespoons cornstarch	1	cup sour cream
2½	teaspoons grated lime peel	1	pie shell, baked
⅓	cup lime juice		Whipping cream
1	cup half-and-half	1-2	tablespoons sugar

◆ Combine sugar with cornstarch and lime peel in medium pan. Add lime juice and stir until smooth.

◆ Blend in half-and-half and butter or margarine. Cook and stir over medium heat until mixture thickens and starts to boil, 10 to 12 minutes.

◆ Remove from heat and let cool, stirring occasionally.

◆ Fold in sour cream and pour into pie shell.

◆ Combine whipping cream and sugar in medium bowl and whip to soft peaks. Spread on top of pie and serve.

Yield: *6 to 8 servings*

Note: *Prepared whipped topping may be used.*

Fresh Fruit Flan *(Dairy)*

So easy and so delicious!

½	cup butter	1	teaspoon vanilla
¼	cup sugar	4	ounces whipping cream
2	cups biscuit baking mix		Sliced fruit such as peaches,
1	(3-ounce) package cream cheese		apples, nectarines, plums
½	cup sugar	½	cup currant or apple jelly

◆ Preheat oven to 375°. Mix butter and sugar. Cut in baking mix until combined, by hand, food processor or mixer.

◆ Press into bottom of lightly greased 10-inch flan pan with removable bottom, or similar pan such as a springform.

◆ Bake until browned, 13 to 18 minutes. Let cool.

◆ Beat cream cheese, sugar, and vanilla in food processor. Slowly add whipping cream and beat until stiff.

◆ Pour into cooled crust and refrigerate several hours or overnight. Place sliced fruit on top of the flan. Melt currant or apple jelly and brush over fruit to make a glaze and prevent fruit from turning brown.

Yield: *12 servings*

Strawberry Rhubarb Pie *(Parve or Dairy)*

2	cups rhubarb chunks	1½	cups sugar
1	cup sliced strawberries	1	(9-inch) pie shell, unbaked
¼	cup water	1	teaspoon orange rind
3	tablespoons cornstarch		

Topping

1	cup flour	½	cup butter or margarine
¾	cup sugar		

- ◆ Preheat oven to 450°. Place rhubarb and sliced strawberries in a large mixing bowl.
- ◆ Mix water, cornstarch and sugar together and pour over fruit. Let sit for 15 minutes.
- ◆ Pour fruit mixture into pie shell; sprinkle orange rind over fruit.
- ◆ Mix flour, ¾ cup sugar and butter in food processor. Cover fruit completely with mixture.
- ◆ Bake for 10 minutes; reduce heat to 350° and bake for 40 to 50 minutes.
- ◆ Cool before serving.

Yield: *6 to 8 servings*

Note: *Vanilla ice cream is delicious with this pie.*

Fresh Strawberry Pie *(Dairy)*

1	(8- or 9-inch) graham cracker crust	3	tablespoons cornstarch
2	pint boxes strawberries	1	teaspoon lemon juice
¾	cup sugar		Whipping cream or light whipped cream
¼	cup water		

- ◆ Line pie crust with 1 pint strawberries, trimmed side down. Crush other pint of berries in a saucepan; add sugar, water and cornstarch. Bring to boil until thick and clear, stirring frequently.
- ◆ Add lemon juice and pour over whole berries in pie shell. Refrigerate 2 hours. Garnish with whipped cream ½ hour before serving.

Yield: *6 to 8 servings*

Mom's Luscious Pumpkin Pie *(Parve or Dairy)*

4	extra large eggs	2	(12-ounce) cans evaporated
1½	cups sugar		milk (3 cups) or 3 cups
1	teaspoon salt		nondairy creamer
4	teaspoons pumpkin pie spice	2	(10-inch) deep-dish pie shells,
3½	cups canned pumpkin		unbaked
	(29-ounce can)		

- ◆ Preheat oven to 425°. In mixer, beat eggs lightly. Stir in sugar, salt, pumpkin pie spice and pumpkin. Mix well; gradually stir in evaporated milk.
- ◆ Pour into pie shells that have been crimped high along edge.
- ◆ Bake for 15 minutes. Reduce temperature to 350°; bake an additional 40 to 50 minutes or until knife inserted near center comes out clean.
- ◆ Cool on wire rack for 2 hours. Serve immediately or chill.

Yield: *8 servings*

Note: *This pie is best served fresh. Do not freeze. To avoid burnt pie edges, crimp strips of foil around edges. Remove foil strips during last 10 minutes of baking.*

Chocolate Tofu Mousse *(Parve)*

Our taster's choice.

1	(12-ounce) package chocolate chips	1	(10-ounce) box silken tofu

- ◆ Melt the chocolate chips in the microwave or in the top of a double boiler. Let cool a bit.
- ◆ Purée the tofu in a food processor. Add melted chocolate and whirl it a bit more until well mixed. Pour into glass bowl.
- ◆ Chill and serve.

Yield: *4 to 6 servings*

Blueberry Tart *(Dairy)*

Crust

1	cup flour	½	cup butter
¼	teaspoon salt	1	tablespoon white vinegar
2	tablespoons sugar		

Filling

1	cup sugar	⅛	teaspoon cinnamon
2	tablespoons flour	4½	cups blueberries, divided

◆ Preheat oven to 400°. Prepare a 10-inch springform pan with vegetable spray. Combine flour, salt and sugar.

◆ Cut in the butter. Mix in the vinegar. Pat the crust on bottom of springform pan and up 1 inch around the sides.

◆ Combine sugar, flour and cinnamon for the filling. Add 2½ cups blueberries and place on top of the crust. Bake for 1 hour.

◆ Remove from oven and put 2 cups blueberries on top. Lightly press in. Cool. Remove pan rim and serve from the bottom of the springform pan.

Yield: *8 to 12 servings*

Note: *Tart may also be made in a 10-inch pie plate.*

Sugar-Free Tofu Mousse *(Parve)*

12	ounces silken tofu	5	teaspoons granulated sugar
8	tablespoons unsweetened		substitute
	cocoa powder	1	teaspoon vanilla

◆ In a food processor, blend tofu until it is smooth. Add cocoa, sweetener and vanilla.

◆ Process until mixture is smooth and creamy. Serve chilled or at room temperature. Serve over fruit if desired.

Yield: *4 to 6 servings*

Chocolate Banana Tofu Dessert *(Parve)*

You'll never know it's tofu!

¾-1 cup semisweet chocolate chips	1 teaspoon vanilla extract
1 (10-ounce) box silken tofu, soft variety	2-3 tablespoons light brown sugar
	¼ teaspoon salt
2 large ripe bananas	1 teaspoon raspberry vinegar

◆ Melt the chocolate chips in a double boiler or in microwave at low power.

◆ Place tofu and ¼ of banana chunks in a blender and purée. Add the remaining banana in small batches and process until mixture is smooth. Add the vanilla, brown sugar, salt, and vinegar while processing.

◆ Pour in the melted chocolate even if it is hot.

◆ Purée one more time until very smooth and uniform. Taste to adjust the sugar.

◆ Transfer the mousse to a container and cover tightly.

◆ Chill for at least 2 hours before serving.

Yield: *6 to 8 servings*

Note: *This recipe contains no eggs. Silken tofu comes in a box and does not need refrigeration until it is opened.*

Chocolate Fondue *(Dairy)*

2 cups sugar	1 teaspoon vanilla
¾ cup cocoa	¼ teaspoon butter flavoring (optional)
2 tablespoons cornstarch	Angel food cake squares
¼ teaspoon salt	Marshmallows
4 cups skim milk	Sliced fruit for dipping
3 tablespoons margarine	

◆ Mix sugar, cocoa, cornstarch and salt in medium saucepan. Add milk, stirring well.

◆ Bring to boil, stirring, over medium heat. Lower heat and simmer, stirring occasionally, for 20 minutes.

◆ Remove from heat, add margarine, vanilla and butter flavoring, if desired.

◆ Serve warm for dipping.

Yield: *5 cups*

Frozen Banana Split Dessert *(Dairy)*

The fudge sauce alone is great over ice cream!

Fudge Sauce

1	cup chocolate chips	1½	cups (12-ounce can) evaporated milk
½	cup butter		
2	cups powdered sugar	½	cup chopped pecans

Crust

1½	cups graham cracker crumbs	3-4	bananas, sliced
⅓	cup sugar	½	gallon vanilla ice cream, softened
½	cup butter, melted		Whipped cream (optional)

◆ Melt chocolate chips and ½ cup butter together. Add sugar and milk and cook until thick. Cool.

◆ Combine graham cracker crumbs and sugar. Add melted butter. Cover bottom of a greased 9x13-inch baking pan with crumb mixture. Pat into place. Chill in freezer for 45 minutes.

◆ Place sliced bananas on top of crust and chill in freezer again for about 10 minutes. Spread softened ice cream over bananas and freeze until firm.

◆ Spread cooled fudge sauce and pecans over ice cream and return to freezer. Remove from freezer 15 minutes before serving. Cut into squares and top with whipped cream if desired.

Yield: *12 to 15 servings*

Bittersweet Chocolate Sauce *(Dairy)*

6	ounces bittersweet chocolate, chopped	2	tablespoons Kahlúa or other coffee-flavored liqueur, orange liqueur or vanilla
3	tablespoons water		
¼	cup heavy cream		

◆ In a double boiler melt the chocolate with the water and cream, stirring until mixture is smooth. Stir in liqueur.

Yield: *1 cup*

Note: *Chocolate can be melted in microwave. Sauce may be made 1 week in advance, kept covered, chilled and reheated. Great for dipping fruit.*

Tiramisu *(Dairy)*

6	egg yolks	2	(3-ounce) packages ladyfingers
¾	cup sugar	¼	cup espresso or strong coffee
⅔	cup milk	2	tablespoons coffee-flavored
1	pound mascarpone cheese		liqueur
1¼	cup whipping cream	1	tablespoon cocoa
½	teaspoon vanilla		

♦ Beat yolks and sugar. Add milk and mix well. In a medium saucepan, heat on top of stove until mixture boils, then reduce heat and stir for 1 minute.

♦ Remove from heat and refrigerate for 1 hour covered with plastic wrap that touches the mix. After 1 hour, mix egg mixture with cheese until smooth.

♦ Whip the cream with the vanilla in a chilled mixing bowl. Line large glass serving bowl with half of the ladyfingers. Drizzle with half of the coffee liqueur and espresso. Spread with half of the cheese mixture and half of the whipped cream, then repeat. Dust top with cocoa.

Yield: *10 to 12 servings*

Schaum Torte *(Parve)*

7	egg whites	1	teaspoon vanilla
⅛	teaspoon lemon juice	1	teaspoon white vinegar
2	cups sugar		

♦ Preheat oven to 250°. Whip egg whites and lemon juice until soft peaks form, about 5 minutes. Add sugar a little at a time, whipping well after each addition, about 8 to 10 minutes. Fold in vanilla and vinegar and blend well.

♦ Pour mixture into greased 8-inch springform pan or pipe out into individual molded shells. Bake for 30 minutes. Turn off oven and let sit in oven for 30 minutes. Cool.

♦ Remove torte by using a knife around the edge of the pan to loosen. Keep bottom of springform pan attached to avoid cracking the torte.

♦ Fill with berries and cream or ice cream topped with hot fudge or fruit.

Yield: *8 to 10 servings*

Pecan Praline Crunch *(Dairy)*

1	(16-ounce) box oat squares cereal	½	cup light brown sugar
2	cups pecan halves	¼	cup butter
¼	cup honey	1	teaspoon vanilla
¼	cup light corn syrup	½	teaspoon baking soda

◆ Preheat oven to 250°. Combine cereal and pecans in a 9x13-inch glass baking pan that has been prepared with vegetable spray.

◆ Combine honey, corn syrup, brown sugar and butter in a large microwavable bowl and microwave on high power for 1½ minutes. Stir.

◆ Microwave again for 1½ minutes until it boils. Stir in vanilla and baking soda. Pour over cereal mixture; stir to coat evenly.

◆ Bake for 1 hour, stirring every 20 minutes. Remove from oven and spread on foil to cool.

◆ Break into small pieces. Store in airtight container.

Yield: *12 to 14 servings*

Scrumptious Toffee *(Dairy)*

You won't believe how easy this is to make!

2	(12-ounce) packages milk chocolate chips	2	(10-ounce) packages almond toffee bits, divided
		1	cup salted peanuts (optional)

◆ In a medium saucepan, melt chocolate chips over medium heat, stirring constantly with rubber spatula until smooth. Remove from heat and add 1 package of toffee bits and peanuts.

◆ Spread mixture evenly in a 10x15-inch ungreased jellyroll pan. Sprinkle remaining package of toffee bits over top and lightly tap into chocolate mixture. Cover with foil and place in freezer for several hours or overnight.

◆ Remove from freezer and defrost for 30 to 45 minutes. Break into pieces.

Yield: *Approximately 72 pieces*

Note: *Store in refrigerator or freezer until ready to use or give away. Toffee will keep for several months.*

Apple Blueberry Crisp *(Parve)*

Filling
1	teaspoon oil	1	teaspoon cinnamon
4	medium Granny Smith apples, peeled, cored, and sliced	¼	cup sugar
		1	cup frozen blueberries
1	tablespoon lemon juice		

Topping
1	cup rolled oats	4	teaspoons oil
⅓	cup flour	½	teaspoon cinnamon
¼	cup brown sugar	1	tablespoon orange juice

- ◆ Preheat oven to 375°. Lightly wipe a 9½x11-inch baking dish with 1 teaspoon oil.
- ◆ Mix sliced apples with lemon juice, cinnamon and sugar.
- ◆ Press into baking dish and sprinkle with frozen berries on top.
- ◆ Mix topping ingredients and sprinkle over blueberry mixture.
- ◆ Bake for 30 minutes until crumbs look lightly browned. Test apples with a fork for tenderness.
- ◆ Serve warm or at room temperature.

Yield: *9 servings*

Never Fail Fudge *(Dairy)*

⅔	cup evaporated milk	1½	cups chocolate chips
1⅔	cups sugar	1	teaspoon vanilla
½	teaspoon salt	1½	cups walnut halves
1½	cups marshmallows (about 16 small)		

- ◆ In medium saucepan slowly heat milk, sugar and salt until it comes to a boil, stirring constantly.
- ◆ Remove from heat and add marshmallows, chocolate chips and vanilla. Stir until melted; add nuts.
- ◆ Spread into 9-inch square buttered pan or glass baking dish. Refrigerate several hours or overnight. Remove from refrigerator and cut into 1-inch squares.

Yield: *81 pieces*

Apple Oat Crunch *(Parve)*

⅔ cup brown sugar, divided	½ cup flour
5 cups peeled apples, cut in 2-inch chunks	½ teaspoon cinnamon
	¼ teaspoon nutmeg
1 cup quick rolled oats	½ cup margarine

- ◆ Preheat oven to 375°. In a bowl combine ⅓ cup brown sugar and apples.

- ◆ In another bowl combine oats, flour, remaining ⅓ cup brown sugar, cinnamon and nutmeg. Cut in margarine with fork.

- ◆ Spoon apples into 9x13-inch pan sprayed with vegetable spray. Top with crumbled mixture. Bake for 50 minutes.

Yield: *12 servings*

Microwave Toffee *(Dairy)*

½ cup butter	¼ cup water
1 cup sugar	2½ ounces sliced almonds
½ teaspoon salt	1 cup chocolate chips

- ◆ Rub the rim of a large 2-quart microwave mixing bowl with the stick of butter. Put remaining butter in bowl and carefully pour the sugar and salt on the butter. Pour water on top. Microwave for 8 minutes on high power. It will not be done at this time. Add additional time in 30 second increments. (You must open the door of oven every 30 seconds and check.) The candy is done when it turns a light to medium caramel color. *Never stir.*

- ◆ Place foil on a cookie sheet. Spread nuts on foil and pour candy over nuts. Don't scrape the bowl. Let sit at room temperature for 15 minutes.

- ◆ Top candy with chocolate chips. Let sit until chocolate melts. Spread chocolate over candy with knife. Chill and break into pieces. Toffee will keep for weeks in an airtight container.

Yield: *12 to 14 servings*

Note: *Every microwave is different. Watch candy so it does not get too dark.*

Traditional Charoset (Parve)

Charoset is always served as part of the Seder service.

3	large apples or 4 small apples	2	tablespoons sugar or honey
1	cup chopped nuts	½	cup sweet red wine
2	tablespoons cinnamon		

- ◆ Peel and core apples and chop them fine. Add chopped nuts and mix with apples.
- ◆ Add cinnamon and sugar. Mix thoroughly. Add red wine and mix again.
- ◆ Chill for several hours and serve.

Yield: *10 servings*

Sephardic Charoset (Parve)

5	Granny Smith apples, chopped fine	1	cup dates, cut up
1	cup golden raisins	¼	cup honey
1	orange peel, grated	2	tablespoons cinnamon
	Juice of 1 orange (½ cup)	1	cup chopped walnuts

- ◆ Combine all ingredients.

Yield: *12 servings*

Note: *You may also use dried figs, dried cherries and/or currants.*

Apricot Kugel *(Dairy)*

Hot or cold, this one is wonderful.

Kugel
2	cups matzo farfel (or 4 crushed matzos)	1	cup sour cream
3	eggs	½	cup margarine, melted
¼	cup sugar	½	cup raisins
2	cups creamed cottage cheese	½	cup chopped dried apricots
		½	cup apricot preserves

Topping
½	cup chopped walnuts	1	teaspoon cinnamon
2	tablespoons sugar		

- ◆ Preheat oven to 350°. Soak matzo farfel in water and immediately squeeze out water.
- ◆ Beat eggs and add sugar. Add remaining ingredients, except topping, and put into a 9x13-inch greased baking dish. Sprinkle on topping and bake for 45 minutes.

Yield: *12 servings*

Matzo Farfel Kugel *(Meat)*

Also makes a great poultry stuffing.

4	ribs celery, chopped	2	eggs
2	large onions, chopped	1½	(10½-ounce) cans chicken broth, or hot water
3-4	cups sliced mushrooms		Paprika, garlic powder, salt, pepper to taste
	Peanut oil or margarine		
1	(16-ounce) box matzo farfel		
½	cup matzo meal		

- ◆ Preheat oven to 350°. Sauté celery, onions and mushrooms in peanut oil or margarine. Remove from heat and add remaining ingredients. Mix well.
- ◆ Put in greased 9x13-inch casserole dish. Bake, covered, for 45 minutes and uncovered an additional 15 minutes.

Yield: *12 servings*

Note: *You may partially bake casserole for 30 minutes and then freeze.*

Passover Potato Kugel *(Parve)*

4	cups cubed potatoes, peeled (approximately 4 medium potatoes)	1	teaspoon salt
		¼	teaspoon pepper
		¼	cup oil
3	eggs	⅓	cup potato starch
1	large onion, quartered	6	sprigs parsley, stems removed

- ◆ Preheat oven to 350°. Put potatoes in blender with water and pulse until coarsely grated. Remove and drain well.
- ◆ Put remaining ingredients into blender in order listed and process until parsley is chopped.
- ◆ Mix batter with drained potatoes and turn into greased 1½ quart casserole dish.
- ◆ Bake for 1 hour or until brown.

Yield: *6 to 8 servings*

Note: *Do not grate potatoes too fine or they'll be mushy. Recipe may be doubled.*

Mock Kishke *(Parve)*

This modern version is just as good as the original.

2	carrots	¾	cup hot water
2	ribs celery	2	cups matzo meal
1	medium onion	1	egg, beaten
½	teaspoon garlic powder	½	cup oil
1	teaspoon parve chicken-flavored soup mix	1	tablespoon sugar

- ◆ Preheat oven to 350°. Place carrots, celery, onion and garlic powder in food processor. Process until fine.
- ◆ Dissolve bouillon in water and combine with matzo meal. Add vegetable purée, egg, oil and sugar. Divide in half and form 2 rolls.
- ◆ Wrap in aluminum foil and bake for 45 to 60 minutes. Slice to serve.

Yield: *12 pieces*

Note: *This may be frozen and reheated.*

Spinach or Broccoli Soufflé *(Parve)*

An elegant and easy side dish.

6	tablespoons margarine, divided	⅓	cup matzo meal
4	cups chopped onions	1½	teaspoons salt
8	eggs, separated	1	teaspoon minced garlic
2	(10-ounce) packages frozen chopped broccoli or spinach (see note)	¼	teaspoon freshly ground pepper

◆ Preheat oven to 350°. In medium skillet, melt 2 tablespoons margarine. Add onions and sauté for 5 minutes. Let cool.

◆ Beat egg yolks. Add onions, broccoli or spinach, matzo meal, salt, garlic, pepper and 2 tablespoons margarine.

◆ In a separate bowl, beat egg whites until stiff and stir into broccoli mixture. Pour into 2-quart casserole or soufflé dish greased with remaining margarine.

◆ Bake for 40 to 45 minutes.

Yield: *6 servings*

Note: *Frozen chopped spinach should be thawed and squeezed dry when used in place of the broccoli.*

Spinach Puffs *(Parve)*

1	tablespoon oil	2	teaspoons minced fresh garlic
½	cup onion, cut in ½-inch cubes	4	eggs, lightly beaten
1	cup sliced mushrooms	½	cup matzo meal
1	cup carrots, cut in ¼-inch rounds	¾	teaspoon salt
2-3	cups cooked spinach	¼	teaspoon pepper

◆ Preheat oven to 350°. In large skillet, heat oil. Sauté onion, mushrooms and carrots for 3 to 5 minutes. Add spinach and garlic and sauté for 2 to 3 minutes.

◆ Place eggs in large mixing bowl. Add vegetable mixture and thoroughly mix together with a wooden spoon.

◆ Add matzo meal and seasonings and stir until well blended.

◆ Pour into greased muffin tins and bake for 45 minutes.

Yield: *12 to 16 puffs*

Vegetable Patties *(Parve)*

1½	cups red and yellow peppers, seeded and chopped	½	pound raw spinach, chopped into small pieces
1	large onion, grated	3	medium potatoes, boiled and mashed
2	tablespoons olive oil		
1½	cups grated carrot	3	eggs
			Salt and pepper

◆ Preheat oven to 350°. Sauté pepper and onion in oil.

◆ Mix all ingredients together. Allow to sit for 30 minutes.

◆ Make patties from the mixture and bake on greased cookie sheet for 10 minutes. Then flip to other side for another 10 minutes.

Yield: *8 servings*

Note: *These pancakes can also be fried.*

Passover Blintzes *(Parve or Dairy)*

Bletlach *is Yiddish for blintz pancake or crêpe.*

6	eggs	½	teaspoon salt
1½	tablespoons sugar	1½	cups water
1	cup potato starch		Margarine or butter for frying

◆ Beat eggs and add sugar. Sift dry ingredients, add to beaten eggs with water and mix well.

◆ In a hot 8-inch omelet pan, spread a little melted margarine with a piece of waxed paper.

◆ Put ½ cup batter in pan and roll around until thin batter sticks to pan. Pour excess batter back into batter bowl. Cook on medium-high heat. When crêpe begins to pull away from side of pan, tap out onto linen dish towel. When cooled, crêpes may be stacked until ready to fill and may be kept in refrigerator or frozen for future use.

◆ Fill crêpes with desired filling.

Yield: *20 crêpes*

Note: *For dairy blintzes, use butter.*

Cheese Filling for Blintzes *(Dairy)*

1	pound dry cottage cheese or farmer's cheese	1	tablespoon sugar, or more to taste
1	egg		Cinnamon to taste (optional)

◆ Mix ingredients together. Blend well. Put rounded tablespoon on prepared crêpe, fold in sides and roll up.

◆ Fry cheese blintzes in margarine or butter until browned on each side or bake in greased pan at 375° for 20 minutes, turning once. Serve with sour cream and jam or sprinkle with cinnamon and sugar.

Yield: *20 blintzes*

Meat Filling for Blintzes *(Meat)*

2	pounds soft cooked beef or chicken	½	teaspoon salt or to taste
2	large onions, diced	½	teaspoon paprika
¼	cup oil		Dash of pepper

◆ Chop meat. Sauté onion in oil. Add seasonings and mix all ingredients.

◆ Place filling just below middle of parve crêpe. Fold up bottom, fold in sides, then roll up.

◆ Meat blintzes should be baked at 350° in greased pan until golden brown, about 45 minutes.

Yield: *Approximately 30 blintzes*

Matzo Lasagna *(Dairy)*

7-8	matzos	¼	tablespoon garlic powder
2	pounds small curd cottage cheese	2-3	(11-ounce) cans tomato sauce
3	eggs	1	pound mozzarella cheese, shredded

- ◆ Preheat oven to 325°. Place matzos in colander and pour hot water over them.
- ◆ In separate bowl, mix cottage cheese, eggs and garlic powder.
- ◆ Coat 9x13-inch pan with oil.
- ◆ To assemble, put tomato sauce on bottom, then matzos, cottage cheese mixture, mozzarella cheese. Repeat in that order until ingredients are used up, about 4 layers.
- ◆ Bake for 45 minutes.

Yield: *8 servings*

Passover Pizza *(Dairy)*

4	matzos	8	slices cheese (mozzarella, American or cheddar)
1	(11-ounce) can tomato mushroom sauce		Chopped onions, olives or mushrooms (optional)

- ◆ Preheat broiler. Place matzos on baking sheet. Spread sauce over each piece. Place cheese and optional ingredients on top. Broil quickly.

Yield: *3 servings*

Grilled Cheese *(Dairy)*

Butter
2 matzos

Cheese
2 slices tomato (optional)

♦ Butter 1 side of matzo. Place cheese and tomato on unbuttered side of matzo and add the other matzo, buttered on top. Brown in skillet, turning once. This can also be made open faced under broiler.

Yield: *1 serving*

Cinnamon Toast *(Dairy)*

Butter
1 matzo

Cinnamon to taste
Sugar to taste

♦ Preheat broiler. Butter matzo. Sprinkle with cinnamon and sugar. Broil quickly. Watch carefully so it doesn't burn.

Yield: *1 serving*

French Dressing *(Parve)*

½ cup sugar
½ cup oil
⅔ cup ketchup
⅔ cup Passover vinegar

1 teaspoon paprika
1 clove garlic, minced
1 tablespoon grated onion

♦ Mix all ingredients together.

Yield: *1½ cups*

Granola *(Parve)*

Great as a breakfast cereal or as a snack.

2½	cups matzo farfel	½	teaspoon salt
1	cup shredded fresh coconut	1	cup raisins
1	cup chopped pecans	1	cup dates, cut up
¼	cup margarine	1	teaspoon cinnamon
¼	cup Passover brown sugar or white sugar		Chocolate chips for Passover (optional)
¼	cup honey		

- ◆ Preheat oven to 325°. Combine matzo farfel, coconut, and nuts in bowl. Spread mixture on lightly greased jellyroll pan. Bake for 15 to 20 minutes, tossing several times until lightly toasted.

- ◆ Meanwhile, in 2-quart saucepan combine margarine, sugar, honey and salt. Bring to simmer for a few minutes, stirring constantly. Remove from heat.

- ◆ Add lightly toasted farfel-coconut-nut mixture to syrup mixture. Mix well, tossing ingredients as if making a tossed salad. Coat everything evenly. Place back on jellyroll pan.

- ◆ Increase oven temperature to 350° and toast mixture for 20 to 25 minutes until ingredients are golden brown. Stir frequently to avoid burning.

- ◆ Transfer granola to large mixing bowl. Stir in raisins, dates, and cinnamon with spatula and break up any large lumps.

- ◆ Cool thoroughly and add chocolate chips. Store in airtight container.

Yield: *7 cups*

Sponge Cake *(Parve)*

10	extra large eggs, separated	½	cup matzo cake meal
1½	cups sugar		Pinch of salt
½	cup potato starch		

- ◆ Preheat oven to 325°. Beat egg whites until they stand in peaks. Add sugar very slowly. Beat well. Gradually add egg yolks to mixture.
- ◆ Sift together dry ingredients and add slowly to wet mixture. Beat for 1 minute or until thoroughly mixed, being careful not to beat too long.
- ◆ Bake in ungreased tube pan for 1 hour. Turn pan upside down over wine bottle to cool. When cool, loosen sides and middle with sharp knife and turn out onto plate.

Yield: *12 servings*

Note: *You may make this cake with 7 or 8 eggs. However, it will not be as high.* **Variations:** *Add juice of 1 lemon or 2 tablespoons wine. Mash a banana and add together with ½ cup finely chopped nuts. Add cocoa to ⅓ of the mixture and place remaining ⅔ of batter into tube pan, slowly swirling cocoa batter into yellow mixture for marble effect.*

Honey Cake *(Parve)*

3	eggs	2	teaspoons baking soda
1	cup sugar	1	teaspoon ginger
1	cup honey	1	teaspoon cinnamon
1	cup hot coffee	½	cup oil
2	cups matzo cake meal	3	tablespoons chopped nuts
½	cup potato starch		

- ◆ Preheat oven to 325°. Beat eggs well, adding sugar gradually. Mix honey with warm coffee and blend into eggs.
- ◆ Sift together all dry ingredients and add with oil and nuts to egg mixture. Blend thoroughly.
- ◆ Pour into greased 9x13-inch pan and bake for 30 minutes.
- ◆ Turn oven up to 350° and bake an additional 15 minutes until toothpick comes out clean.

Yield: *12 to 16 servings*

Passover Nut Crust *(Parve)*

1½ cups pecans   ¼   cup cake meal
3   tablespoons sugar   Dash of cinnamon
2   tablespoons margarine

◆   Preheat oven to 375°. Mix in food processor. Pat into 10-inch springform pan. Bake for 7 minutes.

Yield: *1 crust*

Passover Cookie Crust *(Parve)*

¼   cup margarine, melted   1   cup Passover cookie crumbs

◆   Combine margarine and cookie crumbs. Pat into bottom of pie pan or springform pan.
◆   Chill in freezer for 5 to 10 minutes before filling, or bake at 375° for 6 to 8 minutes before filling. Cool and fill.

Yield: *1 crust*

Macaroon Pie Crust *(Parve)*

1⅓ cups macaroons, crumbled   ¼   cup sugar
½   cup margarine, cut into 8 pieces   ¼   teaspoon cinnamon

◆   Preheat oven to 375°. Place macaroons in work bowl of food processor. Using metal blade, process macaroons until fine crumbs form, about 15 to 20 seconds. Add remaining ingredients and process until well blended.
◆   Press crust into the bottom and up the sides of an ungreased 9-inch pie pan. Bake for 7 minutes or until golden brown.
◆   Cool completely before filling.

Yield: *1 (9-inch) pie crust*

Lemon Meringue Pie *(Parve)*

Crust

1	cup matzo meal	⅛	teaspoon salt
¼	cup margarine, melted	½	teaspoon cinnamon
2	tablespoons sugar	½	cup chopped nuts

Filling

3	egg yolks	6	tablespoons lemon juice
1	cup sugar	2	tablespoons margarine
¼	teaspoon salt	1	tablespoon grated lemon rind
4	tablespoons potato starch	2	cups water

Meringue

3	egg whites	6	tablespoons sugar
	Dash of salt		

- Preheat oven to 350°. Blend ingredients for crust and press into 9-inch pan. Bake for 15 to 20 minutes; cool.

- For filling, beat egg yolks; add sugar, salt and starch, beating in slowly. Add lemon juice, margarine, rind and water.

- Cook slowly in top of double boiler until thick, stirring constantly to avoid lumps. Cool at room temperature.

- Meanwhile, beat egg whites with salt until foamy. Gradually add 6 tablespoons sugar and beat until thick and glossy.

- Put filling into baked pie shell and cover with meringue. Bake at 375° for 15 minutes or until browned.

Yield: *8 servings*

Brownie Pie *(Parve)*

Crust

¼	cup softened margarine	2	tablespoons matzo meal
½	cup sugar	1	cup finely ground walnuts or
1	tablespoon matzo cake meal		pecans

Filling

½	cup margarine	4	ounces semisweet chocolate,
1	cup sugar		melted, or ½ cup chocolate
3	eggs		chips, melted
		⅓	cup matzo cake meal

- ◆ Preheat oven to 325°. For crust, mix all ingredients together and press into a 10-inch pie pan. Chill.
- ◆ For filling, beat margarine with sugar until fluffy. Add eggs one at a time.
- ◆ Add melted chocolate and cake meal.
- ◆ Pour into pie shell and bake for 45 minutes. Cool. Slice to serve.
- ◆ Keep refrigerated.

Yield: *8 servings*

Mandelbread (Parve)

This one is a traditional winner.

Mandelbread

1 cup margarine	2¾ cups matzo cake meal
1½ cups sugar	¾ cup potato starch
6 eggs	

Variations to Add

1 cup chopped nuts or slivered almonds	1 teaspoon orange juice and rind
1 teaspoon almond or vanilla extract for Passover	1 teaspoon lemon juice and rind
	1 cup semisweet chocolate chips
	1 cup raisins

Topping

1 tablespoon cinnamon	2 tablespoons sugar

◆ Preheat oven to 350°. Cream margarine and sugar. Add eggs, one at a time. Add cake meal and potato starch and any combination of the variations.

◆ On an ungreased cookie sheet, form into 2-inch diameter loaves. Combine sugar and cinnamon and sprinkle on top of loaves.

◆ Bake for 45 to 50 minutes. After baking, slice while warm into 1-inch pieces and lay flat on cookie sheet.

◆ Sprinkle lightly with more cinnamon sugar mixture and put back in oven at 225° for 45 minutes.

◆ Toast lightly under broiler on both sides until just browned. Watch carefully, being sure not to burn.

Yield: *70 slices*

Double Chocolate Biscotti *(Parve)*

¾	cup oil	1¼	cups matzo cake meal
⅔	cup sugar	¼	cup matzo meal
½	cup brown sugar	2	tablespoons potato starch
1	teaspoon vanilla	¼	cup ground almonds or
¼	cup cocoa		walnuts
3	eggs	¾	cup semisweet chocolate,
2	tablespoons brewed coffee		chopped, or ¾ cup mini
	Pinch salt		chocolate chips

- ◆ Preheat oven to 350°. Grease cookie sheet.
- ◆ In a large bowl, beat oil, sugars, vanilla and cocoa. Add eggs, coffee, salt, cake meal, matzo meal, and potato starch. Fold in nuts and chocolate.
- ◆ Divide dough into 2 equal portions and pat into 2-inch wide strips on the cookie sheet. Bake for 35 to 40 minutes. Cool slightly.
- ◆ Wrap cookie sheet well in foil and refrigerate for 2 hours to firm loaves up. Remove from refrigerator and with a sharp knife, carefully cut strips into ¼-inch slices.
- ◆ Place slices on baking sheet and bake at 325° for 15 to 20 minutes, turning once midway during baking.

Yield: *Approximately 50 slices*

Chocolate Meringue Cookies *(Parve)*

These are really yummy!

4	egg whites	10	ounces chocolate chips, melted
1	cup sugar		

- ◆ Preheat oven to 350°. Beat egg whites until stiff, gradually adding sugar. Fold in the melted chocolate.
- ◆ Drop by teaspoonfuls on a greased cookie sheet and bake for about 10 minutes. Place on wire rack to cool.

Yield: *48 cookies*

Chocolate Chip Cookies *(Parve or Dairy)*

1½ cups margarine or unsalted butter	2 eggs
1¾ cups brown sugar	1½ cups matzo cake meal
2 tablespoons sugar	¼ cup matzo meal
¼ teaspoon salt	2½ cups semisweet chocolate chips

◆ Preheat oven to 350°. Grease two baking sheets or line with parchment paper.

◆ Mix the margarine or butter with sugars, salt and eggs. Blend in cake meal and matzo meal. Stir in chocolate chips.

◆ Scoop large tablespoonfuls of dough onto baking sheets. Flatten with spoon. Bake until slightly golden, 13 to 15 minutes.

Yield: *48 cookies*

Almond Cookies *(Parve)*

8 ounces ground almonds	Matzo cake meal
2¼ cups sugar	Slivered almonds
5 egg whites	

◆ Preheat oven to 350°. Combine almonds and sugar. Mix well. Add egg whites, 1 at a time; mix until paste is formed. Refrigerate for 10 minutes.

◆ Line cookie sheets with parchment paper. Dust with matzo cake meal. Using a teaspoon, drop cookie dough onto prepared pan, about 1½ inches apart. Place almond sliver on top, pushing down slightly.

◆ Bake for 14 to 18 minutes until slightly browned. Carefully remove from pan with metal spatula. Cool on racks.

◆ Best stored in covered tins.

Yield: *36 cookies*

Toffee Bars *(Parve)*

You'll make these more than once!

1	cup margarine	¼	teaspoon salt
1	cup sugar (may be ½ brown and ½ white)	1	cup matzo cake meal
		10	ounces chocolate chips
1	egg	1	cup chopped pecans
1	teaspoon vanilla		

- ◆ Preheat oven to 350°. Cream margarine and sugar until light and fluffy. Add egg. Beat well. Blend in vanilla, salt, and cake meal.
- ◆ Spread dough in lightly greased jellyroll pan with spatula. Dough will be sticky. Bake for 20 minutes. Remove from oven.
- ◆ Melt chocolate chips by placing over hot baked dough.
- ◆ Cover with aluminum foil for 5 to 10 minutes. Spread chocolate chips when melted. Sprinkle with chopped pecans.

Yield: *24 bars*

Caramel Pecan Squares *(Parve)*

4	matzos	1	cup chopped pecans or walnuts
1	cup margarine	1½	cups semisweet chocolate pieces
1	cup brown sugar, packed	1	cup slivered almonds or walnuts

- ◆ Preheat oven to 350°. Line bottom of well-greased 10½x15½-inch jellyroll pan with matzos, breaking as necessary to fit pan.
- ◆ In medium saucepan over medium-high heat, combine margarine, brown sugar and pecans. Bring to boil, stirring with wooden spoon. Reduce heat to medium and boil for 2 minutes, stirring constantly.
- ◆ Pour over matzos and bake for 7 to 8 minutes.
- ◆ Remove from oven and sprinkle with chocolate.
- ◆ Return to oven and bake for 2 to 3 minutes longer to melt chocolate.
- ◆ Remove again and spread melted chocolate with spatula.
- ◆ Sprinkle immediately with almonds. Pat down while still warm. Cut into 2-inch square pieces and refrigerate for 30 minutes until set.

Yield: *30 squares*

Fantastic Chocolate Brownies *(Parve)*

These disappear fast!

10	ounces semisweet chocolate chips	6	eggs
1	cup margarine	3	cups sugar
3	tablespoons instant coffee granules	¾	teaspoon salt
		1½	cups matzo cake meal
		½	cup chopped nuts

◆ Preheat oven to 350°. Melt chocolate and margarine together in microwave, about 2 minutes.

◆ Mix instant coffee granules into chocolate mixture. Set aside to cool.

◆ Meanwhile, beat eggs, add sugar and beat well. Add the chocolate mixture slowly. Mix thoroughly.

◆ Add salt and cake meal. Mix thoroughly and add nuts.

◆ In a greased 9x13-inch pan, bake for 40 to 45 minutes.

Yield: *12 squares*

Chocolate Passover Brownies *(Parve or Dairy)*

Fabulous!

½	cup margarine or butter	¼	cup potato starch
2	squares unsweetened chocolate	¼	cup matzo cake meal
		1	teaspoon vanilla
2	eggs	6	ounces semisweet chocolate chips
1	cup sugar		

◆ Preheat oven to 350°. In 2-cup glass measuring cup, melt margarine or butter and unsweetened chocolate in microwave. Cool.

◆ Meanwhile, beat 2 eggs with mixer. Add sugar and beat until well mixed.

◆ Combine potato starch and cake meal and add to mixture.

◆ Add cooled chocolate mixture and vanilla. Mix well and add chocolate chips.

◆ In a greased 9-inch square pan, bake for 20 to 25 minutes.

Yield: *9 squares*

Cocoa Brownies *(Parve or Dairy)*

3	eggs	¾	cup cocoa
1½	cups sugar	1	teaspoon vanilla
¾	cup margarine or butter, melted	½	cup nuts (optional)
4½	tablespoons matzo cake meal		

- ◆ Preheat oven to 400°. Beat eggs. Add sugar and beat. Add melted butter or margarine and beat.
- ◆ Mix in dry ingredients, vanilla, and nuts.
- ◆ In a greased 9x13-inch pan, bake for 18 minutes.

Yield: *12 squares*

Apple Squares *(Parve)*

3	large apples	4	tablespoons orange juice or lemon juice
1-2	tablespoons sugar (or more to taste)	½	cup oil
½	teaspoon cinnamon	1	cup matzo meal
3	eggs, separated	½	teaspoon salt
1	cup sugar		

- ◆ Preheat oven to 350°. Peel the apples and slice into a medium bowl. Sprinkle with 1 to 2 tablespoons sugar and ½ teaspoon cinnamon. Toss the apples to coat well. Taste and sprinkle on more sugar if the apples are tart. Set aside.
- ◆ In a medium bowl, beat the egg yolks until light. Gradually add the sugar, beating until thick. Add the juice and oil.
- ◆ Add the matzo meal and salt. Beat at low speed until well blended.
- ◆ In a mixing bowl, with clean beater, beat the egg whites until stiff. Gently fold the whites into the yolk mixture.
- ◆ Spread half of the batter in the bottom of a lightly greased 8-inch square pan.
- ◆ Spread the apples in an even layer over the batter. Cover with the remaining batter.
- ◆ Bake for 45 minutes or until browned. Cool and cut into squares.

Yield: *16 squares*

Note: *You may substitute 1 cup sugared blueberries for the apples.*

Apricot Bars *(Dairy)*

Pastry

½	pound unsalted butter, softened	2	cups matzo cake meal
2	egg yolks	2	teaspoons grated lemon rind (optional)
	Pinch salt	1	teaspoon vanilla
1	cup sugar		

Filling

1	(16-ounce) jar apricot preserves	½	cup chopped nuts
¼	cup lemon juice		Chopped raisins (optional)

◆ Preheat oven to 325°. Combine all pastry ingredients in a food processor.

◆ Spread ¾ of the dough on the bottom of a greased 9x13-inch pan. Bake for 20 minutes. Refrigerate remaining dough until needed.

◆ Mix filling ingredients together. Remove crust from oven. Spread filling mixture over hot crust. Crumble remaining dough on top.

◆ Bake for 30 to 35 minutes. Cut into squares when cool.

Yield: *35 to 40 squares*

Mixed Fruit Cobbler *(Parve)*

3	eggs	8	cups chopped mixed fresh fruit (apple, pear, blueberry, strawberry, raspberry)
¾	cup sugar		
¾	cup matzo meal		
¼	cup oil	3	tablespoons sugar
2	tablespoons potato starch	½	teaspoon cinnamon
¼	teaspoon salt		

◆ Preheat oven to 350°. Mix together eggs and ¾ cup sugar. Add matzo meal, oil, potato starch and salt. Mix well.

◆ Place fruit in greased 9-inch square pan. In a separate bowl mix together 3 tablespoons sugar and cinnamon, then sprinkle over fruit. Spoon matzo mixture over fruit.

◆ Bake for 45 minutes. Serve warm or at room temperature.

Yield: *6 to 8 servings*

Blueberry or Cherry Muffins *(Parve or Dairy)*

⅓ cup margarine or butter
1½ cups sugar, divided
3 eggs
½ teaspoon vanilla
½ cup matzo cake meal, unsifted
¼ teaspoon salt

¼ cup potato starch
1 cup frozen blueberries or
    1 cup pitted cherries, drained
2-3 tablespoons cinnamon
    Lemon rind (optional)

◆ Preheat oven to 350°. Cream together margarine and 1 scant cup of the sugar. Add eggs, 1 at a time, beating after each addition.

◆ Add vanilla, cake meal, salt and potato starch. Fold in blueberries or cherries.

◆ Top with the other ½ cup of sugar mixed with cinnamon, or lemon rind and sugar.

◆ Bake in muffin pan with paper fillers for 45 minutes.

Yield: *12 muffins*

Passover Rolls or Bagels *(Parve)*

⅔ cup oil   *⅓c*
1½ cups water   *1c*
2 cups matzo meal   *1c*

6 eggs   *4*
⅓ teaspoon salt
1 tablespoon sugar

◆ Preheat oven to 375°. In a 4-cup glass measuring cup, bring oil and water to boil in microwave. Mix matzo meal into boiling mixture carefully. Cool slightly.

◆ By hand or in mixer, beat in the eggs, 1 at a time, beating thoroughly after each addition. Add salt and sugar.

◆ Wet hands and shape dough into 2- or 3-inch balls and place on a greased baking sheet.

◆ For bagels, dip finger in cold water and make a depression in the center of each roll.

◆ Bake for 1 hour.   *375 20*
                                      325 30

Yield: *16 servings*

Ingberlach or Ginger Candy *(Parve)*

This is a favorite treat handed down through the generations.

4	cups matzo farfel	2	tablespoons lemon juice
1	egg, beaten	½	teaspoon powdered ginger,
1	pound honey		divided
1	cup sugar	½	cup cold sweet red wine
1	cup chopped nuts, divided		

- Mix matzo farfel with egg and set aside to dry on waxed paper.

- Separate particles and place dried farfel in a heavy 2½ quart pot. Add honey and sugar.

- Boil together, stirring with a wooden spoon until mixture is brown. Be careful not to burn.

- Remove from stovetop and add nuts, lemon juice and ginger. Stir well.

- Put mixture on a wooden board that has been moistened with some wine. Dip hands in cold wine and pat mixture to ¼-inch thickness.

- Sprinkle with additional chopped nuts and ginger. Cool and cut into squares.

Yield: *16 pieces*

Notes

Contributors

Congregation Beth Israel Sisterhood thanks its members, their families and friends who contributed recipes and tested each one. Space limitations made it impossible to include every submission. We sincerely hope that we have not overlooked anyone.

Chef Greg Abbate
Shirley Askot •
Evelyn Balkansky
Maureen Bard
Donna Becker
Lainie Beim
Anne Berger
Shari Berson
Eunice Biller
Rose Burns
Jane Butenhoff
Ruby Carneol
Sharon Cohen
Maxine Cohn
Marcia Colton
Aidee Cooper
Cindy Cooper
Joanne Cremer
Suzanne Davidson
Penny Deshur
Bunny Dolnick
Jed Dolnick
Sy Dolnick
Harriet Dorf
Mindy Edwards
Maureen Eichenbaum
Jennie Elias
Suzy Farkas
Bev Feiges
Lynne Stern Feiges
Phyllis Fink
Ireta Fisher
Flo Fishman
Linda Freeman
Anne Friedman
Brenda Friedman •
Rose From
Ruth Fromstein
Diane Futterman
Charlotte Gellerman
Rosalie Gellman
Susan Glickstein
Sharon Goldberger
Edith Gould •
Jessica & Josh Hamermesh
Jackie Hammes

Vivian Hearst
Judy Hirsch
Marcia Hirschman •
Corky Horn
Gary & Robin Ittigson
Betty Jacobs
Alice Jacobson
Linda Jacobson
Sue Jacobson
Judy Joseph
Lisa Jubas
Bobbi & Larry Kahn
Julie Kahn
Miriam Kahn
Sari Karsh
Linda Keller
Melissa Kerbel
Susan Klapper
Barbara Kohl-Spiro
Judy Kristal
Belle Lane
Esther Lauwasser
Gloria Leeb
Phyllis Lensky
Ellen Leshin
Linda Leshin
Rene Lieberman
June Louis
Cheryl Lubotsky
Mindy Marcus
Rita Marcus
Susan Marcus
Illana & Adam Margolis
Judy Margolis
Rachel Marks
Bobbie Mendelsohn
Chef Dina Menzl-Russo
Shari Messerman
Sue Miller
Terri Minkin
Michelle Missner
Lorraine Mitz
Phyllis Morrison •
Claire Moss
Anita Nagurka
Roberta Newman

Gittle Ort
Annette Paine
Natalie Palay
Eveline Panitch
Barbara Perchonok
Lenore Picus
Mickey Pittleman
Linda Polan •
Susan Rabovsky
Beverly Rice
Carol Richheimer
Rita Rogers •
Vivian Rothschild
Phyllis Rubin
Rena Safer
Jean Saltzman
Sylvia Schecter •
Harriet Schendlinger
Sari Schiff
Lynn Schmelzer
Karen Schumacher
Laura Waldman Schwartz
Nancy Sedloff
Susan Selby
Gladys Shukur
Diana Siegel
Cheryl Siegel-Gajewski
Sharon Siegel-Picus
Lillian Smith
Eileen Staller
Maitzie Stan
Ceil Stern
Sue Strait
Sharon Styler
Bev Ugent
Betty Wallens
Debra Watton
Jodi & Steve Weber
Lois Weber
Patti Weigler
Barbara Weiss
Norma Wells
Judy Wolkenstein
Ardis Zarem
Selma Zeiger

• Of Blessed Memory

Index

G

H

I

P

MAIL ORDER FORM
Congregation Beth Israel Sisterhood
Can't Believe It's Kosher
6880 N. Green Bay Avenue
Milwaukee, WI 53209
Phone: (414) 351-1800   Fax: (414) 351-1803
Toll-Free: (866) 331-1818

Please send me _____ copies of *Can't Believe It's Kosher*   @ $24.95 each $ _____

U.S. Shipping and Handling (Single Copy)   4.00 $ _____

Outside U.S. Shipping (Single Copy)   8.00 $ _____

Additional Charge for Copies to Same Address   2.00 each $ _____

Wisconsin Residents, Please Add $1.40 Sales Tax Per Copy $ _____

Gift Wrap (Per Copy)   2.00 each $ _____

Outside US: Credit Card Orders Only   **TOTAL** $ _____

Please make checks payable to *CBI Sisterhood*   ☐ Check Enclosed

Name: _____ Phone No. _____

Please charge my: ☐ Visa
                    ☐ Mastercard

Account Number: ☐☐☐☐ ☐☐☐☐ ☐☐☐☐ ☐☐☐☐

Expiration Date _____

Cardholder's Signature: _____ Phone No. _____

(Please complete reverse side of form)

MAIL ORDER FORM
Congregation Beth Israel Sisterhood
Can't Believe It's Kosher
6880 N. Green Bay Avenue
Milwaukee, WI 53209
Phone: (414) 351-1800   Fax: (414) 351-1803
Toll-Free: (866) 331-1818

Please send me _____ copies of *Can't Believe It's Kosher*   @ $24.95 each $ _____

U.S. Shipping and Handling (Single Copy)   4.00 $ _____

Outside U.S. Shipping (Single Copy)   8.00 $ _____

Additional Charge for Copies to Same Address   2.00 each $ _____

Wisconsin Residents, Please Add $1.40 Sales Tax Per Copy $ _____

Gift Wrap (Per Copy)   2.00 each $ _____

Outside US: Credit Card Orders Only   **TOTAL** $ _____

Please make checks payable to *CBI Sisterhood*   ☐ Check Enclosed

Name: _____ Phone No. _____

Please charge my: ☐ Visa
                    ☐ Mastercard

Account Number: ☐☐☐☐ ☐☐☐☐ ☐☐☐☐ ☐☐☐☐

Expiration Date _____

Cardholder's Signature: _____ Phone No. _____

(Please complete reverse side of form)

Shipping Information
Please Print Legibly

Sending a copy of *Can't Believe It's Kosher* to a friend is a long lasting reminder of your thoughtfulness. All copies will be sent to your address unless otherwise specified. If you wish books to be sent as gifts, please note below.

Mail Book To:
Name _____

Address _____

City _____

State _____ Zip Code _____

Phone Number (   ) _____

Send Gift(s) To:
Name _____

Address _____

City _____

State _____ Zip Code _____

Name _____

Address _____

City _____

State _____ Zip Code _____

You may enclose your own gift card(s) with this order, or we can include a small gift card with your personal message. Please include your brief message(s) on a separate sheet of paper.

— —

Mail Book To:
Name _____

Address _____

City _____

State _____ Zip Code _____

Phone Number (   ) _____

Send Gift(s) To:
Name _____

Address _____

City _____

State _____ Zip Code _____

Name _____

Address _____

City _____

State _____ Zip Code _____

You may enclose your own gift card(s) with this order, or we can include a small gift card with your personal message. Please include your brief message(s) on a separate sheet of paper.